Native Orchids of Minnesota

Also published by the University of Minnesota Press

Trees and Shrubs of Minnesota
Welby R. Smith

Northland Wildflowers: The Comprehensive Guide to the Minnesota Region
John B. Moyle and Evelyn W. Moyle; photography by John Gregor

Gardening with Prairie Plants: How to Create Beautiful Native Landscapes
Sally Wasowski; photography by Andy Wasowski

Minnesota's Natural Heritage: An Ecological Perspective
John R. Tester

Native Orchids of Minnesota

Welby R. Smith
Minnesota Department of Natural Resources

Illustrations by Vera Ming Wong and Bobbi Angell

University of Minnesota Press
Minneapolis
London

The University of Minnesota Press gratefully acknowledges financial assistance provided by the Minnesota Department of Natural Resources for the publication of this book.

Partial funding for this book was provided by the Minnesota Environment and Natural Resources Trust Fund as recommended by the Legislative–Citizen Commission on Minnesota Resources (LCCMR).

Generous financial support toward the publication of this book was provided by the Minnesota Native Plant Society.

Some material in this book first appeared in *Orchids of Minnesota* by Welby R. Smith, University of Minnesota Press, 1993.

Published by the University of Minnesota Press
111 Third Avenue South, Suite 290
Minneapolis, MN 55401-2520
http://www.upress.umn.edu

Library of Congress Cataloging-in-Publication Data

Smith, Welby R. (Welby Richmond), author.
Native orchids of Minnesota / Welby R. Smith.
Includes bibliographical references and index.
Revision of: Orchids of Minnesota / Welby R. Smith ; illustrated by Vera Ming Wong.—Minneapolis : University of Minnesota Press, c1993.
ISBN 978-0-8166-7823-5 (pb : alk. paper)
1. Orchids—Minnesota. 2. Orchids—Minnesota—Identification. I. Title.
QK495.O64S64 2012
584'.409776—dc23

2011042872

Printed in China on acid-free paper

The University of Minnesota is an equal-opportunity educator and employer.

19 18 17 16 15 14 13 12 10 9 8 7 6 5 4 3 2 1

Contents

Counties of Minnesota

Preface

Nineteen years have passed since publication of *Orchids of Minnesota*. During that time interest in native orchids has not waned. In fact, interest in orchids, and all aspects of Minnesota's natural history, appears to be growing.

When a new edition was first contemplated, it was thought that only small updates were needed, but it soon became apparent that any new edition would have to be entirely rewritten in order to accommodate recent scientific advances and the ever-growing expectations of the public.

The format of this new edition is similar to the first, although significantly expanded. Six orchids have been added (four additional species and two additional varieties), new maps were created, and new photographs were acquired. The text was rewritten with greater emphasis on species identification and habitat.

The orchid drawings of Vera Ming Wong that appeared in the first edition have never been surpassed, so they have been retained in the new edition. Drawings of newly added species have been expertly rendered by Bobbi Angell.

The distribution maps in the first edition were based on a collection of 2,915 herbarium specimens. Maps in the new edition are based on 4,435 specimens, the difference being the number of specimens collected in the intervening time. This should allow a finer depiction of distribution patterns, although there is still much fieldwork to be done.

In spite of my efforts to create a book useful to everyone, the results will not satisfy all users. Space limitations meant that much information was left out, especially taxonomic details, atypical color forms, identification of hybrids, and pollinator ecology. The result is a book that is more than a field guide but less than a textbook.

It is important to acknowledge that this book is built on the accumulated work of many botanists. This includes the contributions of talented laboratory and herbarium scientists from all over the world as well as Minnesota-based field botanists who have been gathering specimen data for 150 years. My own contribution is no greater than that of others except I have been given the rare opportunity to summarize and interpret what is known about Minnesota orchids in a book.

Special recognition must go to Rolf Dahle, who designed the database that produced the state distribution maps and contributed years of dedicated fieldwork; Tom Klein, who constructed the phenology chart and contributed invaluable services with the maps and photos; Shannon Flynn, who provided critical help with the North American range maps; Charles Sheviak and Paul Catling, who answered questions and examined specimens; Anita Cholewa, who curated the specimens in the herbarium of the J. F. Bell Museum of Natural History at the University of Minnesota in St. Paul with great dedication and provided access to the collections; and Carmen Converse, who supported this work in many ways.

Others who have actively contributed directly to the contents or production of the second edition include Karen Myhre, Erika Rowe, Audrey Engels, Scott Milburn, Steve Mortensen, Michael Lee, Lynden Gerdes, Lawson Gerdes, Rebecca Holmstrom, Ethan Perry, Derek Anderson, Stacey Olszewski, Norm Aaseng, Esther McLaughlin, Dave McLaughlin, Jan Wolff, Jared Cruz, Dan Wovcha, Otto Gockman, and Chel Anderson.

Introduction

How to Use This Book—a Few Tips and a Note of Explanation

The scientific study of orchids is a highly technical pursuit, by which I mean serious botanists who study orchids study the fine details such as the interior workings of the flowers, the chemical processes of the cells, and the DNA that passes from generation to generation. That is how scientific advances are made, and that is the science on which this book is based. However, this book skips over most of that to get to the results that can be seen and used by the average person. I have tried my best to keep things simple and yet retain the accuracy and thoroughness that people should expect.

The first step for most people is putting a name to an orchid they have just discovered. While most orchids found in Minnesota can be matched to the photos relatively easily, some cannot, and for these you will need to refer to the keys and descriptions. I have tried to make them clear and easy to use, but you will still encounter terms that are not in everyday use. The glossary at the back of the book will help. Don't be intimidated—everything can be done with a hand lens and a fine-scaled centimeter ruler.

The terminology and descriptions will all make sense fairly quickly, and besides, you can't get far without learning some of the details. For example, each orchid flower has three petals and three sepals—learn to recognize them and learn to look for differences in shape, size, and color from one species to another (Figure I.1).

You will notice that the book is organized alphabetically by the scientific names of the orchids. This is because there are simply too many different common names used for the same species. A word of advice from someone who has been there: get used to using scientific names—there aren't that many, and learning them will make things much less confusing. The use of scientific names for the non-orchid plants mentioned in the text has been minimized as much as possible so as not to distract from the focus of the book. I have put the common names in the glossary—look there for an explanation of the non-orchid plants.

The dot maps are original to this book and represent a great deal of work. They provide a visual summary of almost 150 years of fieldwork by a number of dedicated botanists, both professional and amateur. Each dot represents the location where a herbarium specimen was collected. Collecting voucher specimens is how botanists document their work. Each of these specimens is on deposit in a public herbarium and has been seen and verified by myself. Most of the specimens are in the University of Minnesota herbarium in St. Paul (MIN); a few are at the University of Minnesota Duluth campus (DUL), St. Cloud State University (SCL), and St. John's University in Collegeville (CSB).

Most of the vouchers were collected incidental to general floristic surveys. There has never been a thorough or systematic ground survey of orchids in Minnesota, so there are still some geographic gaps. Once you learn what a particular orchid looks like and what habitat it prefers, you will undoubtedly find it in places where there are no dots on the map.

Open circles on the maps represent specimens collected on or before 1965. Solid dots represent specimens collected between 1965 and 2011. This distinction was made in the hope of revealing trends in orchid populations over time. This succeeded in some cases, but perhaps more often it revealed trends in the population of botanists.

The description of each species includes a range of flowering dates. This is intended to represent a normal range of flowering dates. Extremes are left out. It is easy to find an odd

Figure I.1. Flower structure of a typical Minnesota orchid, *Platanthera orbiculata*

plant that flowers earlier or later than the rest, so do not be surprised if you find an orchid flowering "out of season."

Photographs of the underground structures of orchids are an unusual aspect of this book. Plants were painstakingly excavated and photographed, and the plants were reburied with minimal disturbance. This was done only if it was thought the plant would not be harmed.

Getting Started with Orchids—First Things First

What Is an Orchid?

Not all pretty flowers are orchids, and not all orchids have pretty flowers. So what is an orchid? Basically, an orchid is any plant in the orchid family. That may sound obtuse, but it is a good place to start. Plant taxonomists have arranged all plants into families. These are groupings of plants that have a common evolutionary history. There is the grass family, the lily family, the pine family, the orchid family, and so on. Botanists recognize approximately 500 families of flowering plants (Heywood et al. 2007), and orchids constitute the largest. In fact, there are about 25,000 species of orchids in the world, mostly in the tropics (Dressler 2005). The continental United States has only a small slice of the orchid family, about 208 species (Romero-González et al. 2002), and Minnesota has an even smaller slice with 46 species.

How Can You Tell Orchids from Other Plants?

Orchids are most likely to be confused with members of the lily family; however, there are several things that distinguish orchids from lilies. The basic orchid flower consists of six parts, three petals and three sepals, like the lilies. But in the lilies, the petals and sepals of each species are pretty much the same size, shape, and color, giving each flower a symmetric appearance. Things are different with the orchids. The sepals may or may not look alike, and the petals will definitely not look alike. There will always be one odd-looking petal, called the *lip* or *labellum*. The lip is modified in some way to facilitate pollination. It may be larger, a different color, or more complicated in shape. The lip is most often at the bottom of the flower, and it will usually be obvious. The pouch of a lady's-slipper flower is an example of a lip. The fringe and spur of a *Platanthera* is also the lip.

Basic Orchid Biology—Only As Much As You Need to Know

Mycorrhiza—the Secret Orchids Don't Want You to Know

First, what is meant by the word *mycorrhiza*? It is the process or condition of a close association—a symbiosis between the underground parts of a fungus, termed *hyphae*, and the roots of a plant. This is a living physical connection between a fungus and a plant through which substances pass from one to the other in a two-way flow of water, minerals, and organic compounds. The majority of all land plants, not just orchids, have this association with soil fungi. It is normally a mutualistic association, meaning that both the fungus and the plant benefit from the arrangement (Whigham 2004; Wang and Qiu 2006).

What Is the Purpose of This Association?

Reducing the concept of mycorrhiza to its essence is fairly easy: The fungus provides water and minerals, including nitrogen, to the plant. The plant uses photosynthesis to turn the water, minerals, and carbon dioxide into carbohydrates, which it shares with the fungus (Whigham 2004). Carbohydrates are used by all plants and all fungi for energy, except fungi cannot produce carbohydrates on their own. The result is a very neat system of mutualism.

Orchid mycorrhizae are different in that the fungi supply the orchid with not just minerals and water but also carbohydrates, and the orchid gives very little to the fungus in return. In the case of nonphotosynthetic orchids, the fungi get nothing at all. Since only the orchid benefits, the relationship becomes a sort of parasitism rather than mutualism (McCormick et al. 2006).

If fungi do not produce their own carbohydrates, then where do they get the carbohydrates they give to the orchids? That is the real story.

Fungi can scavenge for carbohydrates among the dead organic material in the soil, or they can get them from living green plants. The plants that supply carbohydrates to fungi include nearly all the plants in a forest, most notably the trees, but not the orchids. In a sense, it is the trees that feed the orchids. But it gets even more complicated.

The mycorrhizal system in the soil of a healthy forest can become an intricately woven network. Individual fungi can be simultaneously associated with several plants, and individual plants can be simultaneously associated with multiple fungi. In addition, both plants and fungi disperse independently, so relationships are constantly shifting (Bruns et al. 2002). Furthermore, there are interactions with other soil organisms, such as earthworms, nematodes, or bacteria. This is all part of the complex functioning of an unseen ecosystem where orchids are at the top of the food chain.

How Dependent Are Orchids on Mycorrhizal Fungi?

Some orchids, like the *Corallorhiza*, have little or no chlorophyll and therefore no capacity to make carbohydrates. It has been shown that they are entirely dependent on mycorrhizal fungi (Rasmussen and Whigham 2002). Also, orchid seeds have no stored carbohydrates and no way to make any until they produce their first green leaf—so orchid seeds and seedlings are also entirely dependent on mycorrhizal fungi (Smith and Read 2008).

Other orchids, those with green leaves, do have the capacity to make their own carbohydrates, at least as adults. And we know that if a green leafy orchid is deprived of sunlight, photosynthesis will cease, and the orchid will eventually die. Therefore it is apparent that the mycorrhizal fungi do not sustain it entirely. But it seems likely that some, if not most, green leafy orchids maintain some sort of mycorrhizal association for their entire life. This is especially true for orchids that occur in deep shade.

How Does Mycorrhiza Work?

The fungal hyphae are designed to pass individually through the cortical cell walls of an orchid root by simple penetration. Apparently, the orchid does not attract the fungus, or at least no special chemical attractant has been discovered. It appears that the fungus enters the orchid while investigating possible sources of food. Orchids allow fungi to enter specific cells of certain underground organs, particularly the roots but also the rhizomes. The orchid has powerful fungicides to protect other parts of the plant because some of the fungi may be pathogenic and could cause harm if they penetrated unprotected tissue. Once inside the orchid cells, the fungal hyphae are rolled into tight coils called *peletons*. Nutrients then pass through the wall of the fungal cells into the orchid cells (McCormick et al. 2006).

An indication of the total commitment of orchids to this strange dependence on fungi can be seen in the highly modified structure of the belowground organs of most adult orchids. They have evolved to take maximum advantage of the mycorrhizal association, and in most cases they cannot function fully without fungi. Therefore, this association is not opportunistic—it is essential. It is a highly evolved trait.

What Kind of Fungi Are We Talking About? Are These Special Fungi?

A large number of unrelated fungi have been found forming mycorrhizal associations with orchids. They belong to at least five major taxonomic groups of basidiomycetes. There appears to be no close taxonomic relationships among these fungal groups, just physical similarities. Some of the fungi appear to specialize in mutualistic mycorrhizal associations, especially with trees. Other fungi are primarily scavengers or decomposers (McCormick et al. 2006). There have been many attempts by botanists to determine the degree of specificity of fungi to orchid, and orchid to fungi. There apparently is a high degree of specificity among the nonphotosynthetic orchids, such as those in the genus *Corallorhiza*, but less specificity among the green photosynthetic orchids (Bruns et al. 2002; McCormick et al. 2006).

More on Life Underground

The discussion of mycorrhiza leads to more questions about the underground life of orchids. The belowground parts are perhaps as intricately evolved as the flowers and deserve every bit as much attention.

The story here begins with the seed. Since orchid seeds possess no stored energy reserves (carbohydrates or fats), they must rely on fungi for the energy to fuel germination. After germination the seed grows into a mass of differentiated cells called a *protocorm*.

The protocorm is essentially the seedling stage of orchids. It is the stage from the time the seed germinates until it appears aboveground. During this stage it is a formless mass of tissue without root or stem, and it is entirely nourished by fungal hyphae. It remains in this stage up to several years.

Eventually the protocorm develops roots and an aerial stem with leaves and flowers. The roots of orchids possess a number of unusual characteristics. They are typically few in number and may be entirely absent. They are often thick, fleshy, and sometimes brittle, owing to the large amount of cortical tissue needed for their life of parasitism on fungi. Another characteristic of orchid roots is they do not branch; each root is formed by the rhizome—the underground portion of the stem. The rhizome may also produce underground storage organs such as a tuber or a pseudobulb, or the rhizome itself may store food.

Very little of what goes on underground has to do with reproduction. With a few exceptions, the underground structures simply replace the old stem with a new one. Actual reproduction, that is, the production of two or more free-living individuals from one, is rarely performed by the underground structures. When it does happen, it is an example of vegetative or nonsexual reproduction, which is essentially a cloning process. Vegetative reproduction is quite rare among Minnesota orchids. In fact, only five species do it with any intent or to any great effect, and never exclusively or aggressively. Those species are *Pogonia ophioglossoides*, *Malaxis paludosa*, and the three *Goodyera* orchids.

The Insect Connection

The primary mode of reproduction in orchids involves seeds produced by sexual union, although there is the strange case of a select group of *Spiranthes* that have figured out how to make fertile seeds without sex. This is a sort of vegetative seed production called *agamospermy*, and *Spiranthes* use it to augment sexual seed production.

Agamospermy notwithstanding, all Minnesota orchids have flowers that can be pollinated by flying insects. Most Minnesota orchids are obligate outbreeders, meaning they require cross-pollination, but some are self-pollinating.

The general story of insect-mediated pollination is that the process benefits both participants. The plant gets its pollen moved from one plant to another, and the insect gets to eat any excess pollen or drink nectar from the flower. Orchids play the game differently: they may or may not give the insect a sip of nectar, and they never give a taste of pollen. Often the insect gets nothing at all. In that case, the orchid is using deceit to repeatedly trick the insect into carrying the pollen. In fact, the insect is sometimes subjected to a torturous experience in the process. It may be trapped, tossed about, turned upside down, and then cast away with a tiny packet of pollen glued somewhere to its body—somewhere the insect can't reach but where the next orchid flower can find it and deftly remove it using its stigma.

Insects can be fooled, to the benefit of orchids, but they are not always reliable. To hedge against this uncertainty, some orchids have developed the ability to pollinate themselves and eliminate the need for insects. This is called *auto-pollination*. The efficacy of the various pollination strategies can be debated, but it must be admitted that orchids are incredibly successful when it comes to devising strategies for pollination. It is sometimes tempting to think of orchids as possessing an evolved intelligence, or at least a cleverness.

When the flower has been pollinated, it begins to develop into a fruit, which is called a capsule. It is a fruit in the strict botanical sense that it is the seed-bearing structure of the plant, but it is not fleshy or sweet like an apple or a berry since the fruit is not intended to be eaten by an animal. It dries on the stalk rather quickly, then splits open, and an incredible number of minute, dustlike seeds are shaken loose by the wind.

Orchid Seeds—Secrets Revealed and Secrets Withheld

Seeds of terrestrial orchids are among the smallest in the plant kingdom, rarely measuring more than 2 mm long and 0.5 mm wide (Rasmussen 1995; Stoutamire 1964). Not only is the seed incredibly small, most of the seed is empty space. Orchids can produce these tiny seeds by the millions. One tropical orchid species has been estimated to produce 3.7 million seeds per capsule (Stoutamire 1964).

I don't believe any Minnesota orchid has entered the record book, but it has been reported that a single ripened seed capsule of our common stemless lady's-slipper (*Cypripedium acaule*) contained approximately 54,180 seeds (Stoutamire 1964). About 526 of these seeds weigh 1 mg. For comparison, a small, poorly fed mosquito weighs a little over 2 mg.

An orchid seed consists of an outer, usually transparent, seed coat and a small round or oval mass of cells composing the embryo. The embryo may consist of a very small number of cells, perhaps as few as ten (Stoutamire 1964).

The large amount of empty space in an orchid seed results in a structure with a large volume-to-weight ratio, which makes it very well adapted to travel on wind currents. It is hard to imagine the seeds of auricled twayblade (*Listera auriculata*), for example, which sits atop a four-inch stem in the lowest part of a dense forest, encountering significant wind currents. And yet it does happen, although perhaps not often. It has been reported that orchids migrate farther than any other wind-dispersed flowering plant (Ridley 1930; Wijaja and Arditti 1983).

But floating on air currents is only part of the process. When the seed reaches its final destination it must then find (or be found by) a suitable fungal host before it can germinate. Joining with a fungus must take place before or shortly after germination.

We have our own examples of long-range orchid dispersal in Minnesota. A number of orchids, including *Liparis liliifolia*, *Platanthera flava* var. *herbiola*, and *Spiranthes casei* var. *casei*, have in recent years been found growing in drained sediment basins on the Iron Range in Itasca and St. Louis Counties. This is far from where they normally occur. These are artificial basins created for the disposal of tailings, which is the mineral residue of iron ore and taconite mining. The tailings are carried to the basins in a slurry of water and eventually they settle to the bottom. When the basin is full, the water is drained, leaving a basin filled with a reddish, powdery "soil."

Initially, a drained basin resembles the surface of the moon—at least it would if the moon were red. In a remarkably short period of time, the basin becomes colonized by common plants from adjacent habitats. Typically, after perhaps twenty or thirty years, a young forest will have developed with scattered stands of trembling aspen, balsam poplar, paper birch, speckled alder, and a variety of common grasses, sedges, and forbs. Most of the colonizers are native forest species or early successional generalists, as well as several species of non-native weeds. During this process of reforestation, the basin habitat becomes very attractive to a variety of native orchid species, some of which are not known to occur anywhere else within a 150-mile radius.

The only way orchids can arrive at these sites is as wind-borne seeds. But the surprising aspect is how quickly and repeatedly it happens, even in basins separated by a number of miles. There are at least three species of orchids that have made this long-distance journey and several others that have arrived from closer by. None of the orchids share any obvious commonalities when their original habitats or points of origin are compared. To the contrary, they are an odd assortment of species from entirely different biomes and habitats. It should be noted that these habitats did not attract orchid seeds; the seeds arrived by chance. This must mean there is an incredible number of orchid seeds floating on wind currents.

Seeds can also float on the surface of water, possibly for weeks (Rasmussen 1995). And since most seeds fall to the ground near the parent plant, they are perhaps more likely to get caught up in nearby water currents than air currents. Reportedly, orchid seeds in the ground can also be dispersed short distances by small creatures that intentionally or unintentionally eat them and then pass them unharmed through their gut—earthworms and millipedes have been cited as examples (Rasmussen 1995).

Can orchid seeds remain dormant in the soil, or must they germinate quickly? There is evidence that seeds of at least some orchid species can remain dormant in the ground for at least a few and possibly several years before they germinate (Whigham et al. 2006). However, seeds of some of our bog orchids seem to germinate almost immediately (Stoutamire 1974).

Orchid Habitat—What You Need to Know to Find an Orchid

A habitat is the place where a species lives. The concept is simple, but describing a habitat in any detail can be tricky. Describing the aspects of a habitat that are important to orchids is even more difficult, and it can get a bit technical. No one tells orchids where they can and cannot grow, so expect surprises.

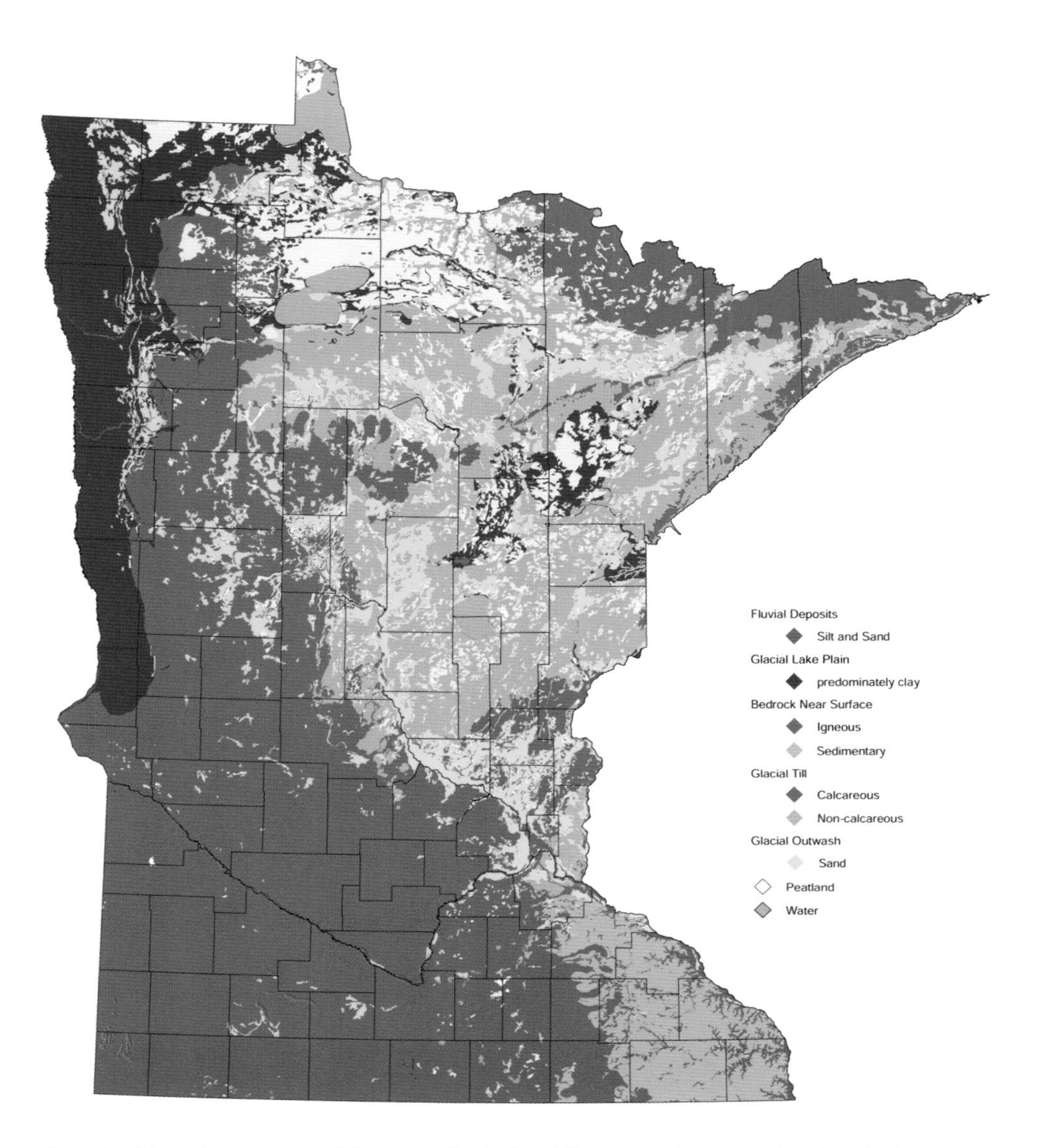

Map I.1. Major substrate types of Minnesota (Agricultural Experiment Station, University of Minnesota, Minnesota Soil Atlas Project, 1969–1981)

Of the forty-nine orchids known to occur in Minnesota, twenty-five occur exclusively or preferentially in permanent wetlands. These places are called *peatlands* because the constantly soggy conditions impede the process of decomposition and allow the slow accumulation of partially decomposed plant matter, *peat*. Peatlands are simply land that is covered with a thick layer of peat. Temporary wetlands do not produce peat because during dry periods the dead plant material becomes exposed to the air, which speeds decomposition. There are approximately 7.2 million acres of peatlands in Minnesota (Malterer et al. 1979). They go by the names swamp, bog, and fen. They can be told apart by vegetation structure, floristic composition, and the chemical nature of the water that saturates them.

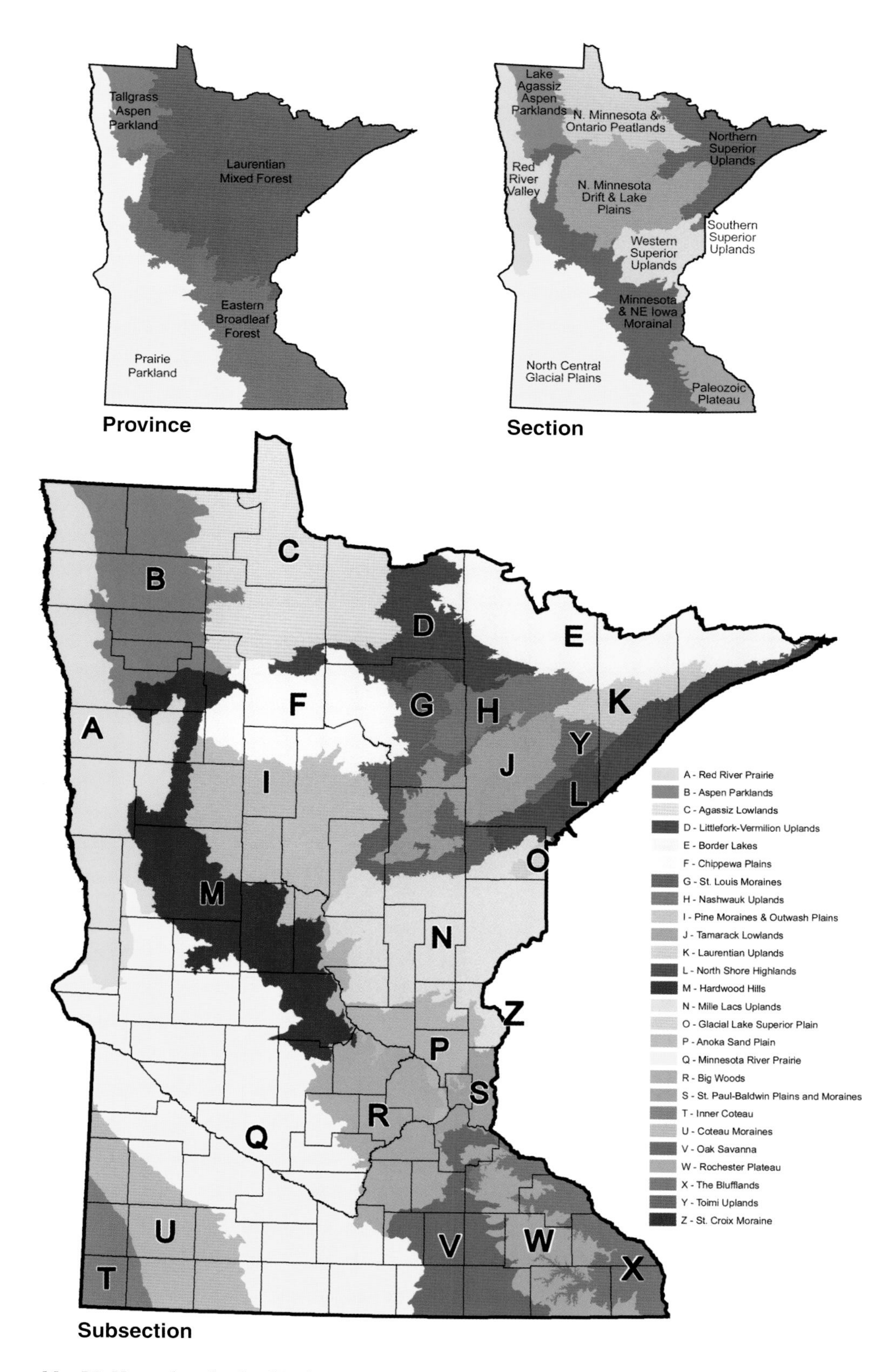

Map I.2. Upper three levels of Ecological Classification System (ECS) in Minnesota

From an orchid's point of view, the most important difference between one peatland and another is the degree of acidity, referred to as the pH, which is measured on a scale of 1 to 14. A pH of 7 is neutral. Anything below 7 is acidic, and anything above 7 is alkaline. Ecologists sometimes use the term *circumneutral* for conditions where the pH is between 5.5 and 7.5. In Minnesota, it is primarily the presence of calcium in the soil that raises the pH above neutral and into the alkaline end of the range, so alkaline soils are often called *calcareous*.

Most Minnesota plants, including orchids, grow in the pH range of approximately 4 to 8. The great bulk of Minnesota orchids occupy a narrower range, perhaps 6 to 7, which is weakly acidic but within the circumneutral range.

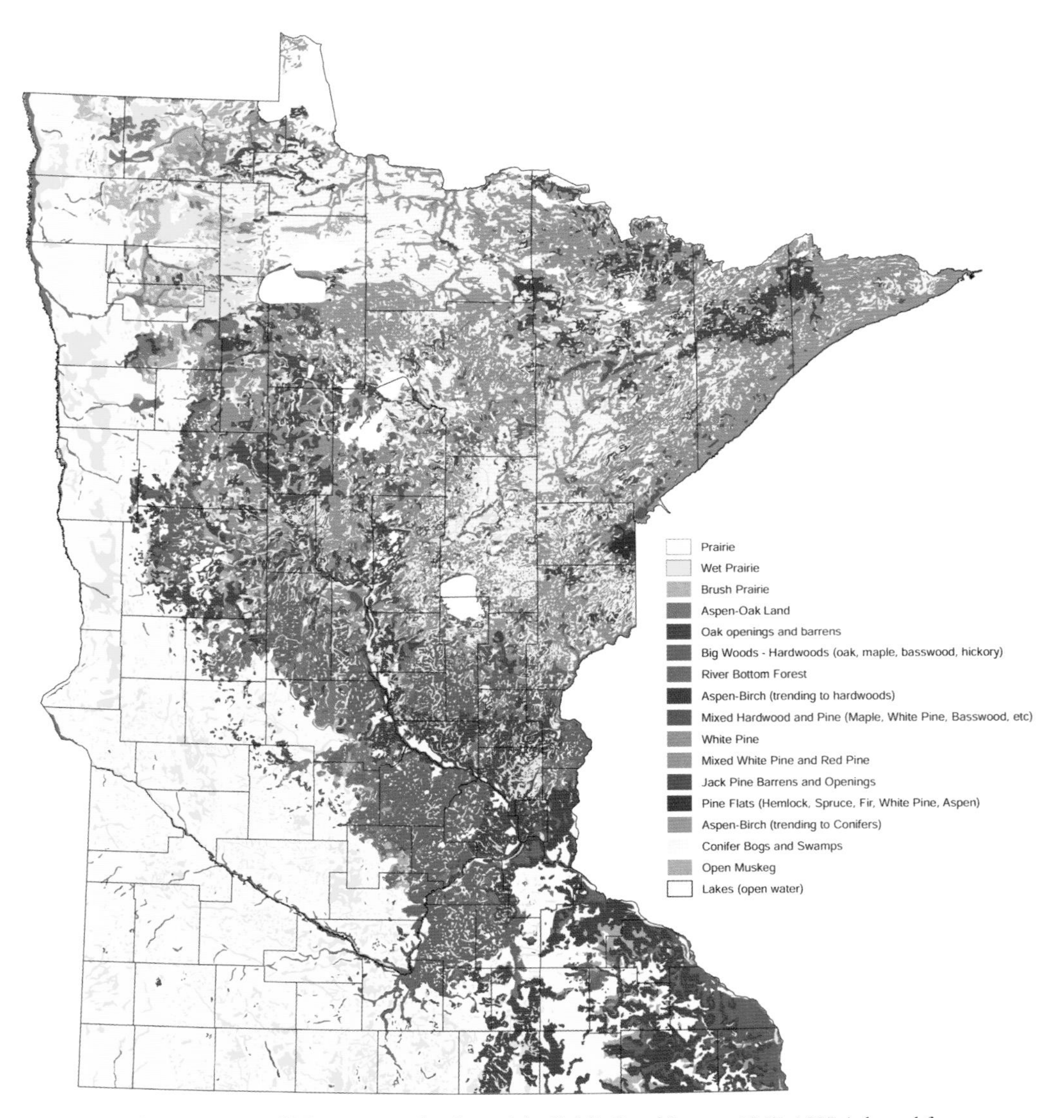

Map I.3. The vegetation of Minnesota at the time of the Public Land Survey, 1847–1907 (adapted from Marschner 1974)

Key to the Genera of Orchids Found in Minnesota

1. Leaves present only at the base of the stem, or leaves absent at flowering time, the stem bearing at most only small vestigial leaves.

2. Leaf 1 per stem or leaves absent.

3. Leaves entirely absent, or at least withered and dying by the time the flowers appear.

4. Flowers uniformly white, spirally arranged in a dense spike.

. . . . ***Spiranthes magnicamporum***

4. Flowers variously colored but not uniformly white, not in an obvious spiral or a dense spike.

5. Flower 1 per stem, flower at least 2 cm long, floral lip with a crest of fleshy yellow bristles.

. . . . ***Arethusa bulbosa***

5. Flowers 2 or more per stem (usually several), flower less than 2 cm long, floral lip without a crest.

6. Stem and a single leaf arising independently from a globular corm (the leaf may be withered by the time the flowers appear).

. . . . ***Aplectrum hyemale***

6. Stem arising from a much-branched coralloid rhizome; leaves entirely absent.

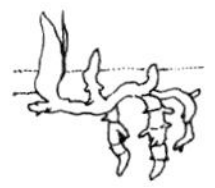

. . . . ***Corallorhiza***

3. Leaf present at flowering time, not withered or dying.

7. Floral lip producing a distinct spur at its base (5–7 mm long).

8. Flowers white with purplish markings, lip 3-lobed; leaf elliptic (widest at the middle).

. . . . ***Amerorchis rotundifolia***

8. Flowers white or greenish white, without markings, lip not lobed; leaf obovate (widest above the middle).

. . . . ***Platanthera obtusata***

7. Floral lip without a spur.

9. Flower 1 per stem; leaf ovate, not more than 3× longer than wide.

. . . . . . ***Calypso bulbosa*** **var.** ***americana***

9. Flowers 2 or more per stem; leaf linear and grass-like, at least 6× longer than wide.

. . . . ***Calopogon***

2. Leaves 2 or more per stem.

10. Floral lip formed into an inflated pouch or "slipper" 3.3–6 cm long.

. . . . ***Cypripedium acaule***

10. Floral lip not an inflated pouch and less than 2 cm long.

11. Floral lip producing a distinct spur at its base (at least 5 mm long).

12. Sepals and petals greenish, yellowish, or whitish, wide-spreading; stems 20–60 cm long; lip no more than 5 mm wide; inflorescence usually more than 8 cm long and consisting of more than 10 flowers.

. . . . ***Platanthera*** (in part)

12. Sepals and petals purple, converging to form a hood that arches over the flower; stem 8–25 cm long; lip at least 6.5 mm wide; inflorescence less than 8 cm long and with fewer than 10 flowers.

. . . . ***Galearis spectabilis***

11. Lip without a spur.

13. Flowers uniformly white; stem arising from a horizontal rhizome or a cluster of stout, fleshy roots.

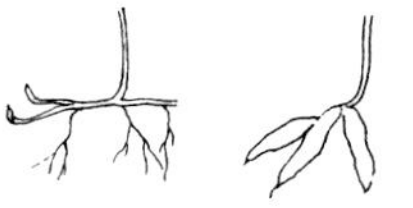

14. Floral lip in the shape of a sac; stem arising from a creeping horizontal rhizome, densely hairy; flowers not in a noticeable spiral arrangement; leaves green with white reticulation.

. . . . ***Goodyera***

14. Lip more or less flat with wavy margins, not in the shape of a sac; stem arising from a cluster of stout, fleshy roots, hairless or hairy only on the upper half; flowers in a spiral arrangement; leaves uniformly green.

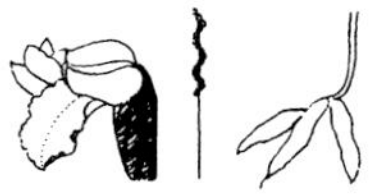

. . . . ***Spiranthes***

13. Flowers greenish or purplish; stem arising from a pseudobulb.

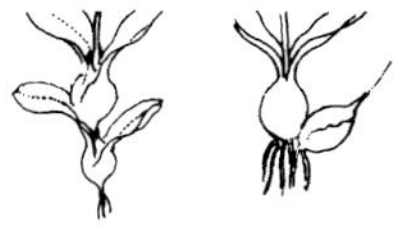

15. Flowers minute, the flower never more than 3 mm long; leaves 2–5 per stem, less than 2 cm long; floral lip widest below the middle.

. . . . ***Malaxis paludosa***

15. Flowers relatively small but not minute, the flower at least 4 mm long; leaves 2 per stem, more than 3 cm long; floral lip widest above the middle.

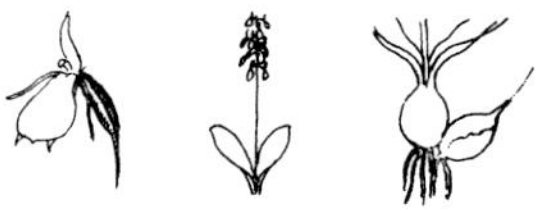

. . . . ***Liparis***

1. Leaves present and not confined to the base of the stem, the stem with 1 or more fully developed leaves clearly attached above the base.

16. Leaves 1 or 2 per stem; if 2, then opposite each other.

17. Floral lip with a distinct spur at base (about 1 cm long).
. . . . *Platanthera clavellata* 

17. Floral lip without a spur.

18. Leaves 2, opposite.
. . . . *Listera* 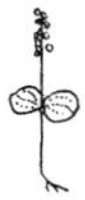

18. Leaf 1.

19. Flowers several per stem, greenish or whitish, minute, each flower less than 3 mm long.
. . . . *Malaxis* 

19. Flower 1 (rarely 2) per stem, pink to purple, more than 1 cm long. 
. . . . *Pogonia ophioglossoides*

16. Leaves 3 or more per stem, alternate.

20. Flowers 1 or 2 per stem; floral lip formed into an inflated pouch or "slipper"; spur absent.
. . . . *Cypripedium* 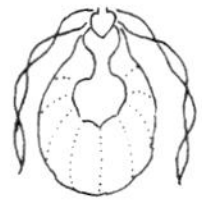

20. Flowers more than 2 per stem; lip not an inflated pouch; spur present at base of lip, or absent in *Epipactis*.

21. Floral spur absent; lip constricted at the middle into 2 parts, the basal part bowl-shaped, the distal part flat.

. . . . ***Epipactis helleborine***

21. Floral spur present; lip not bowl-shaped at base.

22. Floral bracts 2–3× longer than the flowers they subtend (including ovary and pedicel); spur pouch-shaped, less than 3 mm long; tip of the lip with 2 forward-pointing teeth.

. . . . ***Coeloglossum viride***

22. Floral bracts usually less than twice as long as the flowers; spur elongate, more than 3 mm long; tip of lip without 2 forward-pointing teeth. . . . . ***Platanthera***

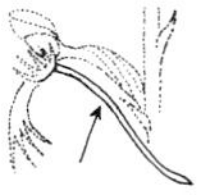

Genera and Species Accounts

Genus *Amerorchis* Hultén

The genus *Amerorchis*, as defined by Hultén (1968), consists of a single species endemic to arctic and boreal regions of North America. It is a woodland orchid that grows from a slender, fleshy rhizome and has a single basal leaf with an inconspicuous petiole. The lip of the flower is deeply three-lobed and has a spur at the base.

It was previously included in the large and often ill-defined genus *Orchis*, but it lacks the tubers of that genus. In fact, the name *Amerorchis* distinguishes it as an American version of the Old World genus *Orchis*. More recently, it has been proposed that *Amerorchis* be incorporated into the existing genus *Galearis* on the basis of evidence derived from nuclear ribosomal internal transcribed spacer (ITS) sequences (Bateman et al. 2009).

Amerorchis rotundifolia

Amerorchis rotundifolia (Banks ex Pursh) Hultén
Round-leaved orchid

[*Orchis rotundifolia* Banks ex Pursh; *Galearis rotundifolia* (Banks ex Pursh) R. M. Bateman]

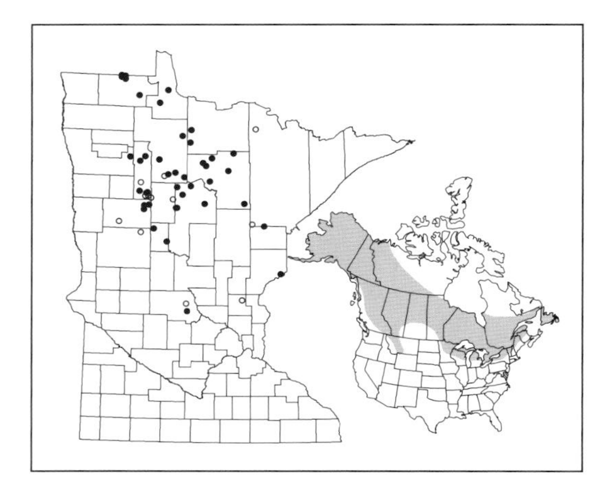

Plants 15–36 cm tall; **stem** leafless above the base, green; **rhizome** slender, fleshy, 2–5 cm long; **roots** 2–4, slender, fleshy, to 15 cm long. **Leaf** 1, essentially basal, broadly to narrowly elliptic, obtuse or blunt-tipped, 5–15 cm long, 2–8.5 cm wide. **Inflorescence** a terminal raceme usually less than 6 cm long, with 4–18 flowers all facing ± the same direction, each flower subtended by a lanceolate bract 4–20 mm long. **Flowers** showy and somewhat conspicuous although not large; **sepals** white to pale pink, ovate, 5–8 mm long; **petals** whitish to pink or purplish, ovate, 4.5–7 mm long, converging with dorsal sepal to form a vague hood over the column; **lip** typically white with purple spots, 3-lobed, 6.5–10 mm long, 4–7.5 mm wide across the lateral lobes, the terminal lobe notched; **spur** about 5 mm long. **Capsules** erect, 1.2–2 cm long. **Flowering** June 5–July 11, mostly the last 2 weeks of June.

White flowers with purple markings appear from about June 5 through July 11 (photograph by Donald Marier).

The first impression of *Amerorchis rotundifolia* is that of a slender naked stem ending with a cluster of small white flowers, each with pink or purple markings. Examined closely, the flowers reveal a distinctive shape. The lip and lateral sepals appear outstretched, while the petals and dorsal sepal converge overhead to form a loose canopy that appears to shelter the "working" parts of the flower.

The single leaf comes from the base of the plant and is present every year, even in years when flowers are not produced, so you will see leaves that have no accompanying flowers. Contrary to the name, the leaf is never actually round.

Each year, *A. rotundifolia* sends off a slender, fleshy rhizome (offshoot) from the base of the stem, which is buried in the moss. The rhizome produces a new stem that angles upward until it reaches the surface of the moss 1 to 4 centimeters from the parent stem. There it waits until the next spring, when it will resume growth

Amerorchis rotundifolia ***A***—Whole plant in flower, ***B***—Portion of the inflorescence, ***C***—Typical flower, exploded view

The typical habitat is a lush carpet of moss in a rich conifer swamp (June 8, Beltrami County).

and produce a leaf, two to four slender fleshy roots, and perhaps flowers. The place on the rhizome where the old stem occurred does not produce a stem or roots again. In fact, that portion of the rhizome will live only about one more year, maybe two, so at any given time there is no part of the plant that is more than two or three years old.

The typical habitat of *A. rotundifolia* in Minnesota is what ecologists call rich conifer swamps. These are permanent wetlands dominated by conifer trees with a substrate of deep, actively forming peat overlain with a carpet of moss. The most abundant tree is usually northern white cedar, with balsam fir, black spruce, and tamarack mixed in.

The water table is usually at the surface of the peat. The mosses, which often form hummocks over tree roots and fallen branches, are just above the water table. The hollows between the hummocks may dip a few inches below the water table.

The moss hummocks are where *A. rotundifolia* is usually found. There will also be scattered clumps of fine-leaved sedges such as *Carex leptalea* and *Carex disperma*. Ferns will be common but not abundant, and there will be a meager component of shrubs such as Labrador tea, alder-leaved buckthorn, red-osier dogwood, or speckled alder. This is the classic orchid "bog" that photographers often seek, so expect to find a number of orchids, in particular

Platanthera obtusata (bluntleaved rein-orchid), *Listera cordata* (heart-leaved twayblade), *Corallorhiza trifida* (early coral-root), and a *Cypripedium* (lady's-slipper) or two.

These conifer swamps are stable communities where fires and floods are rare events. Windstorms are another matter. Anyone who has walked through such a forest knows wet peat doesn't hold tree roots well in a windstorm, a fact given testimony by tree trunks leaning in odd directions or fallen in dense tangles. Surprisingly, "tipped" trees usually survive and continue to grow, adding to the jungle-like feel of these special places.

This type of habitat, or some regional variation, is widespread in northern Minnesota. Yet for some reason *A. rotundifolia* has been found only in the north-central and northwestern counties. It has yet to be found in similar-looking habitats in the northeast, in spite of careful looking.

Plants stand about 6–14 inches (15–36 cm) and have one leaf and four to eighteen flowers (June 9, photograph by Peter Dziuk).

The horizontal structure is the rhizome; the short white structure angling upward is the beginning of a new stem; the two long structures are the roots (July 8).

Genus *Aplectrum* Nutt.

The name *Aplectrum* is from the Greek word meaning "without spur" in reference to the flower. This is a small genus with just two species, one in Japan and one in eastern North America. It is closely related to the genus *Corallorhiza*, but the aerial stem arises from a roundish corm instead of a coralloid rhizome. Actually, the corm stage of *Aplectrum* is sometimes, perhaps routinely, preceded by a coralloid mass resembling the rhizome of *Corallorhiza* (Correll 1950). Remnants of this coralloid stage are rarely if ever seen in mature plants. *Aplectrum* is otherwise distinguished from *Corallorhiza* by the solitary green leaf that appears in the fall and withers the following spring.

At any given time, an individual *Aplectrum* will have two corms side by side, related to each other as parent and offspring, connected by a short rhizome. The offspring corm produces the leaf in the fall and the inflorescence the following spring, during which time the parent corm shrivels and disappears. During the summer, when nothing much seems to be happening, the offspring corm becomes the parent by producing a new corm to renew the cycle (Stevens and Dill 1942). The leaf and the flowers appear to lead independent lives.

Aplectrum hyemale

Aplectrum hyemale (Muhl. ex Willd.) Nutt.

Putty-root

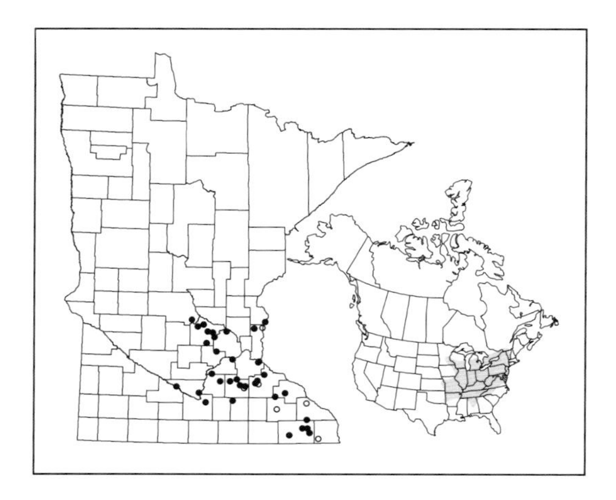

Plants 25–50 cm tall; **stem** leafless, green with pale sheaths loosely enveloping the lower portion; **corm** globular, 2–3 cm across; **roots** coarse and fibrous, several in a cluster at the base of the corm. **Leaf** 1, gray-green with whitish veins, emerging directly from the corm in autumn, persisting through winter, and withering as the plant approaches anthesis the following spring; petiole 3.5–10 cm long; blade elliptic, 8–15 cm long, 2–7 cm wide. **Inflorescence** a terminal raceme 4–12 cm long, consisting of 6–18 flowers, each flower subtended by a lanceolate bract 2–7 mm long. **Flowers** not small, but inconspicuously colored; **sepals** yellowish or greenish, tinged with purple-brown toward the tip, oblanceolate to oblong-spatulate, 9–12 mm long; **petals** similar to sepals but somewhat smaller; **lip** whitish with purple markings, obovate, 7.5–11 mm long, 5.5–8 mm wide, 3-lobed, the middle lobe scalloped on the apical margin; **spur** absent. **Capsule** pendent, 2–2.5 cm long. **Flowering** May 25–June 16.

Each plant produces only one leaf; it appears in the fall independent of the stem (October 30).

The flowers of *Aplectrum hyemale* are mostly pale yellow or yellowish green with purple-brown tips. The lip of the flower is white with purple markings, but it is largely concealed by the petals and sepals. The flowers only appear in dense shade and are very well camouflaged, at least to the eyes of people. To the eyes of the bees that pollinate them they must stand out like beacons since nearly every flower gets pollinated (Hogan 1983). The large seed capsules are usually easier to see than the flowers, and they will remain on the upright stem for a full year.

The leaves of *Aplectrum hyemale* are always more abundant and predictable than the flowers or seed capsules; look for them in the fall after the leaves are off the trees or in early spring soon after the snow melts, then return in early June to see the flowers.

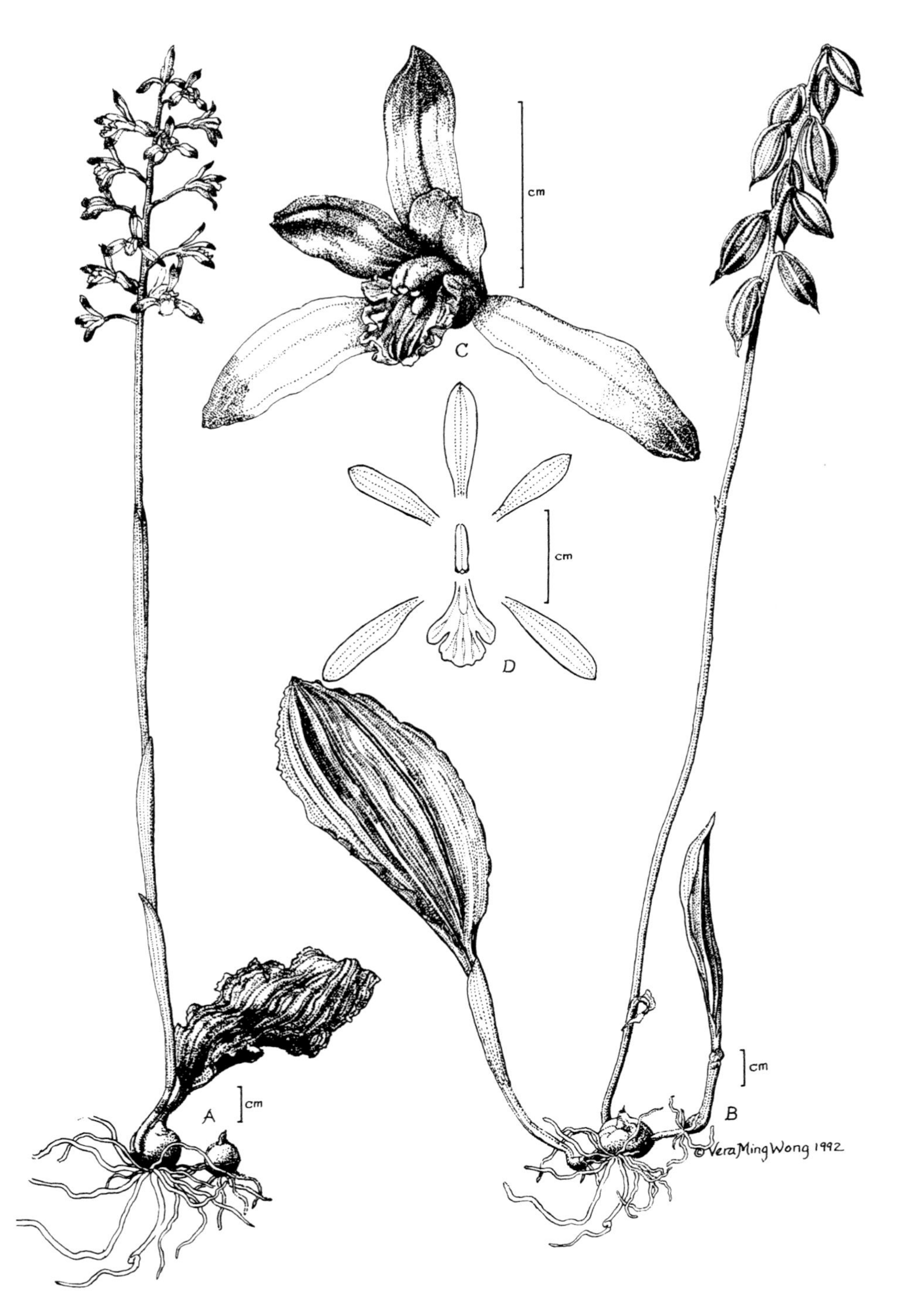

Aplectrum hyemale ***A***—Flowering plant with withered leaf from previous season, ***B***—Fruiting plant with leaf of current season, ***C***—Typical flower, ***D***—Typical flower, exploded view

The whole plant is about 10–20 inches (25–50 cm) tall and easily blends into the background (June 1).

A new corm is produced each year and the old one is discarded; the one on the right was formed the previous summer, the one on the left the year before (May 30).

Expect to find *A. hyemale* in deep shade under a continuous canopy of tall forest trees, particularly in what was historically known as the Big Woods. This was a large block of deciduous forest that at the time of Euro-American settlement covered several counties in southeastern Minnesota. This type of forest is typically dominated by only three tree species: sugar maple, basswood, and red oak, with lesser amounts of American elm, bitternut hickory, black cherry, and green ash. The ground layer is often sparse and consists mostly of shade-adapted seedlings of the canopy trees, a few shrubs, sedges, and forbs. The effects of drought are ameliorated by the fine-textured loamy soils that hold water very well and are kept cool by the dense canopy of trees. The soils have another important characteristic: since they developed from calcareous glacial till, they are alkaline, not acidic. It turns out that *A. hyemale* is one of the few Minnesota orchids that actually prefer (and may even require) alkaline soils.

Another key feature of the Big Woods is the deep shade cast by the dominant trees. Light intensity beneath a closed canopy of sugar maple may be just 0.1–2 percent of direct sunlight (MDNR 2005a), which is below the point at which most plants can make a net energy gain from photosynthesis (Auclair 1972). All the plants in this habitat have some strategy for coping with the darkness. The way *A. hyemale* deals with the shade is to outmaneuver it, which it does ingeniously. When the snow melts in the spring, it reveals still-functioning leaves of *A. hyemale* from the previous year, which immediately begin to perform photosynthesis, even at temperatures as low as 41 degrees F (5 degrees C) (Adams 1970).

The flowers are yellowish green with purple-brown tips; they appear from May 16 through June 16 (photograph by Peter Dziuk).

The pods will shed their seeds during the fall and winter (August 22).

Once the leaves of the canopy trees are fully grown, the leaf of *A. hyemale* becomes useless—too little light for photosynthesis—and it begins to fade. Then the flowers appear. The flowers don't need sunlight, only a pollinator. Since very little else is flowering in the woods in early June, *A. hyemale* gets the undivided attention of any pollinator flying about.

When autumn arrives and the leaves of the canopy trees fall, sunlight once again reaches the forest floor. This is when *A. hyemale* produces another leaf, which stays fresh and green through winter and the following spring. In effect, the season of the leaf is just opposite the season of the flower.

Genus *Arethusa* L.

This genus is named after the river nymph of classical Greek mythology and consists of a single species (*Arethusa bulbosa*) endemic to boreal and north-temperate parts of eastern North America. A similar species (*Eleorchis japonica*) that may belong in the same genus occurs in Japan.

Characteristics of *Arethusa* include an underground corm that produces one stem bearing a single grass-like leaf and a solitary spurless flower.

Arethusa bulbosa

Arethusa bulbosa L.
Dragon's-mouth

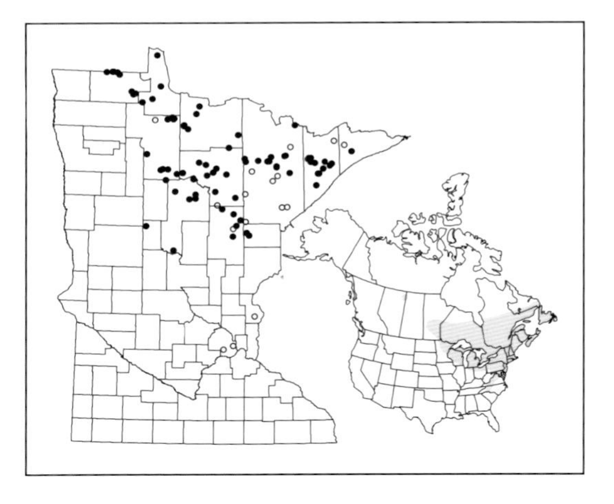

Plants 7–36 cm tall; **stem** arising from a bulbous corm; **roots** 2–4, slender, fleshy, 2–10 cm long. **Leaf** 1, linear-lanceolate, barely developed at anthesis, becoming as much as 18 cm long and 8 mm wide by late summer. **Inflorescence** consisting of a single flower subtended by 2 inconspicuous bracts 2–5 mm long. **Flower** erect, large and conspicuous, pink or rose purple; **sepals** linear-oblong to narrowly elliptic, ± erect, 2.5–4.5 cm long; **petals** similar to sepals but somewhat shorter and proportionately wider, converging to form a vague hood over the column; **lip** pink with rose-purple markings and a crest of fleshy yellow bristles, oblong, 2.6–3.8 cm long, 0.6–1.5 cm wide, curving downward near the middle, the margin of the downward-curving portion irregularly scalloped. **Capsule** erect, 2–3 cm long. **Flowering** May 23–July 23, peaking the second or third week of June.

Flowers are usually pink, sometimes rose-purple, and peak the second or third week of June.

Arethusa bulbosa is not easily confused with anything else. Look for a single brilliant pink flower standing erect at the top of a short naked stem. The single narrow leaf develops later, after the flower is gone.

The flower is designed for a single purpose—to attract an insect pollinator, specifically a large- or medium-size bee, more often than not a bumblebee queen (Stoutamire 1971; Thien and Marks 1972). Apparently bumblebee queens live only one year in Minnesota, so when they emerge in spring they are rather naïve about flowers, and *A. bulbosa* may be the first flower they encounter. The bee is enticed perhaps by a faint scent or a small amount of nectar, but primarily by the conspicuous yellow bristles on the lip that shine brightly in ultraviolet light, which is the wavelength of light bees see best. The bee will actually land on the bristles. Discovering there is no food there, it will take a moment to look around, then eventually crawl toward the back of the flower. After about a minute, it will try to back out of the flower, and in the process it will snag

Arethusa bulbosa ***A***—Whole plant in flower, ***B***—Fruiting plant showing elongated leaf, ***C***—Typical flower, ***D***—Typical flower, exploded view

The heart of the plant is the pea-size corm, which produces one stem and two roots each year (July 8).

a pollinium on the hairs of its back. At that moment it becomes the agent of *Arethusa*, delivering a pollinium to the next *Arethusa* flower it encounters (Thien and Marks 1972).

Although it is the flower that defines *Arethusa* for most people, the heart of the plant is actually a small, irregularly shaped corm, which is the swollen base of the underground portion of the stem. The corm is about 1 centimeter across (the size of a large pea), and lies concealed in the moss. It appears to survive at least two years. During that time it will produce one flowering stem and two fleshy roots each year. When the corm is exhausted, a new corm forms on the stem 2 to 4 centimeters above the old one, and the old one vanishes.

The primary habitat of *A. bulbosa* in Minnesota is nonforested peatlands that fall into the broad category of fen, particularly the rich fens and spring fens that are found in the northern forested region of the state. It does not occur in calcareous fens in the prairie region and certainly not in cattail marshes or hummocky sedge meadows. *Marshes* and *meadows* are terms

This is how the leaf looks when the flower appears in summer; it will grow much longer by fall (July 8).

usually given to wetlands that either flood too often or dry out too often to accumulate much peat, and they will have a completely different flora.

The term *rich* is often used to describe fens that are enriched by the lateral inflow of mineral-laden groundwater from nearby uplands or from groundwater seeping up from below. As a result, the water is only weakly acidic or sometimes nearly neutral (pH 5.6 to 7.0). This is in comparison to "poor" fens, which are isolated from groundwater and any source of inflow, so the water comes only from precipitation. Poor fens contain few mineral nutrients and are very acidic.

Rich fens invariably have a thick cover of mosses, typically *Sphagnum*, which may form a low, fluffy carpet. The habitat is usually too wet for trees to survive, or at least too wet for trees to reach any great height or density. Sedges will thrive here, as well as a few ferns and flowering plants, although it is clearly the mosses that dominate.

A single outsized flower sits atop a 3- to 14-inch (7–36 cm) stem.

Genus *Calopogon* R. Br.
Grass-pinks

Calopogon is a genus of five species endemic to North America, two in Minnesota, and is most closely related to the genus *Arethusa*. The name *Calopogon* is from a Greek word meaning "beautiful beard" in reference to the yellow-tipped bristles on the lip of the flower.

All *Calopogon* species share a similar pollination system, which is based on an elaborate deception (Pijl and Dodson 1966; Thien and Marcks 1972; Stoutamire 1971). It begins when a bee senses the yellow-tipped bristles that are prominently displayed on the upright lip of the flower. Thinking it has found an offering of pollen, the bee lands and attempts, without success, to gather pollen from the bristles. The bristles are only a decoy; they produce no pollen or nectar. The flower does produce pollen, but it is hidden away. If the bee is of suitable size (mainly a *Bombus* or *Megachile* bee), its weight causes the lip, which is hinged at its base, to fall. This drops the bee backward onto the column where the real pollen is hidden. The pollen, in compact packets called *pollinia*, adheres to the back of the bee where the bee cannot reach it. The frustrated bee crawls out and flies away to try another flower, carrying the pollinia on its back. The entire sequence happens within four seconds (Thien and Marcks 1972). The hinged lip quickly springs back to its former position, ready to receive another insect visitor. The bee, determined to get pollen, but having not learned its lesson, flies to another *Calopogon* flower and repeats the process. This time the pollinia carried from the first flower is deposited on the stigma of the second flower.

A Key to the *Calopogon* of Minnesota

1. Lip widened at the end to form the shape of an anvil in outline, the widened portion usually wider than long; stigma positioned perpendicular to the column surface; the single leaf significantly shorter than the inflorescence; corm spherical to ovoid. . . . . ***C. tuberosus***

1. Lip widened at the end to form the shape of a triangle, the widened portion usually narrower than long; stigma typically flat against the column; the tip of the leaf often reaching the inflorescence; corm irregularly shaped, usually with a rounded bulge on one side. ***C. oklahomensis***

Calopogon oklahomensis D. H. Goldman
Oklahoma grass-pink

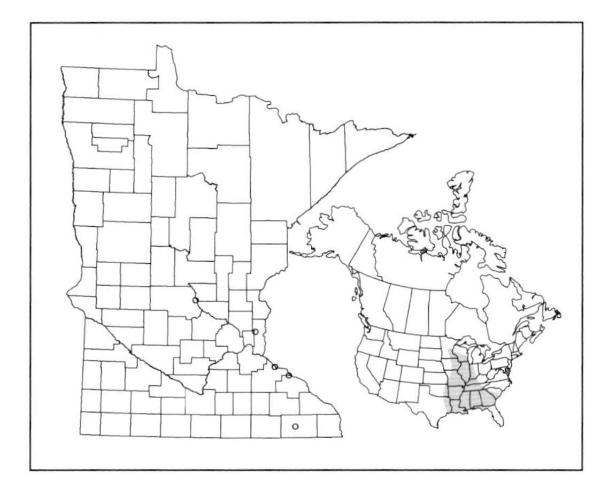

Plants 11–35 cm tall; stem arising from an irregularly elongated corm up to 2.9 cm long; roots few to several, fleshy. **Leaf** 1, attached near the base of the stem, linear-lanceolate and grasslike, 7–35 cm long, 5–15 mm wide, slightly shorter to slightly longer than the inflorescence. **Inflorescence** a terminal raceme with 2 to 7 (11) flowers, each flower subtended by an ovate-lanceolate bract 3–8 mm long. **Flowers** pink to purple or rarely white, fragrant and conspicuous; **sepals** ovate to obovate or elliptic, 1.4–2.5 cm long; **petals** oblong to obpandurate, 1.1–2 cm long; **lip** uppermost of the floral parts (flowers not resupinate) and standing ± erect, 1–1.7 cm long, 0.5–1.2 cm wide, widened at the tip to form a triangular-shaped apex that is usually narrower than long, bearded on ventral surface with yellow-tipped bristles; **column** incurved, winged at apex, 0.9–1.3 cm long; **stigma** semiorbicular, 2–3 mm across, positioned flat against the column surface. **Capsules** erect, up to about 2 cm long. **Flowering** (estimated) June 1–July 15.

The floral lip is at the top of the flower; it displays yellow bristles to attract a pollinator (photograph by Douglas Goldman).

The two species of *Calopogon* that have been found in Minnesota look very much alike. To tell them apart, Goldman (1995) emphasizes the shape of the floral lip. This is the structure at the top of the flower that stands straight up and has a beard of yellow-tipped bristles. Goldman compares the lip of *C. tuberosus* to the outline of an anvil in profile, meaning it has a broad flat top with sides that curve inward to the base. In contrast, the lip of *C. oklahomensis* is described as a triangle where the top is perhaps not so broad and the sides have a straight taper to the base. Both species have a single, slender, grasslike leaf. In *C. oklahomensis* the tip of the leaf often reaches the inflorescence. In *C. tuberosus* the leaf is significantly shorter than the inflorescence. In any case, positive identification is not easy and may require confirmation by a specialist.

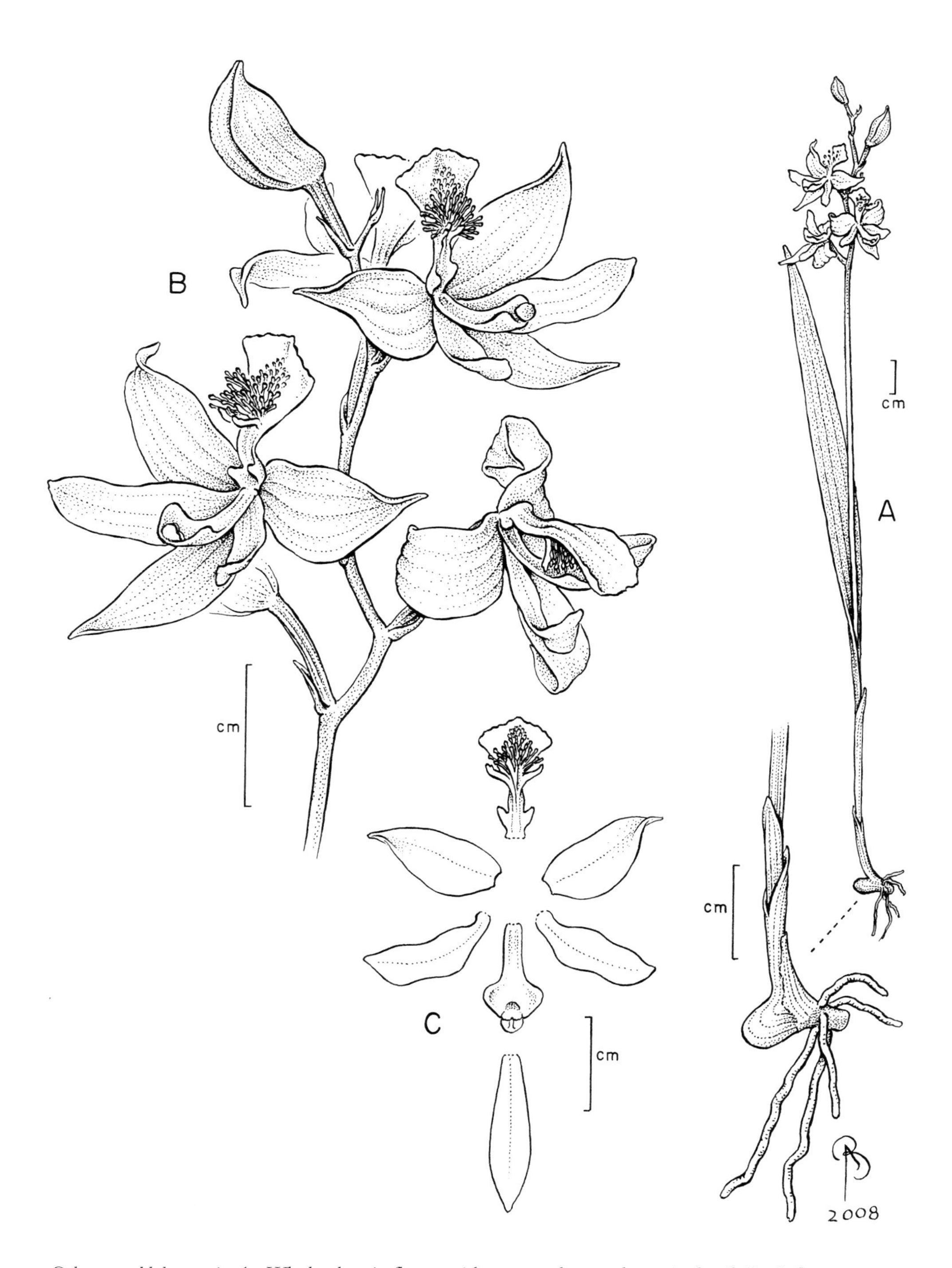

Calopogon oklahomensis ***A***—Whole plant in flower with corm and roots shown in detail, ***B***—Inflorescence, ***C***—Typical flower, exploded view

There is a very good chance that any *Calopogon* found in an upland habitat in the southern third of Minnesota could be *C. oklahomensis*. The most likely habitats would be mesic prairies, dry prairie hillsides, or openings in oak woodlands. Soils would likely be acidic, and might range from sandy to loamy (Goldman et al. 2002; Goldman 1995). The habitat would be very different from the swamp or fen habitat of *C. tuberosus*, and it is almost certain that the two species would not be found growing together in the same place.

The reason there is so much uncertainty about this orchid is because it was not recognized as a distinct species until 1994 (Goldman 1995). Initially it was thought to be restricted to the south-central states, hence its name. But the process of science led to a closer examination of all the *Calopogon* herbarium specimens from a wider area, including Minnesota, to see if any of them might be misidentified specimens of *C. oklahomensis*. In an example of how botanists do their work and the value of herbarium specimens, it was discovered that among the more than seventy-five specimens of *Calopogon* that had been collected in Minnesota over the past 150 years, there were five good candidates for *C. oklahomensis*.

All of the Minnesota candidates had been collected from prairies in the southeastern part of the state, as might be expected, but none more recently than 1884. Everything seems to fit, yet it has been very difficult to get positive identifications of the candidate specimens, and some small doubt remains.

Attempts to rediscover this species in Minnesota have so far failed. It is quite possible, perhaps even likely, that the last prairie habitat of this orchid in Minnesota has been plowed under. In fact, as of 2010, there were only two places in the Upper Midwest where *C. oklahomensis* could still be found: one site in Dane County, Wisconsin, and one site in Will County, Illinois. It is more common farther south but becoming more rare there, too (Goldman, personal communication, 2010).

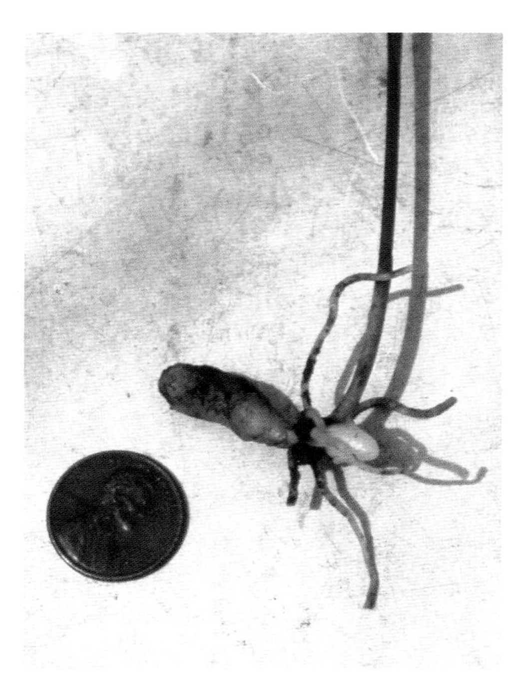

The stem and roots are produced by an elongate corm that is renewed each year (photograph by Douglas Goldman).

The habitat is a dry woodland or prairie, not a bog or swamp (photograph by Douglas Goldman).

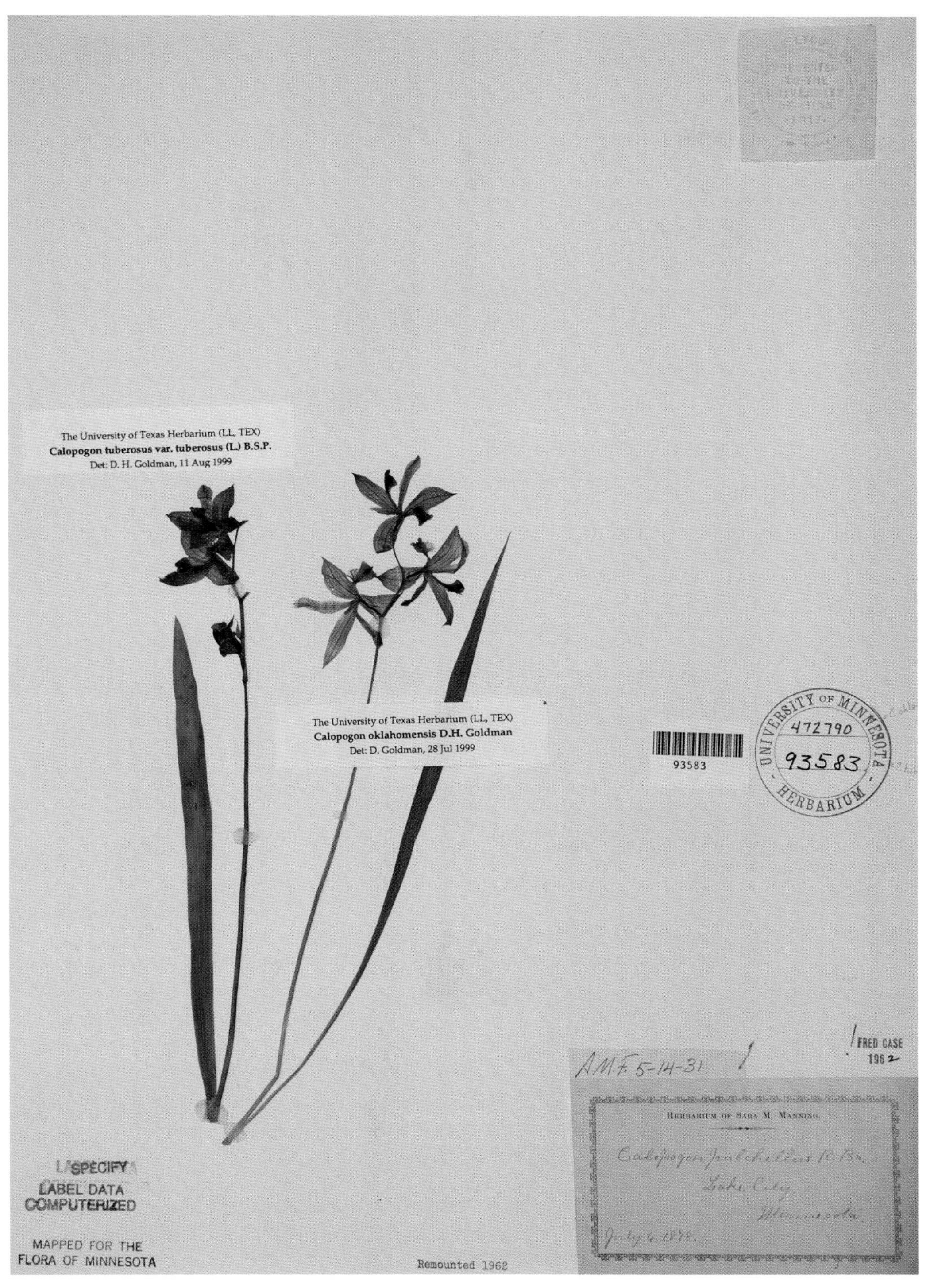

The plant on the right is *C. oklahomensis*, and the one on the left is *C. tuberosus*; the label reads "Lake City, Minnesota, 1878." Photograph courtesy of the J. F. Bell Museum of Natural History, University of Minnesota.

Calopogon tuberosus (L.) BSP. var. *tuberosus*
Tuberous grass-pink

[*Calopogon pulchellus* (Salisb.) R. Br.]

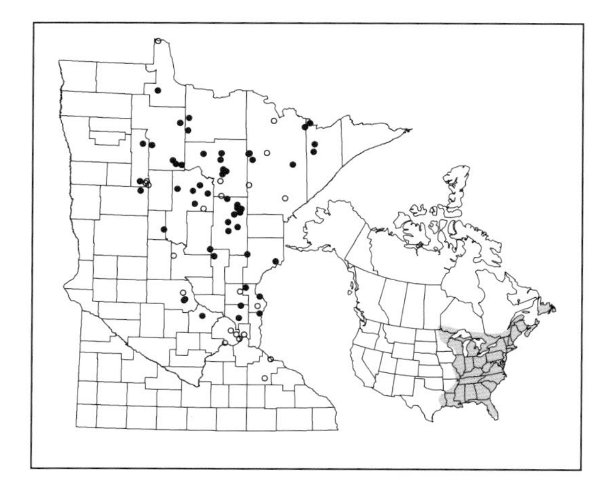

Plants 19–55 cm tall; **stem** arising from a spherical, ovoid, or oblong corm up to about 3 cm long; **roots** few to several, fleshy, 3–10 cm long. **Leaf** 1, sessile, attached on the lower third of the stem, linear and grass-like, 8–35 cm long, 0.2–1.6 cm wide, significantly shorter than the inflorescence. **Inflorescence** a terminal raceme with 2–12 flowers, each flower subtended by an ovate-lanceolate bract 4–8 mm long. **Flowers** conspicuous, pink to purple or rarely white, faintly or not at all fragrant; **sepals** ovate to oblong or elliptic, 1.2–2.4 cm long; **petals** oblong or oblong-elliptic, 1.3–2.4 cm long; **lip** uppermost of the floral parts (flower not resupinate) and standing ± erect, 1.1–2 cm long, 0.6–1.4 cm wide, the tip widened to form an anvil-shaped apex that is usually wider than long, ventral surface bearded with yellow-tipped bristles; **column** incurved, winged at apex, 1.1–1.7 cm long; **stigma** most often perpendicular to the column surface. **Capsule** erect, 1.2–2 cm long. **Flowering** June 18–August 3, peaking in the first 2 weeks of July.

The whole plant will be 7–22 inches (19–55 cm) tall and have a single, grasslike leaf (photograph by Richard Haug).

There are three brightly colored orchids found in open fens in Minnesota: *Pogonia ophioglossoides*, *Arethusa bulbosa*, and *Calopogon tuberosus*. All three species might be found growing together, but they are not hard to tell apart.

Be aware there are two species of *Calopogon* in Minnesota, a northern fen species (*C. tuberosus*) and a very rare southern prairie species (*C. oklahomensis*). They can be difficult to tell apart, but the southern prairie species is so rare it may never be encountered. If you do find a *Calopogon* in a grassland or prairie habitat in southern Minnesota, by all means suspect *C. oklahomensis*. If you think it is a good candidate, contact a specialist.

All habitats of *C. tuberosus* are acidic or circumneutral wetlands of the type called rich fens. There are alkaline fens, called calcareous fens, which occur primarily in the prairie region of the state, but *C. tuberosus* does not occur there. Rich fens include the floating peat mats that sometimes develop at

Calopogon tuberosus ***A***—Whole plant in flower, ***B***—Inflorescence, ***C***—Typical flower, exploded view

Open fen surrounding a small pond in Aitkin County—perfect habitat for *C. tuberosus*

the edge of a pond or a small lake. They are usually carpeted in a thick and continuous layer of *Sphagnum* mosses and feather mosses. This is also the habitat of insectivorous plants like the purple pitcherplant, several species of sundew, and the bladderworts. These tend to be very unstable habitats of the type that makes a person have second thoughts about crossing on foot. It may be too wet or unstable for trees, or there may be scattered, stunted conifers such as black spruce, tamarack, or less often northern white cedar.

The corm is an annual ovoid structure that produces the roots and the stem (July 16).

Not all *C. tuberosus* habitats are floating mats. Good habitats can also be found in small, peat-filled basins and in larger peatlands that develop along linear drainage features. In all cases, the water within the peat will be moderately acidic to circumneutral, with a pH of perhaps 5.5 to 6.5, which is, in part, what makes these fens and not bogs. Bogs, as defined by ecologists, are more strongly acidic. They have a pH of 3.8 to 5.5 and are practically devoid of mineral nutrients.

As far as orchid habitat goes, bogs and fens are totally different. A bog is a very harsh environment for orchids, for all plants in fact. Fens, on the other hand, are very hospitable places and sometimes seem overrun with orchids. Both bogs and fens are common throughout northern Minnesota and are typically found juxtaposed in large peatland complexes where one often grades imperceptibly into the other, although perhaps not imperceptibly to orchids.

The roots of *C. tuberosus* are usually confined to the living moss that grows on top of the peat and are sustained by water wicked upward between the closely packed stems of the moss. This is where the seasonal growth cycle of *C. tuberosus* begins each spring. It starts with a corm, a small roundish structure about the size of a bean. The corm was formed the year before at a point on the stem just above the previous corm—it is created anew each year. Other than the seeds, the corm is the only part of the orchid that survives the winter.

The lip is the "bearded" structure at the top of the flower and is a beacon for pollinators (July 16).

Genus *Calypso* Salisb.

The name *Calypso* honors the mythical sea nymph of Homer's *Odyssey* and means "hiding" or "concealment." It is a distinctive genus, containing a single circumboreal species with a complicated taxonomy.

The intricate flower of *Calypso* produces no nectar and has no scent; the attraction for pollinators is purely visual. In Minnesota, the spring flowering period is synchronized with the emergence of its pollinators, large bumblebee queens. The queens forage close to the ground and encounter *Calypso* flowers head-on. Newly emerged bumblebees are naïve and will investigate anything that seems to offer food, either pollen or nectar. Individual bees rapidly learn to avoid these flowers, although not before a substantial percentage of the flowers are successfully pollinated (Boyden 1982).

Calypso is sometimes considered one of the "slipper orchids" along with the species of *Cypripedium*, but the two genera are not closely related. *Cypripediums* have two fertile anthers, *Calypso* only one—this is a big deal among orchids. Also, the slipper of *Calypso* does not function the same way as the slipper of a *Cypripedium*, which entices an insect pollinator into a large opening, then forces it to pass out of a smaller opening in order to accomplish pollination. The slipper of *Calypso* has only one opening. The pollinator pushes itself into the slipper looking for nectar or pollen, then must back out the same way it entered. In the process, it encounters the single anther where it picks up the pollinia on the dorsal surface of its thorax (Ackerman 1981; Mosquin 1970; Stoutamire 1971).

The structure most people will never see is the corm, which is buried belowground. During the course of a year, it will produce precisely one flower, one leaf, two roots, and finally a replacement corm for the following year. Although only the youngest corm is active, there may be a succession of one to three corms from previous years still attached. On rare occasions a corm will produce two replacement corms, which could lead to two individual plants (Mousley 1925). But vegetative reproduction of this sort is uncommon and probably does not play a major role in the population dynamics of *Calypso*.

Calypso bulbosa

***Calypso bulbosa* (L.) Oakes var. *americana* (R. Br.) Luer**
Fairy-slipper

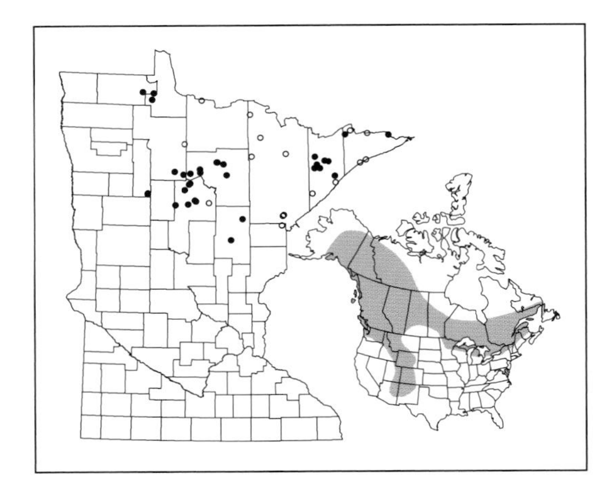

Plants 6–21 cm tall; **stem** leafless, arising from an ellipsoid or ovoid corm about 2 cm long; **roots** 2 per corm, fleshy, descending, 4–10 cm long. **Leaf** 1, arising directly from the corm, overwintering then withering in spring; petiole 1–5 cm long; blade ovate, 3–6 cm long, 1.7–4 cm wide. **Inflorescence** a single nodding flower subtended by a lanceolate bract 8–15 mm long. **Flower** pink or magenta, rarely white, small but relatively conspicuous; **sepals** and **petals** similar, spreading, purplish to pink, linear-lanceolate, 1.3–2.2 cm long; **lip** white to pink, streaked with purple, 1.4–2.2 cm long, 6–11 mm wide, slipper-shaped, the margin expanded forward to form a whitish apron with a crest of yellow bristles, the apron concealing 2 small forward-projecting "horns"; **column** petal-like, suborbicular, more or less covering the opening of the "slipper." **Capsule** erect, 2.5–3 cm long. **Flowering** May 18–June 22, usually the last week in May or first week in June.

There are three varieties of *Calypso bulbosa*, each distinguished by fine details of the flower (Sheviak and Catling 2002b). Europe and Asia have var. *bulbosa*. North America has var. *occidentalis* and var. *americana*. Only var. *americana* occurs in Minnesota.

Calypso bulbosa var. *americana* is a small plant, smaller than people expect, but it is not difficult to spot or difficult to identify. From above, all that is seen are the violet-colored

Each plant produces a single leaf in the summer; it overwinters, then dies back in late spring (May 28).

This is the view that entices a bumblebee queen to enter in search of food (photograph by Donald Marier).

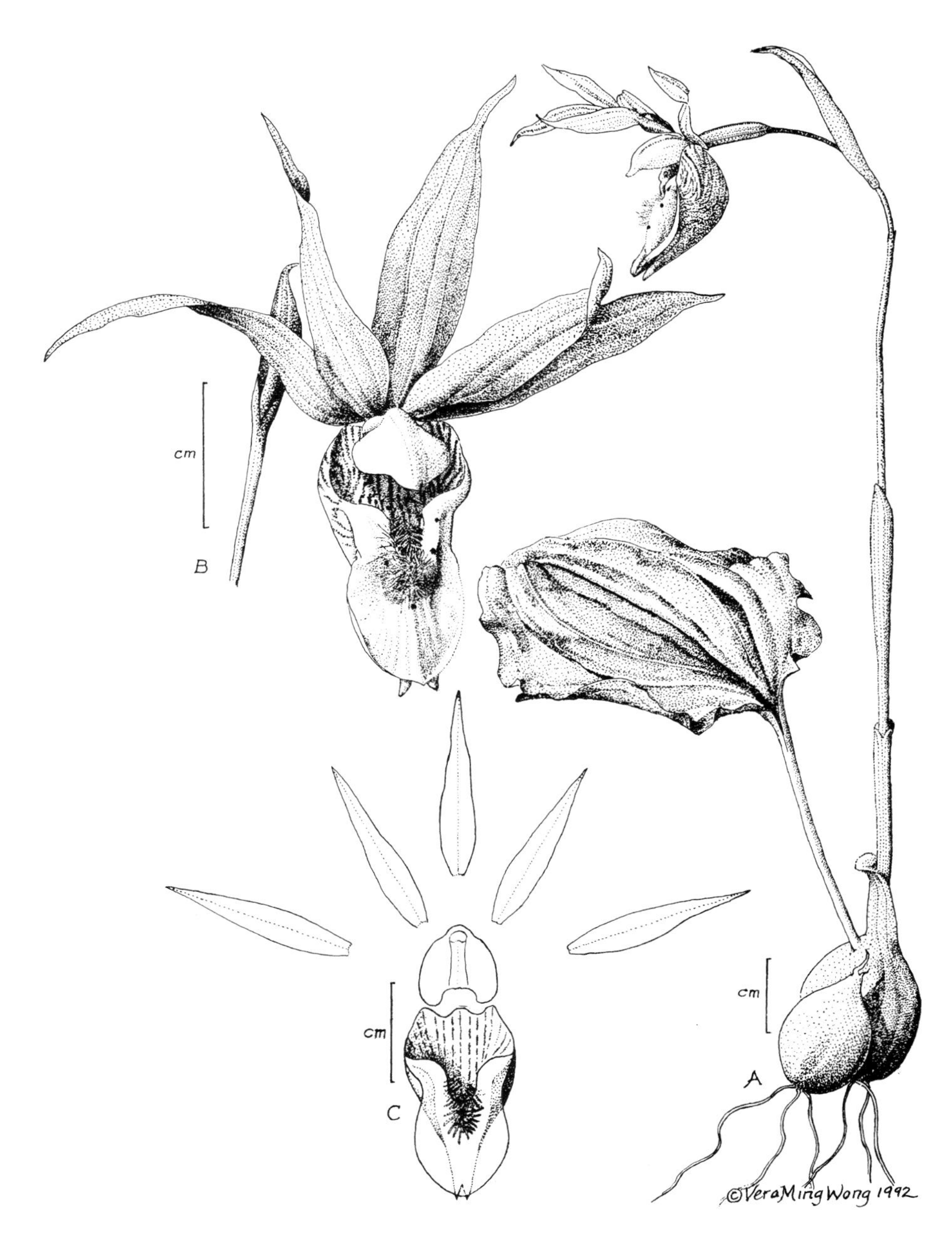

Calypso bulbosa var. *americana* ***A***—Whole plant in flower, ***B***—Typical flower, ***C***—Typical flower, exploded view

A white cedar swamp in Itasca County—prime *Calypso* habitat

sepals and lateral petals radiating outward; the pouch is concealed beneath. The leaf is somewhat dull and has longitudinal creases. It is not thick or fleshy like the leaves of so many other orchids.

In Minnesota, good habitat for *Calypso* is in cool, northern forests. Don't bother to look for it in sunny places. It seems to require a close association with mature coniferous trees, particularly northern white cedar and balsam fir. The best habitats are usually swamps where there is a carpet of mosses and an undulating hummock-hollow microtopography. The hollows are shallow depressions that dip below the water table and have a few inches of standing water. They will support a few hardy aquatic or semiaquatic plants, but no orchids. Any orchids that are present will likely be found on the slightly elevated hummocks of moss that develop over tree roots and fallen logs and at the bases of trees. The rooting zone in the hummocks is somewhat above the water table and remains relatively dry and well aerated. *Calypso* seems to favor these slightly elevated areas, particularly near the bases of large, old white cedar trees. The pH of these habitats is weakly acidic or circumneutral, usually between about 5.0 and 6.5.

A new corm is produced each year; the old one hangs on for a year or two (May 28).

It is also not unusual to find *Calypso* in transitional upland stands of northern white cedar in places where it is not quite swamp and not quite upland. The soil might consist of partially decomposed woody material and moldy cedar leaves, with a patchy covering of non-*Sphagnum* moss. *Calypso* is infrequently found in cool, moist sites under pine.

The peculiar life history of *Calypso* is actually a double life that unfolds over the course of a full year. The flowering stem and the single leaf arise independently from a fleshy, white underground

You will know *Calypso* when you see it, but at less than 8 inches (21 cm) high you might not see it (photograph by Peter Dziuk).

structure called a corm. By the middle of June the flower and leaf are usually done and begin to fade. At this point, nothing can be seen aboveground except perhaps the seed capsule. Underground the corm is in high gear producing a replacement corm for the next year. From this new corm a leaf will arise in late summer and remain green through the winter until the next spring when it will be joined by the flower, and the cycle begins again.

The separate lives of the leaf and the flower have a simple explanation: The leaf is looking for maximum exposure to sunlight; its role is to perform photosynthesis and refuel the corm. The flower is looking for maximum exposure to pollinators; its only role is to produce seeds.

Genus *Coeloglossum* Hartm.

The name *Coeloglossum* comes from the Greek words meaning "hollow tongue," an interesting reference to the shape of the spur, which is a short, roundish, pouch-shaped structure protruding from the base of the lip.

The genus consists of a single, highly variable circumpolar species, *Coeloglossum viride*, occurring across a broad swath of North America and Eurasia. It has confounded taxonomists who have attempted to describe meaningful varieties within the species for more than two hundred years and will likely continue to do so for some time to come. However, the plants that occur in Minnesota appear to be relatively uniform in the taxonomically important characteristics of bract length and orientation, flower color, and general growth habit. They appear to be representative of the common and widespread North American form.

Not only is the status of the species or subspecific taxa likely to change, the placement of the species in the genus *Coeloglossum* has been questioned. Recent molecular research has shown a close evolutionary relationship between *Coeloglossum viride* and species in the genus *Dactylorhiza* (Pridgeon et al. 1997). As a result, *Coeloglossum* has been formally transferred to *Dactylorhiza* in spite of many morphological differences (Bateman et al. 1997). However, the relevance of the molecular data to the taxonomic classification of these two genera is still open to debate (Sheviak and Catling 2002c).

Coeloglossum viride

Coeloglossum viride (L.) Hartm.
Long-bracted orchid

[*Dactylorhiza viridis* (L.) Bateman, Pridgeon & Chase; *Coeloglossum viride* (L.) Hartm. var. *virescens* (Muhl.) Luer; *Habenaria viridis* (L.) R. Br. var. *bracteata* (Muhl.) Gray]

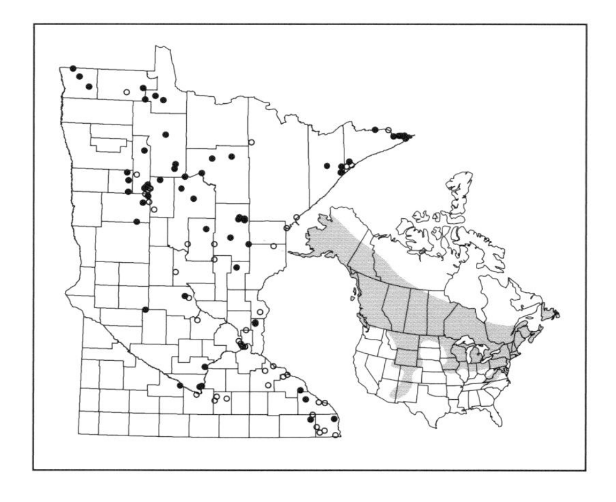

Plants 15–55 cm tall; **stem** leafy throughout or primarily the lower two-thirds; **tuber** palmately branched or bi-forked, to 15 cm long; **roots** 3–6, slender, fleshy, growing laterally for a distance of 10–15 cm. **Leaves** 2–6, the middle and lower leaves elliptic to oblong or obovate, 5–13 cm long, 1.5–6.5 cm wide, gradually decreasing in size upward until grading into the lanceolate bracts. **Inflorescence** a terminal spicate raceme, 4.5–24 cm long, with 11–75 flowers, each flower subtended by a narrow leaf-like bract 1–5.5 cm long, the lower bracts 2–5× longer than the flowers they subtend. **Flowers** greenish to yellowish, typically canted; **dorsal sepal** broadly ovate to nearly elliptic, 3–5.5 mm long; **lateral sepals** ovate, oblique, 4.2–7 mm long; **petals** linear to lance-linear, 3.5–4.5 mm long; **lip** oblong or strap-shaped, yellowish, 4–11 mm long, 0.8–3.5 mm wide, the apex with 2 forward-pointing teeth and sometimes a smaller medial tooth; **spur** pouch-shaped, 2–3 mm long. **Capsule** ± erect, 0.8–1.5 cm long. **Flowering** May 20–August 10, usually peaking the last 3 weeks of June.

The round structure tucked into the back of the flower is the nectar spur (May 27).

Coeloglossum viride is not a small orchid, but it can be inconspicuous. It has no stand-out colors; it is mostly a dark forest green, which allows it to blend very well into its background. It has the long bracts and flower color of *Platanthera flava* var. *herbiola* and the general aspect of *P. aquilonis* and *P. huronensis*. However, the structural details of *Coeloglossum* are quite different. The floral lip is long and strap-like and is tipped with two pointed teeth or horns. Also, the lip tends to be more yellow than the rest of the flower, instead of pointing forward it points backward, and the whole flower is often canted as much as 45 degrees. The defining characteristic that will confirm the identity of *Coeloglossum* is the shape of the spur that is tucked behind the lip.

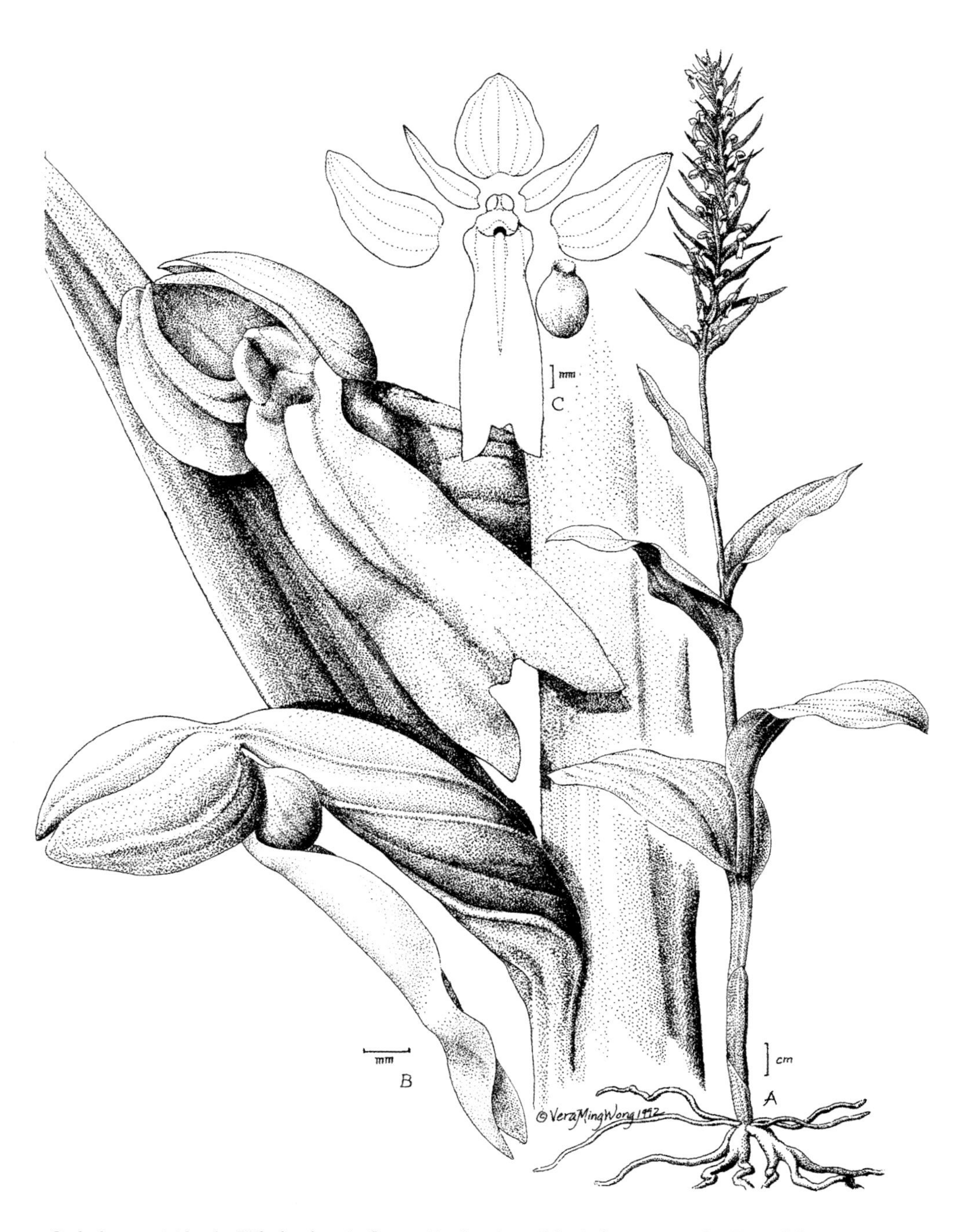

Coeloglossum viride ***A***—Whole plant in flower, ***B***—Portion of the inflorescence, ***C***—Typical flower, exploded view

The flowers are greenish yellow and have a long slender lip (May 27).

It is shaped more like a pouch than a slender tube, which distinguishes it from all the *Platanthera*.

The stem of *Coeloglossum* comes from the top of a peculiar tuber that is unlike the tuber of any other orchid in Minnesota. It has the appearance of a downward-projecting hand with two to five finger-like extensions. There are three to six fleshy roots that come from the top of the tuber and radiate outward. A new tuber is formed each year, which generates a new aerial stem and a new set of roots. The old tuber and roots die away as the new ones take over.

Finding this orchid in Minnesota is not easy. It is not particularly rare, but it occurs so unpredictably and in such low numbers that you would be forgiven for thinking it very rare. You will find it only in upland habitats, primarily in mesic hardwood forests, less often in conifer forests or brushlands. The composition or age of the overstory trees does not matter as much as good, untrammeled

Roots radiate out from the top of a forked tuber (May 27).

forest soil, not soil that was farmed in the past or compacted by cattle. Soil types vary from heavy clay loams to lighter sandy loams and also include loess as well as alluvial and colluvial soils. The pH of the soil seems to range from weakly acidic to distinctly alkaline.

The comings and goings of this orchid are rather mysterious. Minnesota plants have not been studied in their natural habitat. We know next to nothing about population structure, pollination, recruitment, or mortality. However, a study of the same species in the Netherlands found a considerable turnover of plants in successive years, due to both a high mortality rate and high recruitment (Willems and Melser 1998). The longevity of individual plants was reported to be very low. In fact, at the end of the seven-year study, only one plant remained that had been present at the beginning. The percentage of flowering plants in the population they studied was rather high (50 percent), and plants were able to produce flowers their first year aboveground. It is not known how *Coeloglossum* in Minnesota would compare.

At home in a deciduous forest in Aitkin County (May 25)

Genus *Corallorhiza* Gagnebin
Coral-roots

The name *Corallorhiza* comes from the Greek words meaning "coral root" in reference to the appearance of the branching underground rhizome. It is a small genus of eleven species closely related to *Aplectrum*. Except for a single circumboreal species (*C. trifida*), the coral-roots are restricted to North and Central America, with seven species in the United States and four species in Minnesota (Freudenstein 1997).

All coral-roots are leafless, rootless parasites of soil fungi, noted for their general lack of green color and their coral-like rhizomes. Nearly all species have striking color variations that can occur unpredictably in colonies of normal-colored individuals. They appear to be spontaneous mutations. Many of these color variations have been given taxonomic status, usually at the level of form, sometimes as varieties. In this book, I have not attempted to account for all the abnormal color variations that might appear in nature but instead have emphasized the normal color that appears most often and presumably has adaptive value for the plant.

The coral-like rhizome is at the heart of these orchids; it provides the interface with the soil fungi that sustain the plant. The process is quite simple. The fungal hyphae enter the cortical cells of the rhizome where their contents diffuse into the orchid cell. With the exception of *C. trifida*, coral-roots have no other way to obtain energy or nutrients. The superficial structure of the rhizomes varies in small but consistent ways from species to species. For example, *C. odontorhiza* has a whitish rhizome with slender, brittle, pointed branches; *C. maculata* has a larger, sturdier rhizome with round-tipped branches; and *C. striata* has a dense, compact rhizome that is nearly black. The differences in color are fairly consistent and are largely due to the different fungi that are within the cortical cells (Freudenstein, personal communication, 2009).

The tips of the rhizome branches can produce aerial stems with flowers. But not every branch produces a stem every year. In fact, a whole rhizome system can survive an indefinite period without ever appearing aboveground, and many of them probably do. The stem and flowers serve only to produce seeds, which depletes the energy reserves of the orchid. In this way, coral-roots are much like the fungi they prey on; they appear aboveground only to reproduce. Events that stimulate flowering in a coral-root are unknown, but coral-root flowers are uncommonly effective; they typically produce seeds in abundance. Pollination is the key to seed production, and among the coral-roots it is often accomplished through the process of auto-pollination. This is a highly evolved and effective trait that, taken to its extreme, negates the need for an insect partner (Catling 1983; Catling and Catling 1991; Freudenstein 1997; Magrath and Freudenstein 2002).

The subterranean existence of coral-roots raises the obvious question: Can coral-roots reproduce without appearing aboveground? The answer is a definitive maybe. It seems the underground rhizomes are brittle and break apart easily. Physical forces such as frost heave, animal digging, or the force of growing tree roots could cause these rhizomes to fragment, resulting in a form of vegetative reproduction. In fact, it is possible to find such clusters of independent rhizomes at a depth of around 10 centimeters belowground in good orchid habitat, even if no orchids are visible aboveground. Some of these clusters are probably colonies of seedlings, called protocorms, but others may be fragments broken off from an older and larger rhizome. However, there does not appear to be any intrinsic mechanism for this type of vegetative reproduction to occur, and there is no known way for coral-roots to disperse from one place to another other than by seed.

A Key to the *Corallorhiza* of Minnesota

1. Lip of flower 2.5–4 mm long; lateral sepals with 1 vein; petals and sepals 2.7–6.5 mm long; stem and flowers predominantly greenish, greenish yellow, or brown, not brightly colored except for occasional purple spots on the lip; mature capsules 4–14 mm long; column not more than 2.5 mm long.

2. Lip with small lateral lobes near or just below the middle; stems, ovaries, and flowers greenish (often faded in dried specimens); mature capsules 8–14 mm long; base of stems without a noticeable bulge; sepals usually more than 4 mm long; flowering in May and June. . . . . ***C. trifida***

2. Lip without lateral lobes; stems and ovaries brownish or greenish; capsules 5–8 mm long; base of stems sometimes with a noticeable bulge; sepals usually less than 4 mm long; flowers not appearing until August. . . . . . . ***C. odontorhiza* var. *odontorhiza***

1. Lip of flower 4–13 mm long; lateral sepals with 3–5 veins; petals and sepals 5.5–18 mm long; stems and/or flowers with conspicuous red or purple coloring (rarely yellow); mature capsules 10–25 mm long; column more than 2.5 mm long.

3. Lip 4–8 mm long, with a lateral lobe on each side near the middle; petals and sepals variously colored, but not with reddish purple stripes, 5–10 mm long, 1–2.2 mm wide.

4. Lip 1.5–4.5 mm wide, ± uniform in width; floral bracts 0.5–1 mm long. . . . .***C. maculata* var. *maculata***

4. Lip 3–6 mm wide, distinctly wider toward the tip than toward the middle; floral bracts 1–3 mm long. . . . . ***C. maculata* var. *occidentalis***

3. Lip often more than 8 mm long (range of 6–15 mm), without lateral lobes; petals and sepals pale yellowish with 3–7 reddish purple stripes, 8–18 mm long, 1.5–6 mm wide. . . . . ***C. striata* var. *striata***

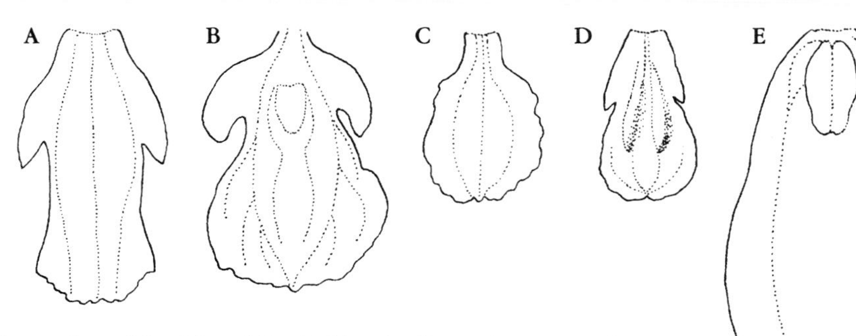

Comparison of floral lips of *Corallorhiza* *A*—*C. maculata* var. *maculata*, *B*—*C. maculata* var. *occidentalis*, *C*—*C. odontorhiza* var. *odontorhiza*, *D*—*C. trifida*, *E*—*C. striata* var. *striata* (all shown approximately 6× actual size)

Corallorhiza maculata (Raf.) Raf. var. *maculata*
Spotted coral-root

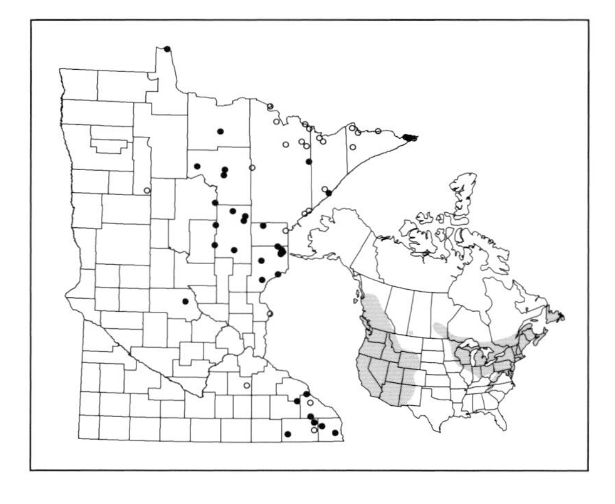

Plants 15–55 cm tall; stems usually some shade of red or purple; **rhizome** white, coralloid, repeatedly and intricately branched, deeply buried, up to 10 cm in length; **roots** absent. **Leaves** reduced to bladeless bracts sheathing the stem. **Inflorescence** a terminal raceme, 3–15 cm long, with 6–50 flowers, each flower subtended by a small lanceolate bract 0.5–1 mm long. **Flowers** relatively small but brightly colored and conspicuous; **sepals** reddish purple, often yellowish near the base, linear to oblong or oblanceolate, 3-veined, 5–10 mm long; **petals** similar to the sepals but often paler and somewhat shorter; **lip** white, unusually spotted with purple, oblong-quadrate, prominently lobed below the middle, somewhat recurved, 4–7 mm long, 1.5–4.5 mm wide, apex expanded slightly or not at all, apical margin undulate. **Capsules** pendulous, 1–2 cm long. **Flowering** July 1–August 10, peaking around the middle of July.

Typically, the stem, petals, and sepals of *C. maculata* var. *maculata* are some shade of red or pink and stand out at a distance. But don't rely too much on colors; they can be variable and unpredictable. The size and shape of the flower parts are more consistent and are definitive. And don't be satisfied identifying this orchid to species—take it one step further and learn to distinguish the two varieties.

The key on page 43 is generally conclusive for varieties; rarely is there much doubt if care is taken. The main difference is the shape of the lip, which is subtle but straightforward. The length of the floral bracts is also a good characteristic but may raise some questions. Look for a bract where the flower stalk joins the stem. In var. *occidentalis* the bract is a narrow, pointed structure, small but easily seen. In var. *maculata* it is measurably smaller and often barely noticeable without magnification. Once you learn to distinguish the two varieties, you will discover they flower at different times, and although the habitats of the two seem very similar, they rarely occur together.

C. maculata var. *maculata* occurs scattered throughout most of the forested region of the state, including the southeastern counties. Where the ranges of the two varieties overlap, var. *maculata* is the less common of the two. The fine-scale distribution of the two varieties within the overlap zone is difficult to decipher. More data, especially from the poorly botanized northwestern counties, may reveal patterns we can't see now.

The primary habitat of *C. maculata* var. *maculata* is deep shade in mesic hardwood forests. In some localities conifers may be present, but the dominant trees are usually sugar maple, red oak, basswood, paper birch, or yellow birch (in the north). Habitats tend to occur in fairly good sites, in terms of ecological integrity. This does not exclude second-growth forests that have been logged sometime in the past, at least not if the logged forest was

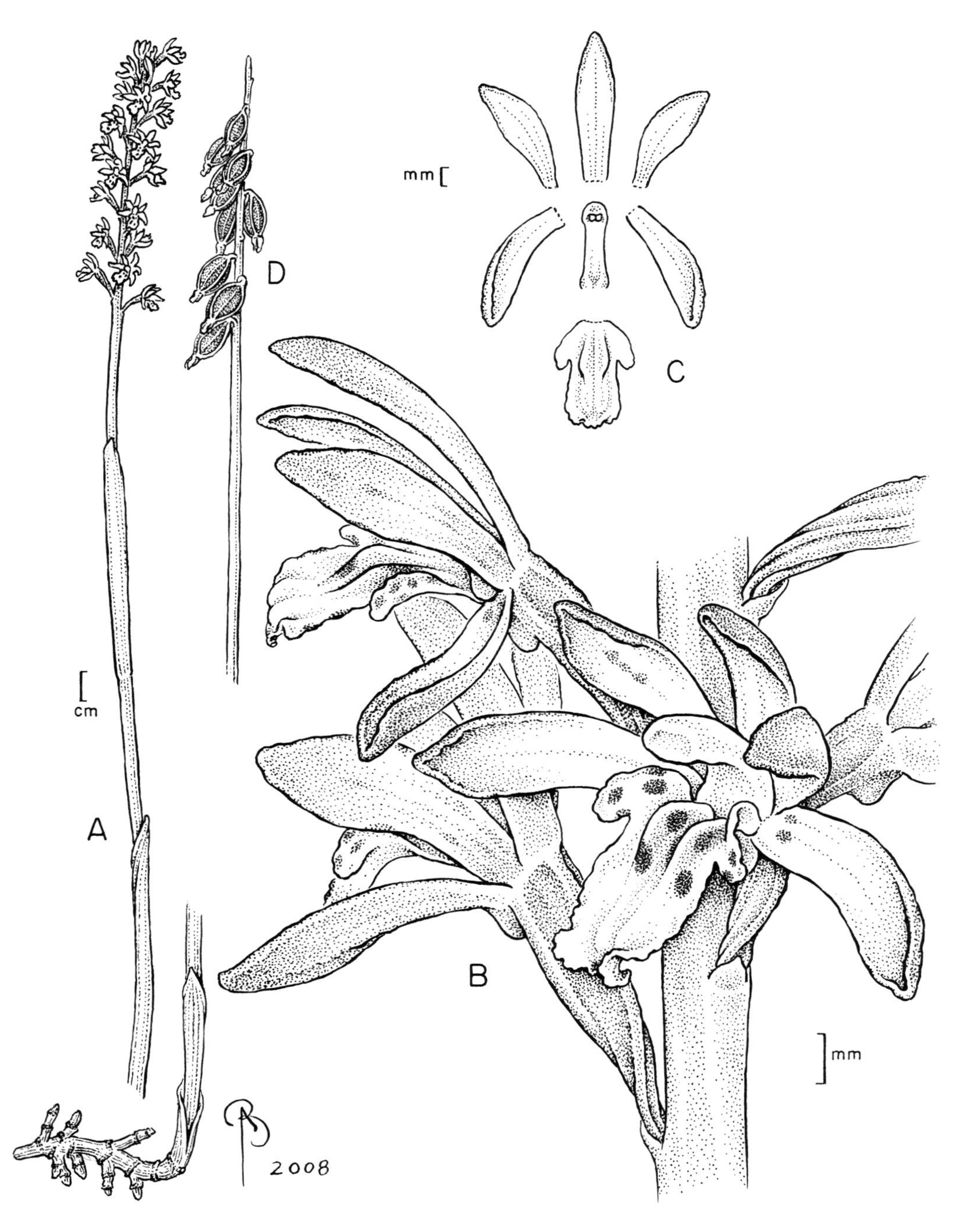

Corallorhiza maculata var. *maculata* ***A***—Whole plant in flower, ***B***—Portion of the inflorescence, ***C***—Typical flower, exploded view, ***D***—Portion of stem with seed pods

A fairly typical rhizome excavated from about 6 inches (15 cm) of soil in Itasca County (July 16)

allowed to recover naturally. When a new canopy has fully formed and the soil has healed, *C. maculata* var. *maculata* may return. In the north, soils tend to be slightly acidic loam and are often rocky. In the south, the soils are similar but more likely to be somewhat alkaline.

Like all the coral-roots, the underground structure of this species is an intricate coral-like rhizome with short, stiff branches. Each branch is capable of producing a flowering stem. Not every branch, however, produces a stem each year. Some years no stems are produced at all. The occurrence of stems aboveground seems to follow no obvious pattern, although it is clearly not random. There is likely some environmental stimulus involved, possibly a deviation in normal seasonal patterns of temperature or rainfall the year before.

Even when no aboveground stems are produced, the plant is not dormant, and it is not in decline. I say this because the popular orchid literature often repeats a claim by Curtis (1941) that this species "is subject to quite violent annual fluctuations in numbers, some years appearing almost everywhere but in others only rarely to be found." This is perhaps correct, when talking about the flowering stems, but the plants themselves seem to be long-lived and form stable populations. Remember, the plants are essentially subterranean and only sporadically emerge aboveground.

Flowering usually peaks in the middle of July but can extend into early August (photograph by Peter Dziuk).

Corallorhiza maculata (Raf.) Raf. var. *occidentalis* (Lindl.) Ames
Western spotted coral-root

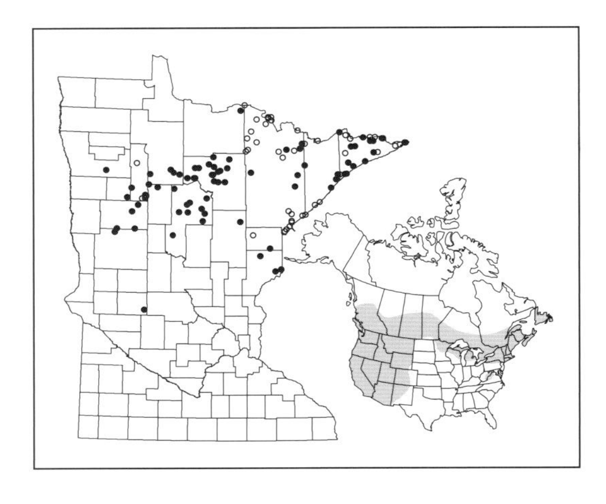

Plants 15–55 cm tall; **stems** usually some shade of red or purple; **rhizome** white, coralloid, repeatedly and intricately branched, deeply buried, up to 10 cm in length; **roots** absent. **Leaves** reduced to bladeless bracts sheathing the stem. **Inflorescence** a terminal raceme, 3–15 cm long, with 6–50 flowers, each flower subtended by a lanceolate bract 1–3 mm long. **Flowers** relatively small but brightly colored and conspicuous; **sepals** reddish purple, often yellowish near the base, linear to oblong or oblanceolate, 3-veined, 5–10 mm long; **petals** similar to the sepals but often paler and somewhat shorter; **lip** whitish, usually spotted with purple, obovate, prominently lobed below the middle, somewhat recurved, 4.5–8 mm long, 3–6 mm wide, apex distinctly expanded, apical margin undulate. **Capsules** pendulous, 1.3–2.2 cm. **Flowering** June 10–July 18, peaking the last 2 weeks of June.

The flowers are small but brightly colored (photograph by Peter Dziuk).

Spotted coral-root, as a species, is fairly well known. Even beginners usually get the identification right. I always encourage people to take the next step and learn the two varieties that occur in Minnesota. It is simple, although not always easy, and worth doing. The two varieties flower at different times (var. *occidentalis* about two weeks earlier than var. *maculata*) and occur in different places; they are distinct entities with little if any hybridization. The two are reliably separated by the width of the lip and the length of the floral bract (see key on page 43). At first it may require a hand lens and a fine measuring scale and getting down on your stomach, but the results are usually unambiguous; I have seen few if any intermediate specimens.

The fact that each variety has a differently shaped flower and a different flowering time hint at separate

Corallorhiza maculata var. *occidentalis* ***A***—whole plant, ***B***—Portion of the inflorescence, ***C***—Flower, exploded view.

The seed pods hang straight down and will shed seeds during the fall and winter (August 6).

pollinators. This situation is called pollinator isolation and is typically how one population of plants becomes genetically isolated from another. This leads to separate evolutionary pathways and eventually separate species.

It appears that var. *occidentalis* is fairly common in the northeastern counties and in some of the north-central counties. It seems to be more common than var. *maculata*. Both varieties show an obvious and unexplained gap in the northwest and far north-central counties. The gap may have a biological basis, or it may just be an absence of data. The apparent absence of var. *occidentalis* from the southeastern counties is likely real.

In essentially all cases, the habitat of *C. maculata* var. *occidentalis* is mesic upland forests, typically under mature hardwood trees but occasionally under conifers. The most often recorded canopy species are paper birch, trembling aspen, balsam fir, and sugar maple. These are among the most common trees in the region, meaning, in one sense, that this orchid occurs in everyday forests, but only in more or less "good" sites, meaning rather extensive tracts of forest that have retained some reasonable semblance of their original diversity of tree and herbaceous plant species and a healthy soil biota. These are not always old-growth forests; in fact, most are probably not. Many of the sites have had the older trees selectively removed by logging sometime in the past but were allowed to recover naturally rather than converted to single-species plantations.

In general, habitat conditions where you might find *C. maculata* var. *occidentalis* seem to reflect ambient forest conditions in northern Minnesota, but things are changing. Forestry practices, and land use in general, are intensifying. In fact, very little forestland in northern Minnesota is not in some sort of management regime, usually timber or fiber production.

The habitats of both var. *occidentalis* and var. *maculata* appear, at least superficially, to be similar, but it is rare to find both varieties growing together. One variety or the other seems to be more common in a particular area. Neither the tree species nor soil types seem to offer any obvious clue. Soils tend to be acidic or about pH neutral, with a high organic content and a high water-holding capacity. They tend to stay moist all summer, even in dry years. The rhizome is often buried quite deep in the soil, which may mitigate some of the effects of weather variability.

A single interconnected rhizome

C. odontorhiza var. *odontorhiza* doesn't usually appear until September (photograph by Peter Dziuk).

trees, particularly sugar maple, basswood, oaks, or aspens. Occasionally the canopy includes pines, usually naturally occurring pines. However, there are at least two known cases in Minnesota where *C. odontorhiza* var. *odontorhiza* was found in pine plantations that were established on sites of cleared oak forests. Soils are usually moist but not wet and have a loamy or sandy loam texture. There are also records from gravelly soil, alluvial soil, and loess. In most cases it has been found in intact forest soils, but not always. In one case it was found among tree saplings in soil that had been used for agriculture only fifteen years before.

Corallorhiza striata Lindl. var. *striata*
Striped coral-root

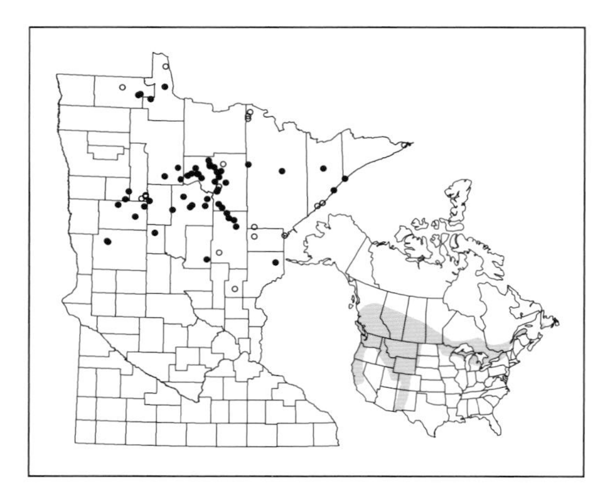

Plants 12–50 cm tall; **stems** reddish to brownish, leafless; **rhizome** coralloid, blackish, densely and thickly branched, deeply buried, up to 8 cm in length; **roots** absent. **Leaves** reduced to 2–4 overlapping bladeless sheaths. **Inflorescence** a terminal raceme, 5–23 cm long, with 7–26 flowers, each flower subtended by a bract 1.5–6 mm long. **Flowers** large and conspicuous; **sepals** with 3–7 conspicuous reddish purple stripes on a yellowish or whitish background, linear-oblong to narrowly elliptic or somewhat obovate, 8–18 mm long; **petals** similar to the sepals; **lip** predominantly dark purple, with pale yellowish bands on lower (basal) portion, obovate to elliptic, unlobed, 6–15 mm long, 3.5–8 mm wide, margins entire, appearing to hang downward. **Capsules** pendulous, 1.5–2.5 cm long. **Flowering** May 20–July 20, primarily the first 3 weeks of June.

The striped petals and sepals seem to droop, but the large purple lip hangs straight down (June 10).

There are believed to be three distinct varieties of this species, although that is the subject of ongoing research, and the taxonomy will likely change (Freudenstein 1997). The plants that occur in Minnesota are relatively uniform and are considered to be representative of the typical variety, which is the reason for the seemingly redundant use of the epithet var. *striata* (Magrath and Freudenstein 2002).

The flowers of *C. striata* var. *striata* are considered the largest and most visually striking of all the coral-roots. Especially striking is the large purple or reddish lip that hangs straight downward. When in full flower this orchid is easily seen and easily recognized. Even late in the season when the flowers are dried and shriveled, it is usually possible to get accurate enough measurements of the flower parts to confirm the identification.

In Minnesota, *C. striata* var. *striata* is normally found in undisturbed soil and in the shade of mature forest trees. Without

Corallorhiza striata var. *striata* ***A***—Whole plant in flower, ***B***—Portion of the inflorescence, ***C***—Typical flower, exploded view

chlorophyll, *C. striata* var. *striata* is probably indifferent to the presence of shade or light, but it would be acutely aware of the presence of trees. Like all *Corallorhiza*, it is indirectly linked to the trees through the fungal hyphae that transport nutrients. The trees feed the fungi and the fungi feed the orchids, and it all depends on a healthy soil environment.

Ideal conditions for *C. striata* var. *striata* are found most often in the interior of mesic hardwood forests of the type often called northern hardwoods. The tree canopy is usually formed by typical forest species such as sugar maple, basswood, paper birch, and trembling aspen. The soils are typically a friable organic loam with a pH in the acidic end of the spectrum. On occasion the soil will be sandy or something in the category of noncalcareous glacial till, but always acidic.

It is also not unusual to find *C. striata* var. *striata* under pine trees where the soils tend to be drier and lower in nutrients. This would be no impediment to *C. striata* var. *striata*, which relies on its fungal lifeline to access the moisture and nutrients stored in the massive tree roots. As long as the trees survive, *C. striata* var. *striata* will have little to worry about. The rhizome is buried so deep it would even be oblivious to ground fires that might burn through the organic layers of the soil. The rhizome is sometimes as deep as 20 centimeters, which is considerably deeper than the roots of most forest plants.

Less often, but not exceptionally, *C. striata* var. *striata* can be found in forested swamps under wetland conifers such as northern white cedar or balsam fir. It would not likely be found in the wettest part of a swamp; instead, it would probably be near an upland edge or in an area that is slightly elevated above the water table. There may be a thick carpet of moss on the surface, but *C. striata* var. *striata* would be "rooted" in the damp peat beneath the moss.

The rhizome of *C. striata* var. *striata* is stout, compact, and black (May 29).

C. striata var. *striata* is the most visually striking of all the coral-roots (Beltrami County, June 10).

Corallorhiza trifida Chat.
Early coral-root

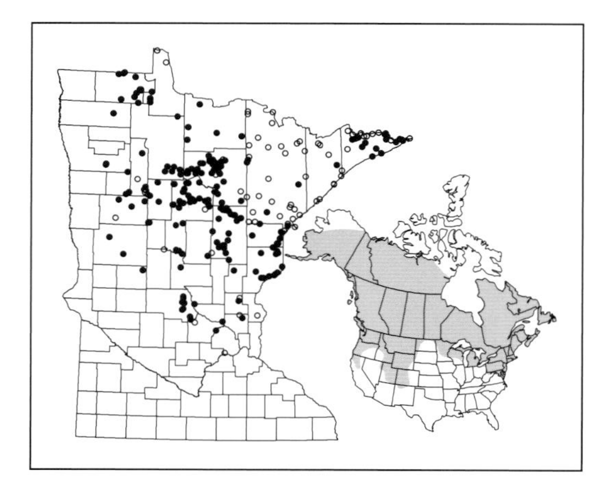

Plants 10–36 cm tall; **stems** greenish to greenish yellow; **rhizome** delicately coralloid, whitish or yellowish, repeatedly and intricately branched, deeply buried, up to 10 cm in length; **roots** absent. **Leaves** reduced to 2–3 bladeless bracts sheathing the stem. **Inflorescence** a terminal raceme, 2.5–8 cm long, consisting of 4–19 flowers, each flower subtended by a bract 0.5–1 mm long. **Flowers** overall whitish-looking, small and inconspicuous; **sepals** yellowish green, linear to oblong, single-veined, 3.2–6.5 mm long, the dorsal sepal somewhat wider than the lateral sepals; **petals** yellowish green, occasionally with purplish spots, linear-oblanceolate, 1–3-veined, 2.7–5 mm long; **lip** white, sometimes with purple spots, oblong-quadrate to obovate, with a short upturned lobe or tooth on each side near or just below the middle, triple-veined, recurved, 2.5–4 mm long, 1.5–2.8 mm wide, the apical margin undulate. **Capsules** pendulous, 8–14 mm long. **Flowering** May 14–June 25, mostly the last week in May and first week in June.

The flower is yellowish green except for the white lip (photograph by Peter Dziuk).

Most *Corallorhiza* tend to be reddish or dark earth-toned in color. But *Corallorhiza trifida* has an overall greenish or yellowish look, not withstanding the white floral lip, which may or may not stand out. In fact, the stem and ovaries of *C. trifida* are distinctly green, which indicates the presence of chlorophyll and a capacity to perform photosynthesis.

Apparently, all coral-roots contain at least trace amounts of chlorophyll, but *C. trifida* is the only one with enough chlorophyll to perform photosynthesis, which it can do even in diffuse sunlight (Rasmussen 1995). In this way it can obtain significant amounts of nitrogen and carbon from a source other than fungi, which is a radical departure from the usual lifestyle of a *Corallorhiza*. One study showed *C. trifida* obtained only about half its total nitrogen and three-quarters of its carbon from fungi; the rest was obtained through the same processes other plants use (Zimmer et al. 2008).

In another departure from the norm, *C. trifida* is the only species of *Corallorhiza* that occurs outside of North and Central America. It is, in fact, found throughout Europe and northern parts of Asia, including high arctic habitats—north to the tree line and even into the treeless tundra.

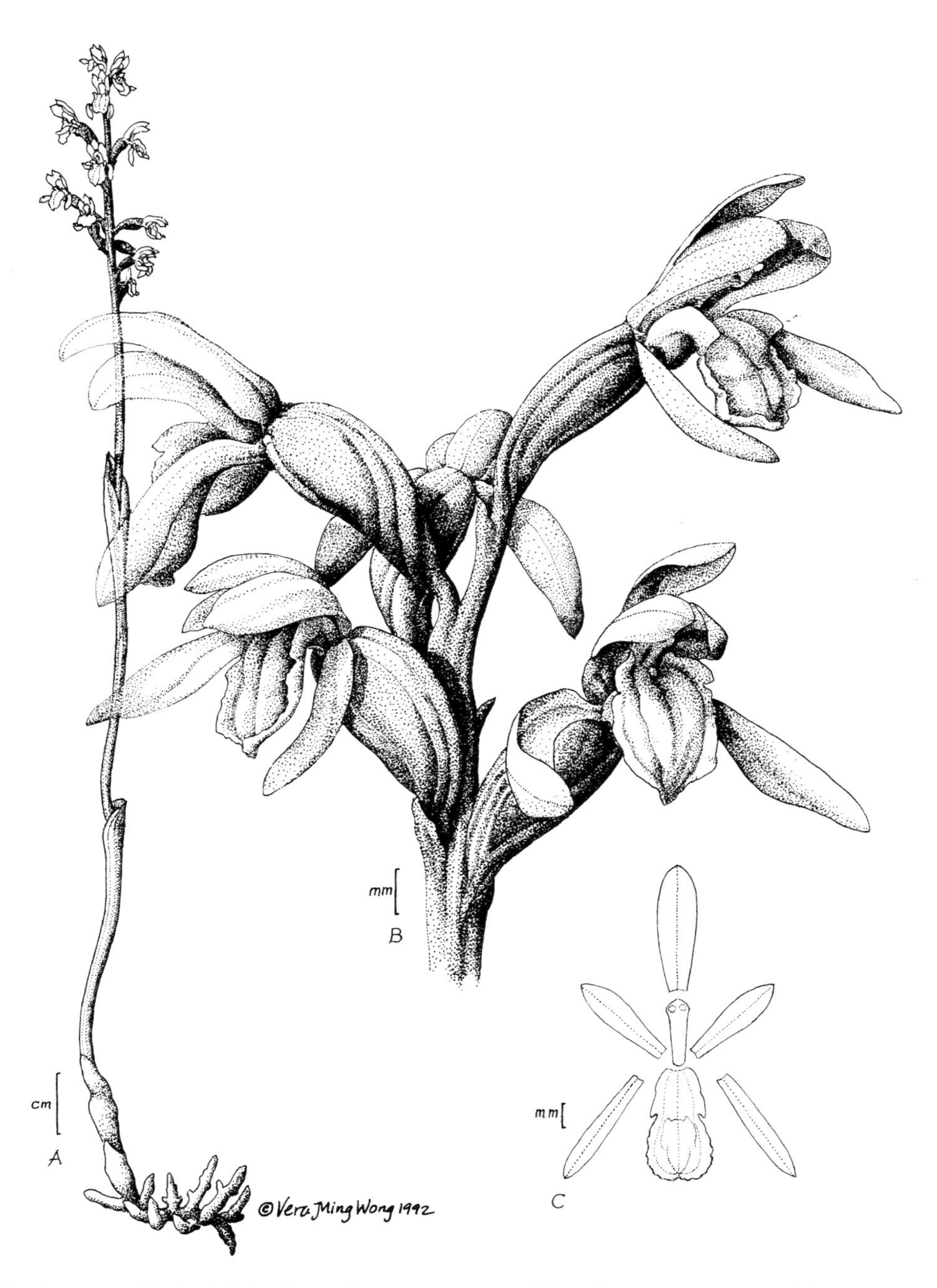

Corallorhiza trifida ***A***—Whole plant in flower, ***B***—Portion of the inflorescence, ***C***—Typical flower, exploded view

When it is in fruit, the whole plant is green (August 5).

Each branch of the rhizome can produce a stem, but rarely does (July 28).

In Minnesota, it seems *C. trifida* does not occur in the open; it is always in the shade of trees or sometimes large shrubs. The best habitats seem to be moist upland forests under either hardwoods or conifers and in mossy swamp forests where it would be "rooted" in wet or damp peat.

Habitats include stable old-growth forests as well as young forests that have lost their old trees to logging but otherwise survived with minimal damage. Soils can be badly damaged by certain forestry practices and can take a very long time to heal, especially the damage done to the biological component of the soil. Healthy soils are soils that provide good habitat for an entire community of organisms, not just tree roots and not just the mycorrhizal fungi that feed them and that, not insignificantly, feed *Corallorhiza*.

Soil health is important for *C. trifida*, but the soil type does not seem critical. It occurs in loam, peat, sand, decomposing wood, and occasionally talus. In nearly all cases, soils are acidic, and they tend to be loose, not compacted, and moist throughout the growing season. Also, *C. trifida* tends to be in stable soils rather than soils that are actively eroding or accumulating water-borne sediments.

In spite of whatever habitat limitations might confront *C. trifida*, it is relatively common in Minnesota. In fact there are more records of *C. trifida* from Minnesota than any other orchid (*Cypripedium acaule* comes in second). This is in spite of the fact that *C. trifida* is a small plant and is not immediately recognized by most people.

Only 3–6 inches (7–15 cm) of the stem appears aboveground; it has a yellowish-green color (June 10).

Genus *Cypripedium* L.
Lady's-slippers

The name *Cypripedium* is from the Greek meaning "Aphrodite's shoe" or "Venus's slipper," in reference to the inflated, slipper-like shape of the lip. There are about forty-five species of *Cypripedium*, primarily in temperate regions of Eurasia and North America (Sheviak 2002a). More than half of the species occur in eastern Asia and Siberia, twelve species occur in North America, and one occurs in western Europe (Stoutamire 1967).

The flowers of all *Cypripedium* have a lip that is in the shape of a pouch with an obvious opening on the top—obvious, at least, to the insects that pollinate them. The insect, in most cases a bee, is initially attracted by the color and form of the flower and ultimately guided by the fragrance. The bee willingly enters the opening, but the pouch is a trap. The bee is unable to crawl out the same way it entered because of the incurved margins of the opening and the smooth, slippery inner walls. Once inside the pouch, the insect investigates the interior and is lured into following dark lines and rows of long, stiff hairs that lead to the exit at the rear of the pouch. The bee soon realizes that escape is possible only by forcing its way through one of two small openings, one on each side of the column, at the rear of the pouch. This route requires the insect to first crawl under and rub against the stigma. If it is carrying pollen from a previous visit to another *Cypripedium* flower, it is deposited on the stigma. Then it pushes its way beneath an anther where it picks up a new mass of sticky pollen on the top of its head or thorax (Catling and Catling 1991).

If a flower is successfully pollinated, the ovary will become ripe with seeds by September. The ripened ovary, called a capsule, will split open and begin to expose the seeds to any small wind current. Before the end of winter, all the seeds will have been released. Some portion of the seeds will germinate the next spring; some might wait until the following spring. Most will die.

Details vary from species to species, but the first foliage leaves of a wild *Cypripedium* seedling typically emerge the third or fourth spring following germination of the seed (Curtis 1943). Prior to emergence it lives underground as a formless protocorm in close association with a mycorrhizal fungus, reportedly showing a strong fidelity to the fungal family Tulasnellaceae (Shefferson et al. 2007). The fungal association continues after emergence but diminishes as the plant matures. It has been estimated that our common species of *Cypripedium* require from eight to sixteen years between seed germination and the production of the first flower (Curtis 1943).

All *Cypripedium* species have a perennial belowground rhizome that grows horizontally at a depth of about 10 centimeters. The rhizome may have two or more branches, each with an actively growing tip. Every year, each branch produces two buds near the tip; the larger of the two buds will produce a shoot the following year. If the shoot is destined to be a flowering shoot, the bud will already contain the flower primordium. The point where the bud emerges will become a new node on the rhizome. On average the new node forms between 0.5 and 1 centimeter from the node of the previous year. Roots, perhaps two to eight, will be produced on the new internode segment of rhizome. Each of the white, fleshy roots will continue to grow for two to four years unless the growing tip is damaged. The roots spread laterally from the rhizome and eventually resemble strands of spaghetti 20 to 50 centimeters in length. Each root will live for many years, often as long as the portion of the rhizome to which it is attached. This results in a huge mass of roots accumulating over a period of years. Stoutamire (1991) calculated that each flowering stem of *Cypripedium candidum* in his study population was supported by a total root length of about 4 to 5 meters. This must be the greatest root-to-shoot ratio of any Minnesota orchid.

The second bud on the rhizome tip, the smaller of the two, is usually held in reserve. If it does start growing the first year, the result will be paired stems (Stoutamire 1991), which is quite unusual. Instead, the reserve bud may start growing the second year or several years later, but usually it stays dormant until it dies or until the portion of the rhizome to which it is attached dies. When it does start growing, it initiates a new branch of the rhizome. All *Cypripedium* rhizomes have the capacity to form branches in this way, but the frequency of branching varies between species and possibly with growing conditions. It is usually possible to see a succession of nodes and trace the history of the rhizome back fifteen to twenty years, but beyond that point the rhizome is usually too worn and weathered to see any structure. By tracking the nodes, it can be determined that the rhizomes of *C. candidum* and *C. parviflorum* var. *makasin* branch most often, typically every three to five years. The rhizome of *C. acaule* branches least often and less predictably, on average perhaps every ten to fifteen years. Since each branch produces a shoot at its tip, the more branches there are, the more shoots are produced—that is why *C. candidum* and *C. parviflorum* var. *makasin* tend to form dense clumps with many stems, and *C. acaule* produces small clumps or more often no clump at all—only a single stem.

For a time, all the stems in a clump are connected to each other via the underground rhizome branches. But as the tip of each branch continually grows forward, the rear parts gradually die away and decay. The time comes, sooner or later, when the progressive death of the rear part reaches the fork of the branch, and the two branches become separate individuals. This is the only way *Cypripediums* can reproduce vegetatively; it is a form of clonal reproduction. Since the rhizome keeps renewing itself at its growing tip, there is no intrinsic reason it can't keep growing indefinitely. Indeed, clones of *C. calceolus* in Europe (a close relative of our *C. parviflorum*) as large as 70 centimeters in diameter have been identified by isoenzyme analysis (Kull 1999). The older parts of such a massive rhizome system will have long since died, so determining the age of such a clone is not directly possible, but it is easy to believe that such a large fragmented clone could be centuries old.

A Key to the *Cypripedium* of Minnesota

1. Leaves 2 per stem, occurring only at the base of the plant; opening of the pouch concealed in a deep longitudinal fissure on the upper surface.
.... *C. acaule*

1. Leaves 3 or more per stem, not confined to the base; opening of the pouch ± circular and clearly visible from above.

2. The 2 lateral sepals are separate and appear on either side of the pouch (resulting in 6 distinct perianth parts); pouch 1–2 cm long, with a conspicuous downward conical projection at the tip; leaves 5–10 cm long and 1.4–3 cm wide.
.... *C. arietinum*

2. The 2 lateral sepals are fused into a single "synsepal" appearing directly below the pouch (resulting in a total of only 5 distinct perianth parts); pouch 1.7–6 cm long, without a downward projection at the tip; leaves 5–25 cm long and 2–16 cm wide.

3. Pouch white or pink or some combination of both.

4. Pouch white, 1.7–2.5 cm long; petals and sepals greenish yellow; flowering stems 10–35 cm tall. .... *C. candidum*

4. Pouch white streaked with pink (rarely pure white), 3–5.5 cm long; petals and sepals white; flowering stems 25–100 cm tall.
.... *C. reginae*

3. Pouch yellow.

5. Pouch 1.6–3 cm long; dorsal sepal 2–4 cm long; lateral sepal (synsepal) 1.9–3.6 cm long; petals 2.5–5 cm long; petals and sepals dark red or reddish brown, usually with yellowish-green streaks.
.... *C. parviflorum* var. *makasin*

5. Pouch 2.2–6 cm long; dorsal sepal 3.5–7 cm long; lateral sepal (synsepal) 3.5–7 cm long; petals 4.5–9.5 cm long; petals and sepals mostly yellowish green with reddish-brown streaks.
.... *C. parviflorum* var. *pubescens*

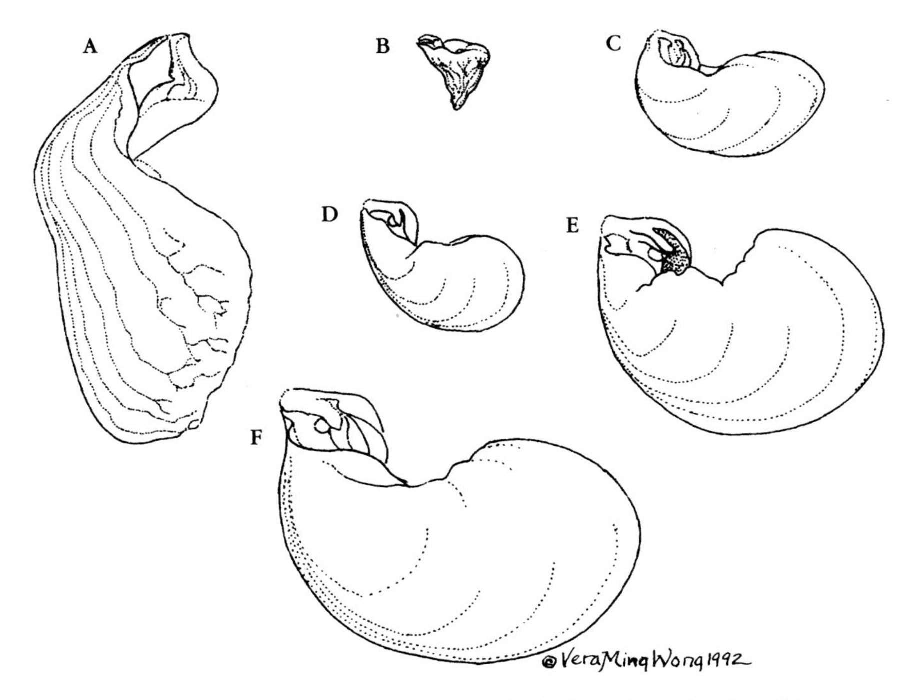

Floral lips (with columns) of *Cypripedium* spp. ***A***—*C. acaule*, ***B***—*C. arietinum*, ***C***—*C. candidum*, ***D***—*C. parviflorum* var. *makasin*, ***E***—*C. parviflorum* var. *pubescens*, ***F***—*C. reginae* (all shown actual size)

Cypripedium acaule Ait.

Stemless lady's-slipper; pink lady's-slipper; moccasin-flower

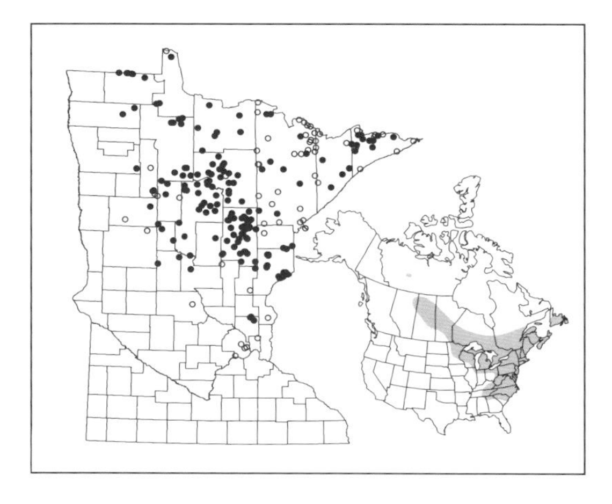

Plants 14–50 cm tall; the "**stem**" is actually a stout, erect, leafless peduncle; **rhizome** reaching a length of about 20 cm, with internodes of about 1 cm, occasionally or infrequently branched; **roots** fleshy or cordlike, to 35 cm long. **Leaves** 2, basal, elliptic, apex obtuse or subacute, 9–23 cm long, 2.5–10 cm wide. **Inflorescence** a single nodding flower subtended by a green lanceolate bract 2.3–4.5 cm long. **Flower** large and conspicuous; **sepals** elliptic to lance-elliptic, yellowish green to brown or purple, 2.5–4 cm long, the two lateral sepals fused to form a single synsepal located directly below the lip; **petals** lanceolate to lance-linear, similar in color to the sepals, 2.8–4.5 cm long; **lip** an inflated pouch, pink to purple, obovoid, 3.3–6 cm long, the opening concealed in a deep longitudinal fissure on the dorsal surface. **Capsule** ascending, 2–4 cm long. **Flowering** May 24–July 10, normally peaking the first 2–3 weeks of June, but peaking late May if an early spring.

A jack pine forest on sandy soil in Hubbard County—excellent habitat for *C. acaule*

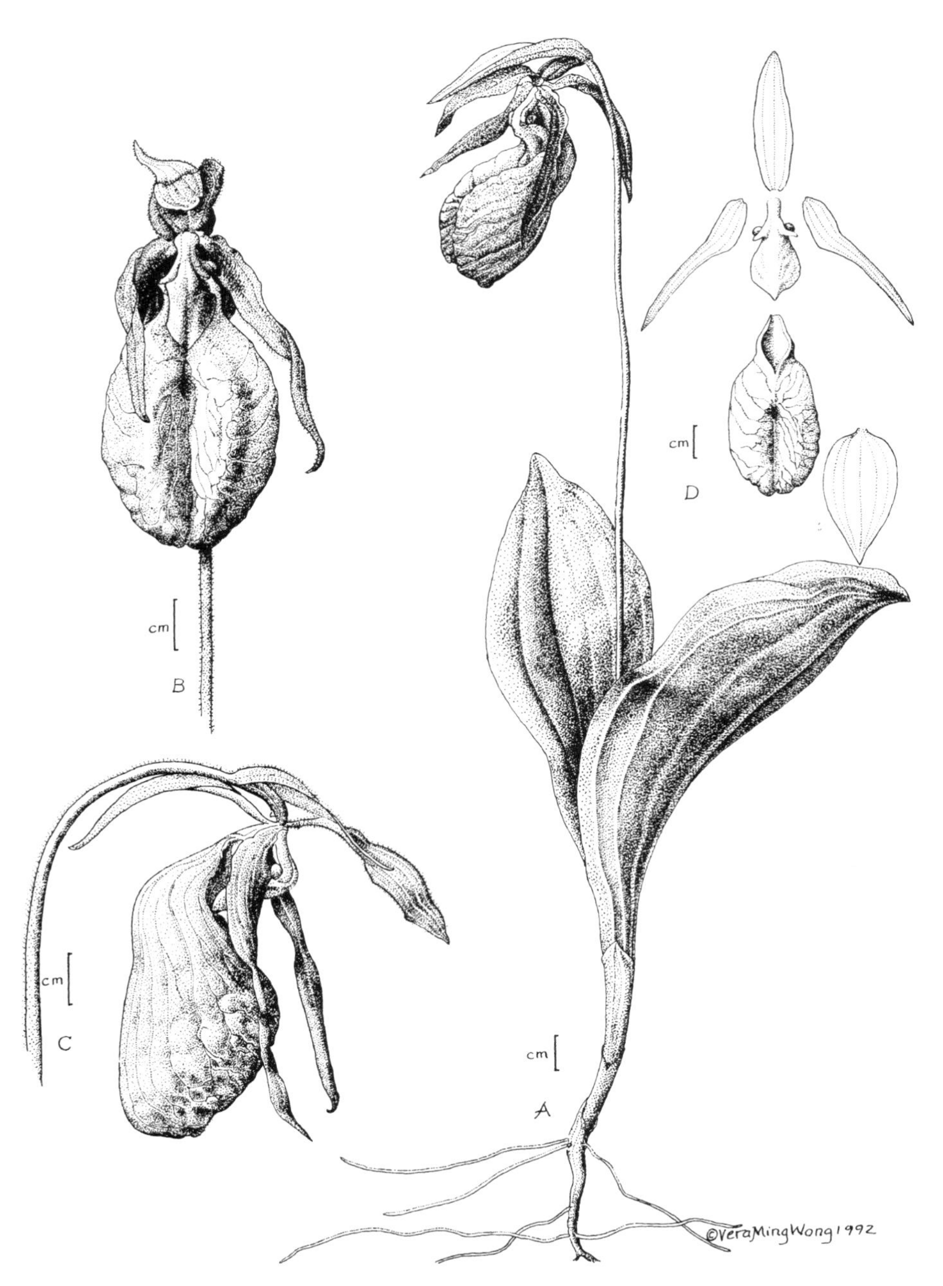

Cypripedium acaule ***A***—Whole plant in flower, ***B***—Typical flower, front view, ***C***—Typical flower, side view, ***D***—Typical flower, exploded view

There are always two leaves, and they come from belowground.

Don't be confused by the name "stemless" lady's-slipper; there is a stem, but it is so condensed it does not extend aboveground. What looks to most people like a stem is really the flower stalk (the peduncle). You can find the actual stem by tracing the leaves back to their point of attachment a short distance belowground.

Another peculiarity of *C. acaule* is the pouch. Unlike the pouches of other *Cypripedium* species, which have a round opening, this one has a slit that runs down the front of the pouch. A bee looking for pollen or nectar can't simply walk in; it takes a strong bee, such as a bumblebee queen, to force its way into the pouch (Stoutamire 1967, 1971). Also, be aware that the pouch is always white or pale when just emerging but typically turns pink or purple by the time it is fully formed. Occasionally, not often, the pouch stays white.

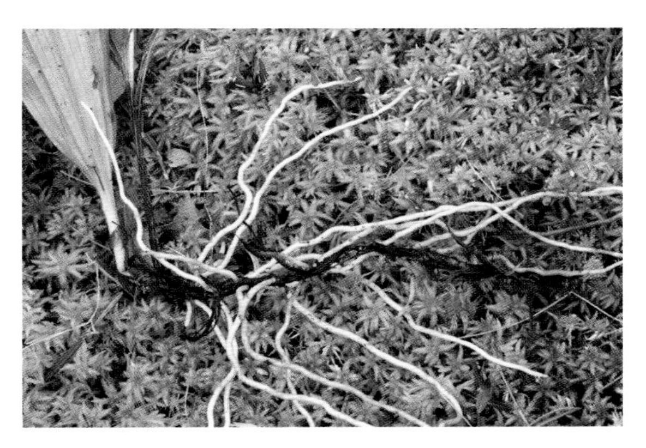

The long black rhizome can be 8+ inches (20+ cm), and the white roots can be 14+ inches (35+ cm).

Often *C. acaule* will produce no flower at all, just a pair of leaves. One study reported that out of 2,500 records, only one plant flowered every year for ten years (Gill 1989). Many people have tried to make sense of the seemingly random and erratic appearance of flowers, but it seems there is no flowering synchrony.

Each seed pod can hold more than 50,000 seeds.

Most records of *C. acaule* seem to fall neatly into two distinct and seemingly unrelated habitat types. The more common of the two (by a ratio of five to two) is bogs and swamps. These are perennially wet habitats with a layer of deep acidic peat and a thick covering of mosses. These habitats may be forested with conifers, or they may be treeless. The most extreme bogs may have a pH as low as 3.8 and will be practically devoid of mineral nutrients. The only way minerals enter the system is through wind-borne dust or in precipitation. This makes true bogs the most species-poor major habitat in Minnesota. In spite of covering a minimum of thirty thousand acres in Minnesota,* a total of only twenty-five plant species have been found growing in these bogs. One of them is an orchid, *C. acaule* (MDNR 2003).

At the other end of the moisture spectrum, you can find *C. acaule* growing in dry upland habitats. Soils may be deep sand or just thin layers of mineral residue over bedrock. These are soils that hold little moisture and have practically no organic material. Trees, if any, are likely to be jack pine or red pine. There may also be bracken fern, bearberry, trailing arbutus, and a number of other drought-tolerant specialists. Like bogs, these dry habitats are acidic and nutrient-poor, but unlike bogs they are very prone to drought, which does not seem to inconvenience *C. acaule*.

* The 224 largest bogs identified by the Minnesota DNR total 29,162 acres (Malterer et al. 1979). Using this number, bogs account for 1.8 percent of the 7.2 million acres of peatlands in Minnesota. The rest are various types of swamps or fens.

Cypripedium arietinum R. Br.
Ram's-head lady's-slipper

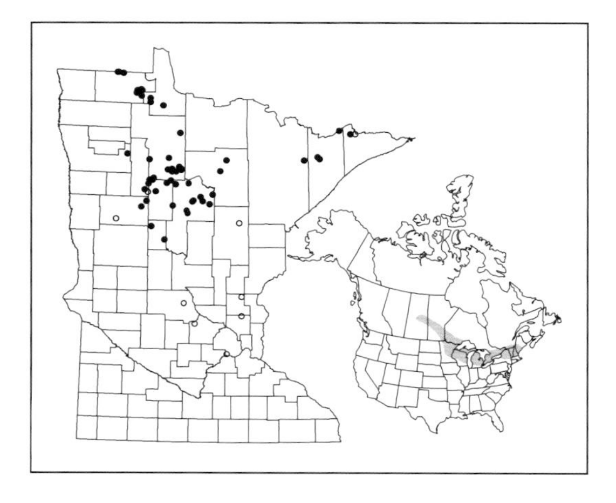

Plants 15–32 cm tall; stem leafy, primarily in the middle third; **rhizome** up to about 7 cm long with internodes no more than 5 mm, occasionally branched; **roots** slender, fleshy, to about 30 cm long. **Leaves** 3–5, elliptic, 5–10 cm long, 1.4–3 cm wide. **Inflorescence** 1 flower subtended by a leaf-like bract 2.5–6 cm long. **Flower** small, intricately patterned, rather inconspicuous; **dorsal sepal** greenish to purplish, ovate to lance-ovate, 1.2–2.6 cm long, **lateral sepals** separate, greenish to purplish, lance-acuminate, 1.2–2.1 cm long; **petals** similar to the lateral sepals; **lip** an inflated pouch 1–2 cm long, whitish or pinkish with prominent purple veins, sometimes entirely white, the apex with a conspicuous downward conical projection, the opening of the pouch surrounded by white silky hairs. **Capsule** ascending, 1.5–2.5 cm long. **Flowering** May 20–June 26, peaking during the first 2 weeks of June in an average spring.

The flower is named for its resemblance to the head of a charging ram.

The form and color of the flower are striking and distinctive, although most people are surprised by its small size and the difficulty in spotting it from directly above. The leaves are also small, rarely more than 10 centimeters long and 3 centimeters wide. This puts it in the range of a very small *C. parviflorum* var. *makasin*. Indeed, without flowers it can sometimes be hard to tell the two species apart with certainty. And in any given year, most individuals in a population of *C. arietinum* will not produce flowers, only leaves. Most of these nonflowering plants are younger plants that will flower in years to come, although some are likely to be seriously stressed older plants approaching the end of their lives.

The relatively large number of records depicted on the map is somewhat misleading. This is actually a rare species in Minnesota and is very hard to find without help. Because it is so rare, a number of populations are being censused annually, usually by counting stems or flowers. This method of census is quick and easy, but the results are very difficult to

Cypripedium arietinum ***A***—Whole plant with two flowering stems, ***B***—Typical flower, ***C***—Typical flower, exploded view

Filtered sunlight in a mature northern forest is the most common habitat (photograph by Erika Rowe).

interpret. For example, there is never more than one flower per stem, but some stems have no flowers at all, and it is clear that one plant may have two or more stems. So counting flowers or stems does not reveal the true number of plants or the demographic structure of the population. Changes in stem count from year to year may not mean much, or at least may not indicate trends, which is the intent of most monitoring. Having said this, the largest populations in Minnesota contain more than one thousand stems.

Habitats of *C. arietinum* include a number of northern forest types. Perhaps the most common habitat is swamp forests, which tend to be dominated by northern white cedar and black spruce and have a substrate of saturated peat overlain by a carpet of *Sphagnum* moss. The moss cover will, in places, be broken by shallow, water-filled hollows that have soft, mucky bottoms (familiar to anyone who has stepped into one). The water in the hollows marks the top of the water table. Expect to find *C. arietinum* in somewhat raised mossy areas where its roots are a distance above the water table.

This rhizome was about 4 cm long and fifteen years old; it was safely reburied.

A dense tangle of roots emanating from a long, tough rhizome

after the snow melts. Sometimes *C. candidum* is found in calcareous prairie fens where the soil is saturated peat. This is sedge-derived peat, not *Sphagnum*-derived peat.

It might seem incongruous, but *C. candidum* also occurs in thin, dry loess soils over dolomite and sandstone bedrock. You see this on steep south- or west-facing prairie slopes in the southeast corner of the state. The habitats are locally known as goat prairies. These high and dry habitats are perhaps not typical habitat for this orchid, but they should not be discounted.

In nearly all cases, *C. candidum* is found in fragments of high-quality habitat that exist in roughly their original form. That is, they have not been plowed, grazed by domestic livestock, sprayed by herbicide, relentlessly mowed for hay, overused, or otherwise abused. *C. candidum* is very sensitive to those things, as are all species of *Cypripedium*.

Cypripedium parviflorum Salisb. var. *makasin* (Farw.) Shev.
Northern small yellow lady's-slipper; lesser yellow lady's-slipper

[*Cypripedium pubescens* Willd. var. *makasin* Farw.]

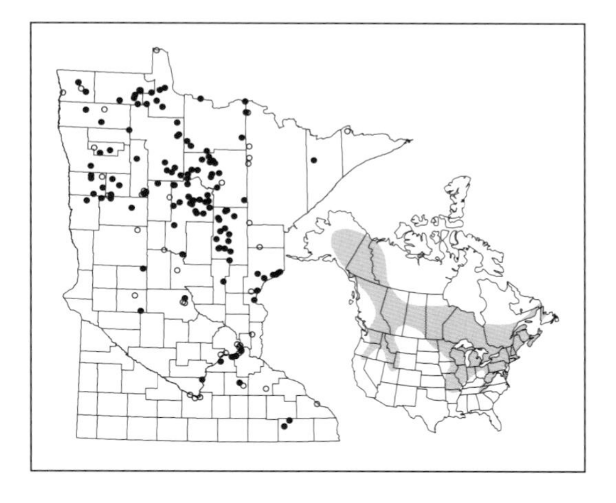

Plants 12–43 cm tall; stems leafy throughout or only on the lower half or two-thirds; **rhizome** branching repeatedly and frequently, the branches up to about 10 cm long with internodes of 0.5–1 cm; **roots** slender, fleshy, to more than 30 cm long. **Leaves** 2–5, elliptic, 6–16 cm long, 2.5–8 cm wide, the apex acute. **Inflorescence** 1 flower (occasionally 2) subtended by a leaf-like bract 2.4–7 cm long. **Flower** not large, but brightly colored and conspicuous; **dorsal sepal** ovate, dark red or reddish brown, often with streaks of yellowish green, 2–4 cm long; **lateral sepals** fused to form a single synsepal found directly below the lip, shallowly notched at apex, otherwise similar to the dorsal sepal but somewhat smaller; **petals** lance-linear, often spirally twisted, the same color as the sepals, 2.5–5 cm long; **lip** an inflated pouch, yellow, obovoid, 1.6–3 cm long. **Capsule** erect, 2.5–3 cm long. **Flowering** May 20–June 30, peaking June 5–June 15.

Note the mahogany-colored sepals at the top and bottom of each flower and the spirally twisted petals at the sides (June 20, Beltrami County).

The existence in Minnesota of both a large-flowered variety and a small-flowered variety of the common yellow lady's-slipper has been long accepted. The situation is somewhat complicated by the existence of a third variety, also a small-flowered variety, that occurs in the southeastern United States and apparently does not reach Minnesota.

All the varieties have undergone a number of name changes and taxonomic interpretations leading to widespread confusion. It seems that no two field guides agree on names or distinguishing characters. The concept that is used here was developed by Charles Sheviak (1993, 1994, 1995) and should provide some much-needed clarity.

Cypripedium parviflorum var. *makasin* ***A***—Whole plant in flower, ***B***—Typical flower, ***C***—Typical flower, exploded view

Although size is most often used to tell the two Minnesota varieties apart, and it usually works, be aware that all the size characteristics overlap. Learn to look first at the color of the sepals. The sepals of pure var. *makasin* are a striking mahogany color; the sepals of var. *pubescens* are basically yellow, especially when viewed from a distance.

Also be aware that wherever *C. parviflorum* var. *makasin* grows in close proximity to *C. candidum* you will likely find hybrids, which are called *C.* ×*andrewsii* nothovar. *andrewsii*. In general, the hybrids look intermediate between the two parents in flower color, but not always. The pouch may be creamy, ivory, or yellow (Sheviak 2002a).

In Minnesota, *C. parviflorum* var. *makasin* occurs in a number of different habitats but most often in rich conifer swamps with a mix of tamarack, northern white cedar, black spruce, or balsam fir. The substrate is typically saturated peat covered by an undulating carpet of *Sphagnum* mosses or feather mosses. In comparison to upland habitats, swamps are more acidic and nutrient-poor and support fewer plant species, but this varies greatly depending on how and where the swamp formed. The particular swamps that this orchid inhabits are at the high end of the nutrient scale, and the pH is only weakly acidic.

The records of *C. parviflorum* var. *makasin* from the lower Minnesota Valley are from calcareous fens, which are alkaline wetlands, not acidic. Calcareous fens lack *Sphagnum* moss and, generally, lack trees. Other common habitats where you can find this orchid include hardwood swamps and upland hardwood forests.

Some of the best habitats for *C. parviflorum* var. *makasin* are in the Aspen Parkland region in the northwestern corner of the state and consist of wet prairies, wet meadows, and wet aspen woods, with the operative word being "wet." These are usually high-quality remnant habitats that have not been plowed, grazed by livestock, or overtaken by brush. Soils are usually loamy glacial till or clayey lake sediments. These are also the habitats of *C. candidum* and *C. parviflorum* var. *pubescens*. Of the three orchids, *C. parviflorum* var. *makasin* favors the wetter sites, but all three orchids can sometimes be seen intermingled. In this milieu the three orchids hybridize freely, so pure forms of anything can be very hard to pick out.

This is likely a single plant with all the stems connected underground.

Cypripedium parviflorum Salisb. var. *pubescens* (Willd.) Knight
Large yellow lady's-slipper

[*Cypripedium calceolus* L. var. *pubescens* (Willd.) Correll]

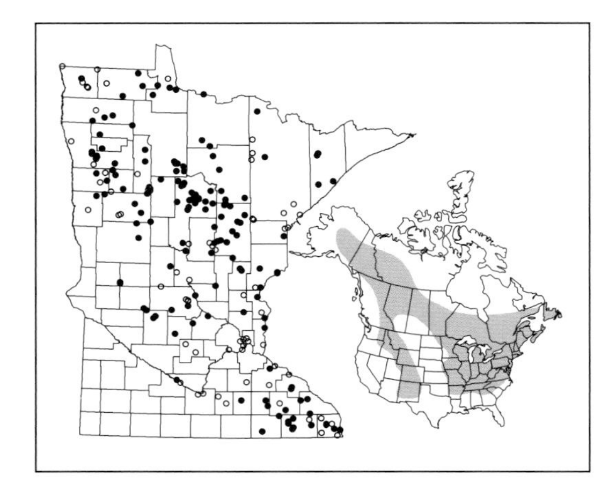

Plants 18–65 cm long; **stems** leafy throughout or only on the lower half or two-thirds; **rhizome** branching occasionally to frequently, the branches up to about 18 cm long with internodes of 0.5–1 cm; **roots** slender, fleshy, to 20 cm or more long. **Leaves** 3–6, elliptic, 8–22 cm long, 3.5–12 cm wide, the apex acute to subobtuse. **Inflorescence** 1 flower (occasionally 2) subtended by a leaf-like bract 4–12 cm long. **Flower** large and conspicuous; **dorsal sepal** ovate, yellowish green, usually with reddish brown streaks, 3.5–7 cm long; **lateral sepals** fused to form a single synsepal located directly below the pouch, shallowly notched at the apex otherwise similar to the dorsal sepal; **petals** lance-linear, often spirally twisted, the same color as the sepals, 4.5–9.5 cm long; **lip** an inflated pouch, yellow, obovoid, 2.2–6 cm long. **Capsule** erect, 3–4 cm long. **Flowering** May 10–July 10 statewide, normally peaking June 5–June 20 in the north, May 20–June 1 in the south.

This plant used to be classified as a variety of the Eurasian *C. calceolus*, a name used since the time of Linnaeus (Correll 1938). It is now widely accepted that the North American yellow lady's-slipper is a separate species known as *C. parviflorum* (Sheviak 1992, 1994). There are three varieties of *C. parviflorum* currently recognized. Two of these varieties occur in Minnesota: var. *pubescens* and var. *makasin*.

The two varieties are easily recognized in their extreme forms. One is big with yellow sepals (var. *pubescens*), and the other is small with reddish sepals (var. *makasin*). Unfortunately, many plants are not so easy to place. There seems to be a continuous gradation of size and sepal color from one extreme to the other (Sheviak 2002a). One interpretation of allozyme data suggests that intermediate-looking plants are genetically indistinguishable from var. *pubescens* (Case 1993). Perhaps everything that is not clearly var. *makasin* should be called var. *pubescens*.

The process of identification offers further challenges. Along the prairie-forest border, *C. parviflorum* var. *pubescens* sometimes comes into contact with the prairie-dwelling *C. candidum* and forms the hybrid named *C.* ×*andrewsii* nothovar. *favillianum*. This hybrid may have characteristics intermediate between those of its parents, or it may have one feature of one parent and another feature of the other parent. In particular, the pouch of hybrids can vary from yellow to off-white (Sheviak 2002a).

Throughout its range in Minnesota, *C. parviflorum* var. *pubescens* occurs most often in upland hardwood forests, usually in deep or moderately deep shade under sugar maple, red

Cypripedium parviflorum var. *pubescens* ***A***—Whole plant in flower, ***B***—Typical flower, ***C***—Typical flower, exploded view

A perennial rhizome connects the two stems and produced the dense tangle of roots.

oak, or basswood. Soils are typically mesic loams that developed from glacial till and have a pH perhaps somewhat acidic or somewhat alkaline but not too far from neutral. On occasion, *C. parviflorum* var. *pubescens* can be found in swamp forests, growing in weakly acidic peat, usually associated with *Sphagnum* moss and conifers like tamarack or black spruce or sometimes black ash. Swamp habitats are more typically where you would find var. *makasin*, but sometimes var. *pubescens* seems quite at home there.

A somewhat different situation exists in the northwestern part of the state. In that region it is fairly common to find both varieties of *C. parviflorum* growing side-by-side in wet prairies, wet brush prairies, and sedge meadows. Habitats are usually in full sunlight or partial shade, and soils vary from fine-textured clayey loams to coarser-textured sandy loams. These are usually high-quality native habitats, but both varieties sometimes appear in roadside ditches. Actually, it seems this is where most people first see lady's-slippers. It can be difficult to convince people that ditches are just another habitat, at least from the point of view of orchids. Ditches that escape the attention of road crews for long enough can develop soil and moisture conditions similar to native habitats. In time they may become colonized by a variety of native plants, including a handful of orchid species, but only if conditions are just right.

The pouch is large, and the petals are yellowish—compare with var. *makasin*.

Cypripedium reginae Walt.
Showy lady's-slipper

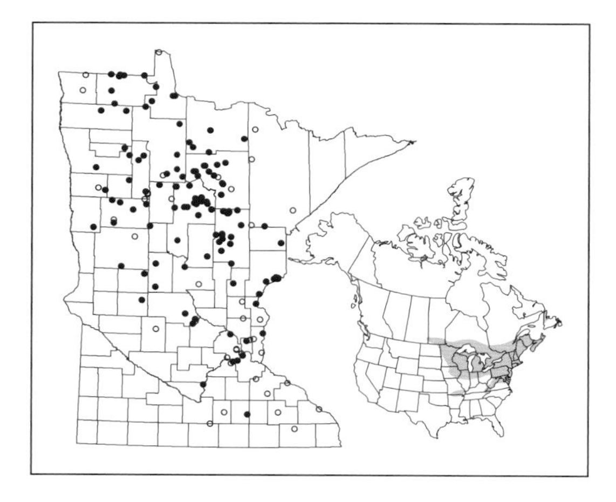

Plants 25–100 cm tall; **stems** leafy throughout; **rhizome** coarse and knotty, branching occasionally to frequently, branches and internodes relatively short; roots slender and fleshy, to 40 cm or more long. **Leaves** 4–12, broadly elliptic, 12–25 cm long, 5–16 cm wide, the apex acute to subobtuse. **Inflorescence** with 1–2 flowers, each flower subtended by a leaf-like bract 6–14 cm long. **Flower** large and conspicuous; **dorsal sepal** broadly elliptic, white, 3–5 cm long; **lateral sepals** fused to form a single synsepal located directly beneath the lip, similar in appearance to the dorsal sepal; **petals** oblong, white, 3–4.2 cm long, ± flat (not twisted); **lip** an inflated pouch, predominantly white with streaks of pink, or occasionally entirely white, subglobose, 3–5.5 cm long. **Capsule** erect, 3–5 cm long. **Flowering** June 12–July 15, peaking around July 1.

For many people this is *the* lady's-slipper (often called "showys"). Identification is rarely in doubt, although people are sometimes confused by the occasional white-flowered specimen. Such specimens are uncommon but not rare.

Minnesota's official state flower (July 8, Beltrami County)

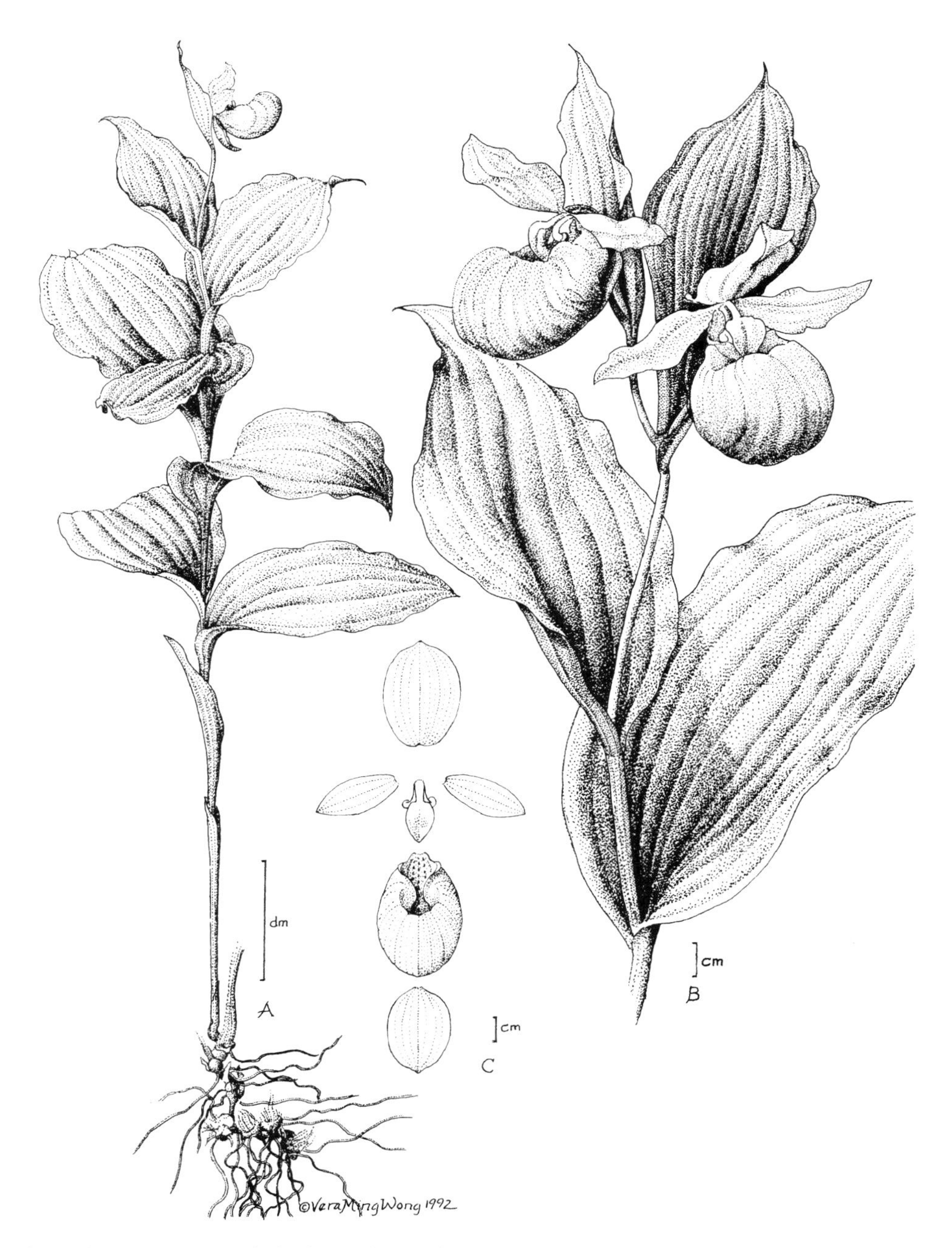

Cypripedium reginae ***A***—Whole plant with a single flower, ***B***—Portion of a two-flowered plant, ***C***—Typical flower, exploded view

Habitats are varied, but are typically associated with permanent wetlands that are kept saturated by a stable and reliable source of groundwater and where conditions range from weakly acidic to weakly alkaline. Expect the soils to be relatively firm peat or occasionally loam of some type. Showys do best in partial shade or direct sunlight, not in deep shade. You will most often find these conditions in a mossy, forested swamp under a thin canopy of conifers, or sometimes in a not-so-mossy swamp under hardwoods or tall shrubs. Sometimes showys can be found in open wetlands such as seepage fens or sedge meadows. Into this last category I would put the odd roadside ditch where showys sometimes make a brief appearance. I say brief because roadside habitats tend to get scraped or graded on a regular basis.

Populations in stable habitats easily survive for decades, probably centuries. But to thrive, showys need fairly large, diverse habitats where ecosystem functions provide a counterbalance to the inevitable (and fateful) perturbations of nature. Ecosystem functions include things like the ability of a forest to regenerate a lost or damaged tree canopy, repel invasive species, build and maintain healthy soil, cycle water and nutrients, and support healthy populations of insect pollinators. These ecosystem functions can usually buffer showys from all but the worst calamity. A small patch of woods that is isolated by roads, clear-cuts, agricultural fields, or buildings can't perform these functions and quickly goes out of balance. Any resident showys will be among the first species to feel the effects.

This often leads to one of the most commonly asked orchid questions received at the MDNR. It usually comes in the form of a frantic plea rather than a question: All the lady's-slippers in my woods have disappeared—what happened? What can I do about it? If all the showys seem to disappear in one year, the culprit is probably deer. No one can know the mind of a deer, but they seem to derive great satisfaction from eating lady's-slipper flowers just as they reach their peak. Eating the flowers does little harm to the plants, but if the deer are still hungry they will then go to the leaves, then the stems. Healthy plants, even

Multiple stems, likely coming from a single rhizome system, can reach 40 inches (100 cm) in height.

The habitat is a black spruce swamp (photograph by Erika Rowe).

if eaten down to the ground, easily recover and come back the next year. But after two or three years of repeated assaults, the plants are weakened and could take eight to twelve years to recover—if the deer give them a chance (Gregg 2004). Unfortunately for lady's-slippers, deer have a great memory for their favorite foods and will keep coming back.

If showys seem to dwindle slowly over a period of several years, suspect some gradual change in the habitat, particularly changes in the normal movement of water through the soil, including the slight rise and fall of the groundwater with the seasons. Often the changes are too subtle to see—almost imperceptible to people, but not to showys. Changes can be caused by beaver activity, the unintended consequences of logging, road or ditch maintenance, or new culverts. There is rarely anything that can be done unless the source of the problem is found and corrected.

Genus *Epipactis* Zinn
Helleborine

Epipactis is the ancient Greek name used by Theophrastus for an unknown plant that was used to curdle milk. In 1757, Zinn adopted the name for this genus, which now encompasses about twenty-five species, mainly Eurasian. All *Epipactis* have leafy stems that grow from perennial rhizomes. One species is native to North America and two are naturalized (Brown and Argus 2002).

The only native North American species is giant helleborine (*E. gigantea*), which is found in marshes and streamside habitats in the western third of the United States. There is very little chance it will ever be found in Minnesota. Of the two nonnative species, *E. atrorubens* is apparently naturalized only at one site in Vermont. The other is *E. helleborine*, which has spread across the continent (Brown and Argus 2002).

Epipactis helleborine

Epipactis helleborine (L.) Crantz
Broad-leaved helleborine

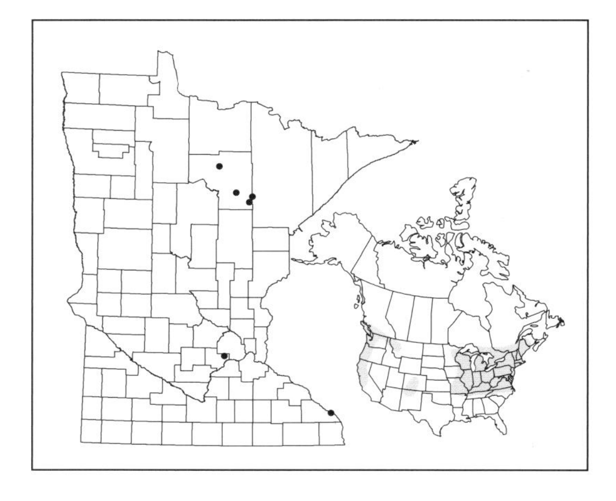

Plants 20–80 cm tall; **stem** leafy throughout or primarily in the middle third; **rhizome** short with condensed internodes, infrequently branched; **roots** in a dense cluster, fleshy, to 15 or more cm long. **Leaves** 3–10, ovate to elliptic or ovate-lanceolate, sharply and often narrowly pointed, 5–15 cm long, 2–9 cm wide, gradually decreasing in size upward until finally grading into the bracts. **Inflorescence** a terminal raceme, often somewhat 1-sided, 4–30 cm long, with 10 to 40 (50) flowers, each flower subtended by a leaf-like lanceolate bract 1.5–6 cm long. **Flowers** somewhat small and inconspicuously colored but numerous enough to be easily noticed; **sepals** triangular-ovate, greenish or suffused with purple, 10–13 mm long; **petals** pale green, pinkish or purplish, triangular-ovate, 9–11 mm long; **lip** 10–15 mm long, 5–6 mm wide, constricted at the middle into 2 parts: the basal part bowl-shaped, purplish to brown inside, lighter outside; the distal part usually pinkish, broadly triangular-ovate, recurved. **Capsules** pendulus, 1–1.5 cm long. **Flowering** July 5–August 18.

Epipactis helleborine growing in the deep shade of a sugar maple forest (July 6, Carver County)

Broad-leaved helleborine is a green leafy orchid that stands about knee-high. It is not particularly small, but it easily blends into the background. When first seen in a shady forest it might be mistaken for *Coeloglossum viride* or perhaps one of the *Platanthera*. But a quick look at the flower tells you it is something different. Certainly, the lip of the flower is unique, with a peculiar bowl-shaped base and triangular tip. Flower color can be quite variable, sometimes very pale or even white. There is even an albino form in which the entire plant, including the leaves, is white (Brown and Argus 2002).

This is the only "wild" Minnesota orchid that is not actually native to Minnesota. It is not even native to North America. It was brought here from Europe for use as a medicinal herb or possibly as a garden ornament. It was first discovered to be growing outside of cultivation near Syracuse,

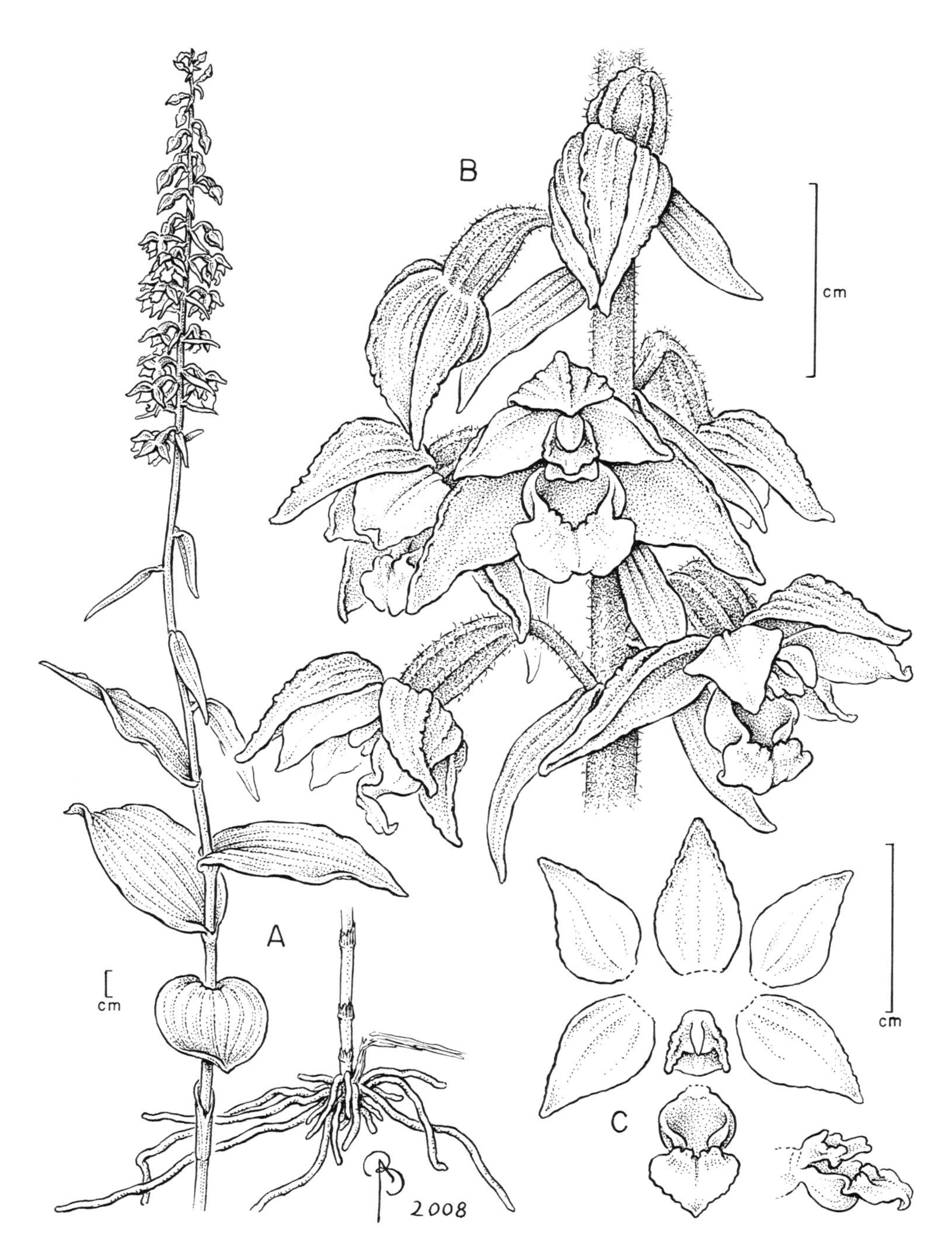

Epipactis helleborine ***A***—Whole plant in flower, ***B***—Portion of the inflorescence, ***C***—Typical flower, exploded view

The roots and stem originate from a short perennial rhizome.

At the base of each flower is a long, leaf-like bract.

New York, in 1879 and has been moving westward ever since (Luer 1975). It is now wild in at least thirty-one states and seven Canadian provinces. It was first found in Wisconsin in 1930 and in Minnesota in 1993.

How it moves about so easily is not entirely clear. It likely moves from one garden to another, intentionally or not, when garden soil containing rhizomes or seeds is moved about. It also seems to have no difficulty spreading on its own. The first plant may arrive by pure chance, a single seed carried for miles on a gust of wind. If conditions are right, a solitary plant can reproduce explosively. Cross-pollination with another plant is not needed to produce fertile seeds. It is self-compatible, even self-pollinating (Catling and Catling 1991). A perennial rhizome is produced, but the rhizome is rather small and short-lived, normally producing only one or two stems and a cluster of fleshy roots each year. The rhizome does not creep about or spawn new plants. Reproduction is limited to seeds, but each flower can produce thousands.

The seed capsules are green in summer, become brown and dry in autumn (August 11).

In Minnesota, *E. helleborine* is at least nominally invasive, meaning it can appear quickly in suitable habitat where it doesn't belong. This can be an annoyance to gardeners, but it becomes an ecological problem when *E. helleborine* escapes into native habitats. In North America it truly is a weed in the sense that it can degrade native habitats by reproducing unchecked and ultimately outcompeting native species, perhaps even native orchids. In fact, in parts of the eastern United States a considerable amount of effort is expended to eradicate it from natural habitats.

There is no obvious pattern of occurrence, so it is hard to predict where it might turn up next. It does not seem to follow human activities the way agricultural weeds do, and it reportedly has a wide tolerance for soil type and pH (Rasmussen 1995). It seems most likely to be found in a deciduous forest, even in the deep shade of an undisturbed sugar maple forest. There are also some indications it could survive in a swamp. So far, it's only been found a few times in Minnesota, but it seems almost certain that there are several, perhaps many, undiscovered populations.

The floral lip has a bowl-shaped base and a triangular-shaped tip (July 6).

Genus *Galearis* Raf.
Showy orchis

The name *Galearis* is from the Latin word meaning "helmet," in reference to the helmetlike structure formed by the sepals and petals.

Galearis is a small genus containing only two species, one in North America and one in east Asia (Sheviak and Catling 2002d). It has been proposed that the genus be expanded to include the genus *Amerorchis*, which contains a single species, *A. rotundifolia*. This proposal is based on evidence derived from nuclear ribosomal internal transcribed spacer (ITS) sequences (Bateman et al. 2009).

Galearis spectabilis

Galearis spectabilis (L.) Raf.
Showy orchis

[*Orchis spectabilis* L.]

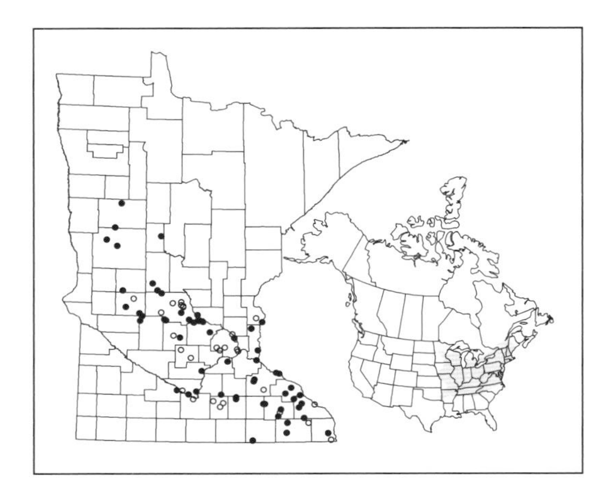

Plants 8–25 cm tall; **stem** smooth and rather stout, distinctly angled in cross section; **tuber** slender, tapering, vertical, 4–10 cm long; **roots** 2–8, fleshy, growing laterally to a length of 15 cm. **Leaves** 2, basal, somewhat succulent, obovate to elliptic or nearly orbicular, 8–20 cm long, 2–9 cm wide, the uppermost of the 2 somewhat narrower and more pointed than the lower. **Inflorescence** a terminal raceme, 4–8 cm long, with 2–10 flowers, each flower subtended by a leaf-like bract 2–6.5 cm long. **Flowers** conspicuous, especially in dense assemblages; **sepals** purple, elliptic to ovate, 1.2–2 cm long, converging with the petals to form an arching hood; **petals** purple, linear, 1–1.8 cm long; **lip** white, ovate to orbicular, constricted near the base, hanging downward, 1.1–2 cm long, 6.5–12 mm wide; **spur** club-shaped (clavate), 1.2–1.8 cm long. **Capsules** erect, 1.5–2.5 cm long. **Flowering** May 11–June 10, typically peaking in the last 2 weeks in May.

Flowering usually peaks during the last two weeks of May (photograph by Peter Dziuk).

The flowers of *Galearis spectabilis* are uniquely colored. They typically have a white lip with purple petals and sepals. Rarely the flower will be entirely white in *f. gordinieri* or entirely purple in *f. willeyi*.

In Minnesota, *G. spectabilis* is the first orchid to flower in the spring, usually about the middle of May. This is about two weeks after the peak of the spring ephemerals and perhaps one week after the start of the morel mushrooms. It is often found without flowers or stem, just a pair of rather broad, succulent, parallel-veined leaves. Both leaves will originate from the same place in the ground and will lack an obvious petiole.

The leaves emerge from the top of a slender tuber that stands in a vertical position just beneath the soil surface. The leaves are quickly followed by a stem of white and purple flowers, which are

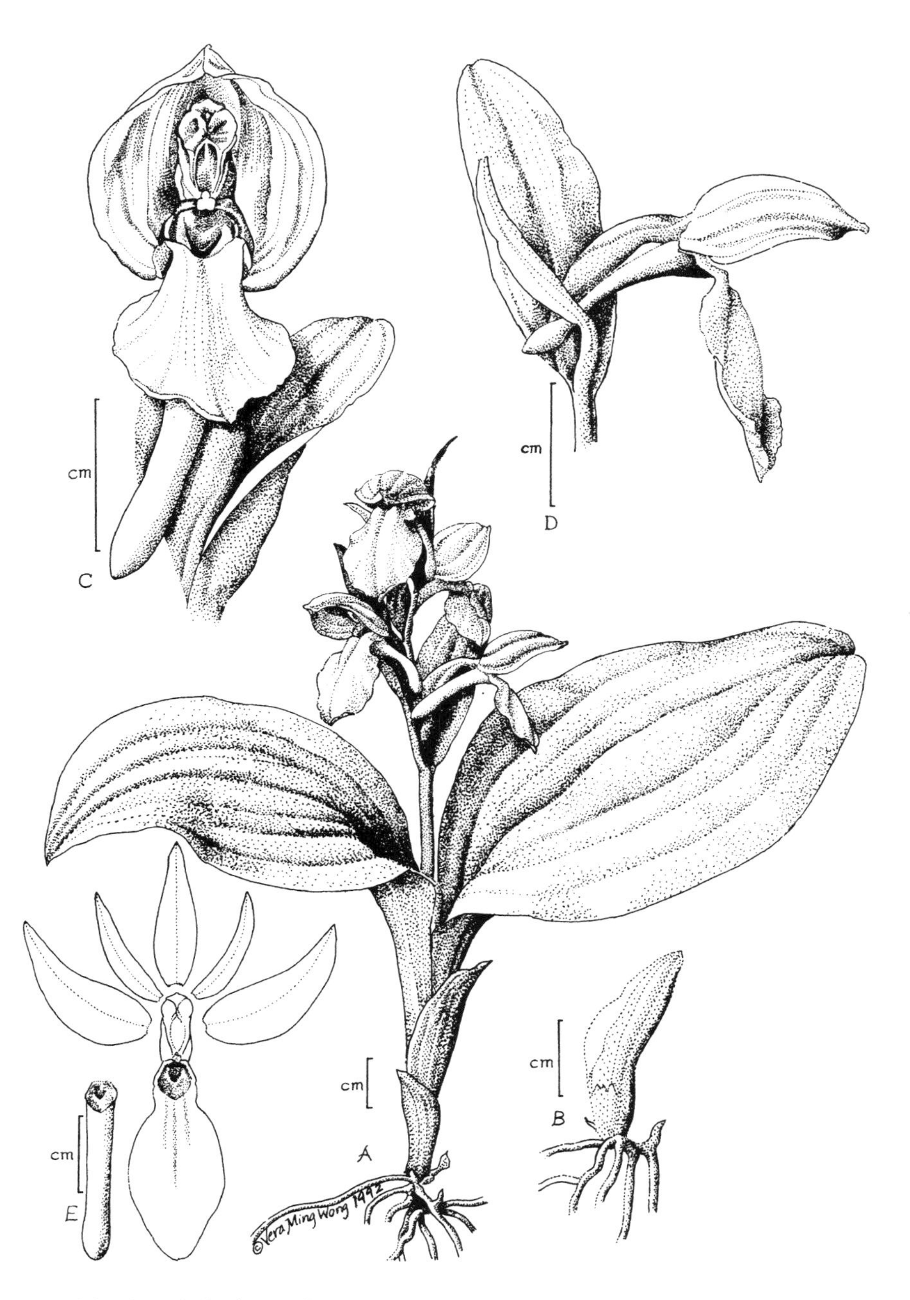

Galearis spectabilis ***A***—Whole plant in flower, ***B***—Portion of the tuber with roots, ***C***—Typical flower, viewed looking upward from the front, ***D***—Typical flower, viewed from the side, ***E***—Typical flower, exploded view

The vertical structure is a tuber, the horizontal structures are roots (May 15).

pollinated by long-tongued bees, including *Bombus* queens (Dieringer 1982). In June the tuber begins to produce an identical replacement tuber, which by fall will have grown to full size and have two to eight fleshy roots radiating outward. For a time in the fall, both generations of tuber and roots can be seen side by side, but by spring only the new tuber and the new roots remain to begin the process over again.

The seed capsules will mature over the summer and shed their seeds by autumn. Most seeds succumb to gravity and fall within a few inches of the parent plant. A lucky few will survive the winter and germinate the following spring (Rasmussen and Whigham 1993). No one knows how long it takes a seedling to appear aboveground—maybe one year, maybe more. The first showing of each new plant is a single leaf, usually right next to the parent plant.

During the next four to six years each new recruit will gain strength, build a series of progressively larger tubers, add a second leaf, and, if ultimately successful, produce flowers. Individual plants apparently don't live long after reaching the flowering stage, perhaps only a few years, but the actual population of plants is more permanent. If a familiar patch of plants dwindles, make a wider search and you might find a new arrival some distance away.

It's not unusual to find *Galearis* growing in a close family group (photograph by Richard Haug).

A mesic oak forest in Wright County—ideal *Galearis* habitat

The region of the state where *G. spectabilis* occurs is what ecologists call the Eastern Broadleaf Forest Province (MDNR 2005a). This is an area of hardwood forest that runs diagonally through the state from the southeast to the northwest. Habitats within this region vary quite a bit, but *G. spectabilis* consistently occurs in deep or moderately deep shade of mature forest trees, particularly, in order of frequency, basswood, sugar maple, red oak, bur oak, trembling aspen, and black ash. Soils are typically moist but well-drained loam, often fine-textured calcareous glacial till or wind-deposited silt. The pH ranges from weakly acidic to moderately alkaline.

Not too long ago, *G. spectabilis* was described as "occasional to frequent" and "found easily . . . around the Twin Cities metropolitan area" (Smith 1993). That may have been true then, but as habitat has become scarce, it is becoming more and more difficult to find this orchid.

Genus *Goodyera* R. Br.
Rattlesnake-plantains

Species in the genus *Goodyera*, named for John Goodyer (1592–1664), an English botanist, are clonal perennials with basal rosettes of evergreen leaves and a spicate inflorescence of small white flowers. The leaves are variously marked with white or pale-green tissue along the veins, forming a reticulate or checkered pattern, which is distinctive to *Goodyera*. There are no other wildflowers in Minnesota with a similar leaf pattern. *Goodyera* also have the distinction of being the only north-temperate orchids that are evergreen (Stoutamire 1974), meaning the leaves survive for at least one full year. Leaves of *Calypso* and *Aplectrum* are considered winter green; the other orchids would be called summer green.

There are an estimated forty to one hundred species of *Goodyera* distributed nearly worldwide, primarily in Southeast Asia (Kallunki 2002). There are four species in the United States, of which three are known to occur in Minnesota. The fourth species, *G. oblongifolia* (giant rattlesnake-plantain) has been reported to occur in Minnesota (Luer 1975) but without supporting evidence. It is known to occur in adjacent portions of Wisconsin, Ontario, and Michigan (Isle Royale), and it is possible that undiscovered populations exist in upland forests in northeastern Minnesota. It is most similar in appearance to *G. tesselata*, but instead of the familiar white reticulate pattern on the leaf, it has only a white band along the midrib.

The flowers of *Goodyera* are regularly and systematically visited by bumblebees (Kallunki 1981), which pick up the pollinia on their tongues when extracting nectar. Since all our species of *Goodyera* are interfertile, at least experimentally, the foraging habits of bees could result in hybrids within mixed populations. This likely happens with *G. repens* and *G. tesselata*, but the larger flowers and later phenology of *G. pubescens* make cross-pollination with that species unlikely (Kallunki 1981).

The reproductive strategy of *Goodyera* does not rely entirely on seeds. All our species of *Goodyera* can reproduce vegetatively via leafy offshoots from the rhizome, which is a horizontal structure on or near the surface of the ground. These offshoots will grow into independent rhizomes that are genetically identical to the parent, but they appear only at the end of the life of the parent rhizome. When a plant reaches a certain size, it produces leafy offshoots and a flowering spike, then dies the following year. Each plant flowers only once.

A Key to the *Goodyera* of Minnesota

1. Inflorescence essentially 1-sided (secund), that is, all the flowers point in the same direction or at least within a single 180-degree arc perpendicular to the axis of the stem.

2. Flowering stem not more than 19 cm high; inflorescence 3–7 cm long, with fewer than 25 flowers; leaves (including petiole) usually less than 3 cm long (range of 1.5–3.6 cm), dark green; floral lip globe-shaped, essentially spherical (exclusive of beak); perianth less than 4 mm in length; beak of rostellum 0.2–0.6 mm long.
. . . . ***G. repens***

2. Flowering stem usually more than 19 cm high; inflorescence 5–17 cm long, often with 25 or more flowers; the largest leaves (including petiole) more than 3 cm long, bluish green; floral lip more elongate, longer than wide; perianth 4 mm long or longer; beak of rostellum 0.6–1.7 mm long.
. . . . ***G. tesselata***

1. Inflorescence not distinctly 1-sided, the flowers radiating equally in all directions perpendicular to the stem.

3. The lowest 5 cm of the inflorescence typically with 15 or more flowers; leaves bright green, the larger ones usually 2 cm wide or more; floral lip essentially spherical (excluding beak). .... ***G. pubescens***

3. The lowest 5 cm of the inflorescence typically with 15 or fewer flowers; leaves bluish green, usually 2 cm wide or less; floral lip more elongate, longer than wide or high. .... ***G. tesselata***

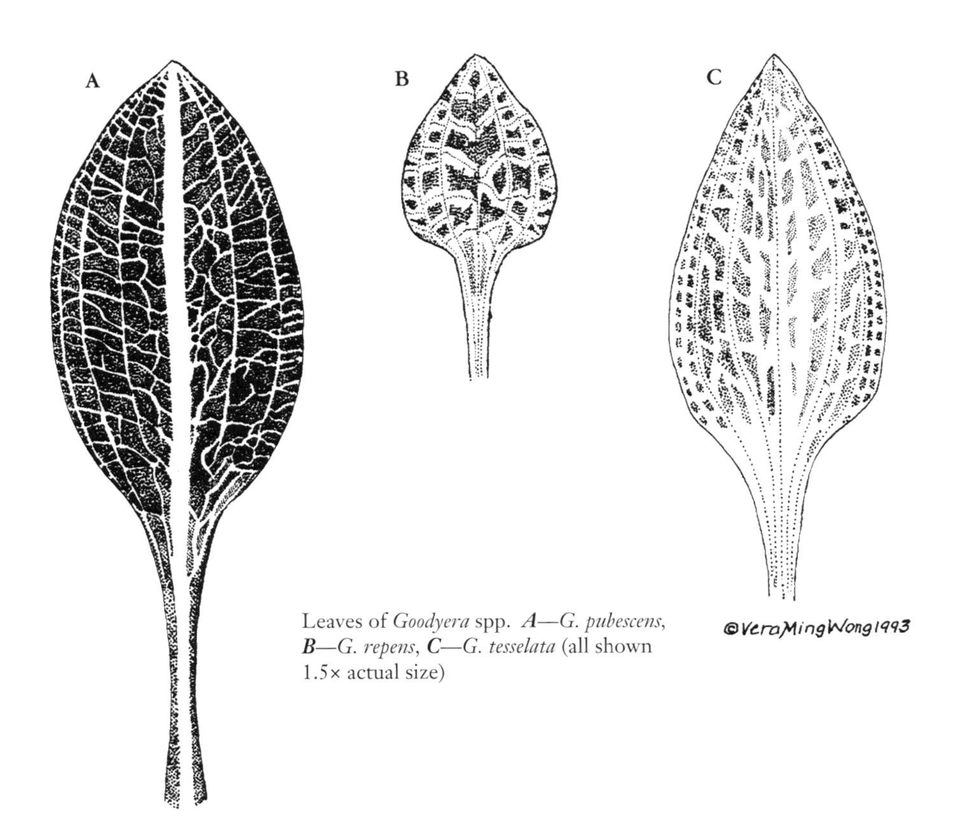

Leaves of *Goodyera* spp. *A—G. pubescens*, ***B***—*G. repens*, ***C***—*G. tesselata* (all shown 1.5× actual size)

Goodyera pubescens (Willd.) R. Br.
Downy rattlesnake-plantain

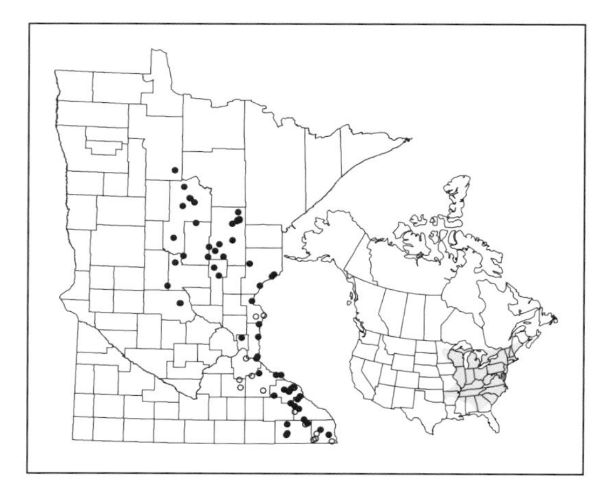

Plants 24–40 cm tall; aerial stem with 5–12 slender-tipped bracts scattered between the base and the inflorescence, otherwise leafless; **rhizome** superficial or shallowly buried, branching, 1–12 cm long; **roots** few, fibrous, rather coarse, 3–12 cm long. **Leaves** 3–10, essentially basal and forming an evergreen rosette; the blade elliptic to ovate or lance-ovate, 2.5–6.2 cm long, 1.3–3 mm wide, bright green with white reticulation along the mid-rib and veins. **Inflorescence** a dense spicate raceme, cylindric, 5.5–14 cm long, with 28–52 white flowers, each flower subtended by a lanceolate bract 4–10 mm long. **Flowers** small and rather inconspicuous; **sepals** ovate to oblong-elliptic, 4–5.5 mm long; **petals** oblong-spatulate, 5–6 mm long, converging with the dorsal sepal to form a hood over the lip; **lip** bowl-shaped, 3.3–4.5 mm long, 3–3.5 mm wide, contracted below the apex to form a short downward-curving beak. **Capsules** ascending, 6–10 mm long. **Flowering** July 30–September 1, peaking about the middle of August.

The reticulate leaves of *G. pubescens* are evergreen and can be seen all year.

This is the most distinctive of the three *Goodyera* species that occur in Minnesota. Compared to the other two, the leaves of *G. pubescens* are larger and the reticulate pattern is more strongly pronounced. Also note that the spike is dense with flowers that point outward in all directions, a full 360 degrees perpendicular to the axis. The flowers of the other two *Goodyera* species tend to point in roughly the same direction.

Habitats of *G. pubescens* are primarily in mesic deciduous forests, typically in the shade of mature sugar maple, basswood, or red oak. It occurs less often under white pine, bur oak, or northern pin oak. Actually, when it comes to predicting where this orchid might occur, the composition of the tree canopy may be less important than the origin of the soils.

The soils preferred by *G. pubescens* are fertile loams derived from noncalcareous glacial till or from wind-deposited silt (loess). These are loose, fine-textured soils with

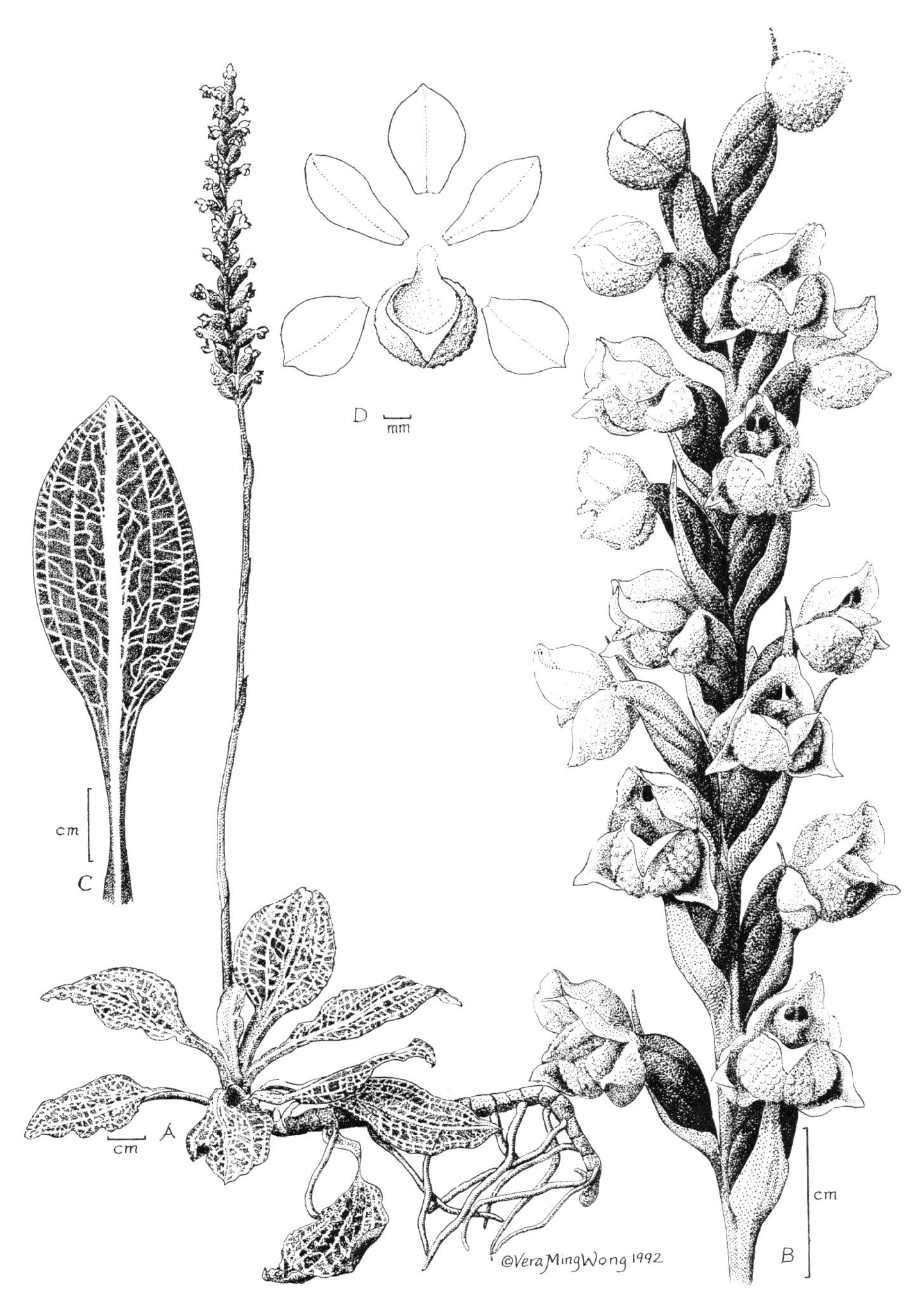

Goodyera pubescens ***A***—Whole plant in flower, ***B***—Inflorescence, ***C***—Typical leaf, ***D***—Typical flower, exploded view

The rhizome creeps over the surface of the ground and sends its roots down into the humus.

Each plant flowers once then dies (August 13).

high water-holding characteristics. They tend to be somewhat acidic, and this seems to be important. Rarely, if ever, is this orchid found in soils derived from calcareous glacial till of the Des Moines Lobe (late Wisconsin glaciation), which are alkaline, not acidic.

A unique feature of all the *Goodyera* orchids is the central role of the peculiar rhizome. In the case of *G. pubescens*, the rhizome is a thick greenish structure that creeps over the surface of the ground like a giant centipede with a few coarse roots serving as anchors. It grows at the rate of 3 to 5 centimeters per year and accumulates evergreen leaves in a

Shady understory in an Aitkin County forest, home to a large colony of *G. pubescens*

spiral whorl. In Minnesota, the leaves seem to live about a year and a half (two summers and one winter), with new leaves produced each year. When the rhizome has reached an age of four to eight years, it will produce its first, and last, flowering spike (Reddoch and Reddoch 2007). The following year the rhizome will produce one to three slender vegetative offshoots, then die. The offshoots will survive and begin to grow as independent rhizomes, producing their own leaves and small roots each year, just as their parent did. After four to eight years, each new rhizome will be ready to produce its first and last flowering spike and vegetative offshoots, repeating the cycle (Reddoch and Reddoch 2007).

Seedlings also enter the population as small creeping rhizomes, indistinguishable from the offshoots. They reportedly grow more slowly than the offshoots and take longer to reach flowering stage; otherwise they function the same (Reddoch and Reddoch 2007). Over several decades, large colonies of rhizomes can develop as a result of offshoot growth and local seedling establishment.

The pearly white flowers are pollinated by bumblebees (August 13).

In one study, only about 7 percent of the rhizomes produced flowers in any given year. This pattern was interrupted every two to four years by mass flowerings that involved up to 30 percent of the rhizomes (Reddoch and Reddoch 2007). These episodic events were found to be synchronous within colonies, among colonies, and between populations, sometimes over large areas. The phenomenon was apparently triggered by extensive periods of warm, dry weather during May of the previous year (Reddoch and Reddoch 2007).

Goodyera repens (L.) R. Br.
Lesser rattlesnake-plantain

[*Goodyera repens* (L.) R. Br. var. *ophioides* Fern.]

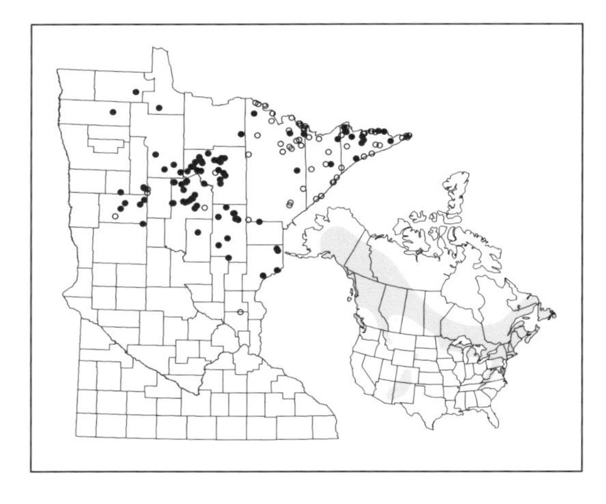

Plants 8–19 cm tall; aerial **stem** with 2–4 lanceolate bracts scattered between the base and the inflorescence, otherwise leafless; **rhizome** reaching a length of about 8 cm; **roots** few, fibrous, 2–6 cm long. **Leaves** 3–8, essentially basal and forming an evergreen rosette; the blades ovate to lance-ovate, 1.1–3.2 cm long, 0.7–1.7 cm wide, dark green with white or pale green reticulation along the veins. **Inflorescence** a dense to loose spicate raceme, 3–7 cm long, ± one-sided (secund), with up to 25 white flowers, each flower subtended by a lanceolate bract 4–8 mm long. **Flowers** small and inconspicuous; **sepals** ovate to oblong or elliptic, 3–3.5 mm long; **petals** oblong-spatulate, 3–3.5 mm long, converging with the dorsal sepal to form a hood over the lip; **lip** bowl-shaped, 2.7–3.5 mm long, about 2 mm wide, contracted above the middle to form a downward-curving beak. **Capsules** ascending or divergent, 3–7 mm long. **Flowering** July 12–August 20, mostly the last 2 weeks in July and the first week in August.

Typically, *G. repens* has no more than twenty-five flowers, on just one side of the stem (photograph by Peter Dziuk).

Older plant manuals often append the name var. *ophioides* to plants that have the familiar white reticulate leaf pattern, and var. *repens* to those without (Smith 1993). Recent studies have discovered so much variability in leaf pattern that recognizing varieties is no longer recommended (Kallunki 2002).

Of the three species of *Goodyera* in Minnesota, people seem to catch on to *G. pubescens* quickly but struggle with *G. repens* and *G. tesselata*. For a convenient handle, think of *G. repens* as the smaller one that lives in wet conifer swamps and *G. tesselata* as the larger one that lives in dry pine forests. This distinction holds true most of the time, although it does not always work in the three northeastern counties where habitat differences between the two species tend to blur, as do differences in their appearance. Intermediate specimens may be hybrids, and they can be very difficult to identify. Fortunately, "pure" examples of both species outnumber hybrids.

Goodyera repens ***A***—Whole plant in flower, ***B***—Portion of the inflorescence, ***C***—Typical leaf, ***D***—Typical flower, sagittal section, ***E***—Typical flower, exploded view

Although habitats of "pure" *G. repens* do vary somewhat by region, in essentially all cases the soil will be moist or wet, acidic rather than alkaline, and shaded by mature coniferous trees. This usually translates into rich swamp forests, although in the three northeastern counties it includes upland forests with loamy soil or woody humus that is relatively moist but not wet. It can also be found on mossy boulders and sheltered rock ledges.

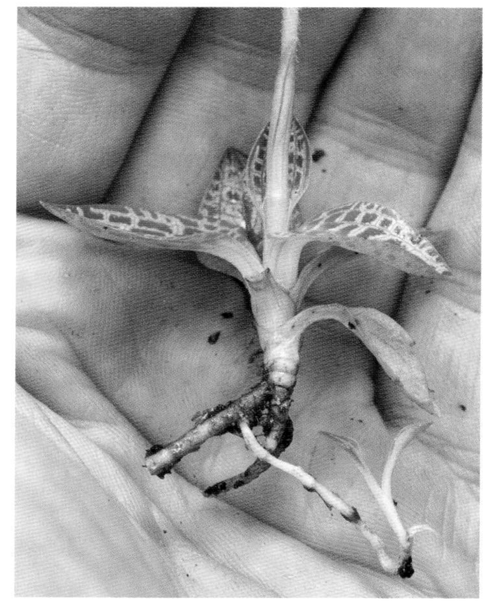

Notice the small leafy offshoot coming off the rhizome (July 14).

G. repens does not live as long or grow as large as *G. pubescens*, but it has a similar life history that revolves around the rhizome—a modified type of stem that lies just beneath the surface of the ground. The rhizome can originate in one of two ways, as a seedling or as a vegetative offshoot from a parent rhizome. Regardless of its origin, the progression of a newly formed rhizome to adulthood is always the same.

During the year in which offshoots are still attached to the parent rhizome, they 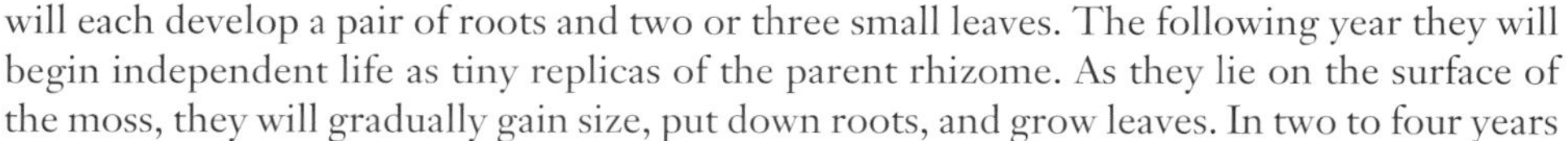 will each develop a pair of roots and two or three small leaves. The following year they will begin independent life as tiny replicas of the parent rhizome. As they lie on the surface of the moss, they will gradually gain size, put down roots, and grow leaves. In two to four years they will be large enough to send up a flowering spike just as their parent did and, like their parent, will send out one to four slender offshoots and then die, leaving the next generation of offshoots to fend for themselves. For a *Goodyera* orchid there is no second chance.

The reticulate leaf pattern seems to be consistent on Minnesota specimens (July 14).

The early life of a *G. repens* seedling is a bit of a mystery. Seedlings probably take a few years longer to reach flowering size than the offshoots, but the end is the same. In this way a population will contain plants of both seedling origin and clonal offshoots. Perhaps this is a hedge against the uncertainty of weather and pollinators.

The whole plant rarely reaches 8 inches (20 cm) tall (July 14).

Goodyera tesselata Lodd.

Tessellated rattlesnake-plantain

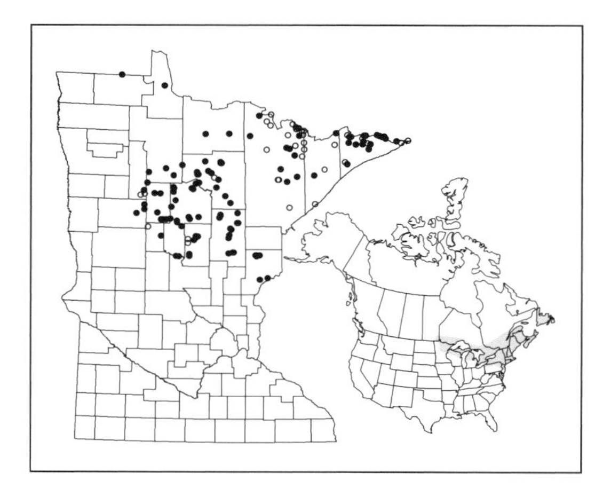

Plants 18–36 cm tall; aerial **stem** with 3–5 lanceolate bracts scattered between the inflorescence and the base, otherwise leafless; **rhizome** shallow, 1–7 cm long; **roots** few, fibrous, rather coarse, 3–10 cm long. **Leaves** 3–8, essentially basal and forming an evergreen rosette; the blades elliptic to ovate or lance-ovate, 2–5 cm long, 1.2–2.5 cm wide, bluish green with white or pale green reticulation. **Inflorescence** a spicate raceme 5–17 cm long, usually 1-sided (secund), partially spiraled or cylindric, with 15–40 white flowers, each flower subtended by a lanceolate bract 5–12 mm long. **Flowers** small and rather inconspicuous; **sepals** elliptic-oblong to ovate-lanceolate, 3.5–6.3 mm long; **petals** spatulate, 3.5–5.8 mm long, converging with the dorsal sepal to form a hood over the lip; **lip** 3–4.5 mm long, 3–3.5 mm wide, deeply concave to bowl-shaped, the apex usually pointed and somewhat recurved. **Capsules** ascending, 5–9 mm long. **Flowering** July 12–August 10, peaking in the last 2 weeks of July.

Trace the six roots back to the rhizome, the heart of the plant (August 6).

In central Minnesota, the ranges of three species of *Goodyera* overlap, but the species are distinct and fairly easy to tell apart. Usually the size and color of the leaves, and the number and arrangement of the flowers, are all that is needed (see key on page 104). Using habitat as an identifying characteristic usually works, with experience, but is not foolproof. If uncertainty lingers, locate the rostellum deep within the flower and measure the length of the tip, or "beak," under a microscope.

The situation is somewhat different in the northeast where *G. repens* and *G. tesselata* tend to blend together. This appears to be the result of hybridization brought about by a close juxtaposition of the two species, a shared pollinator, and overlapping flowering dates. Most of the plants found in the northeast do appear to be genetically pure, but apparent hybrids and backcrosses are not hard to find.

Hybridization may vex people trying to nail down the identification of a plant, but it is often

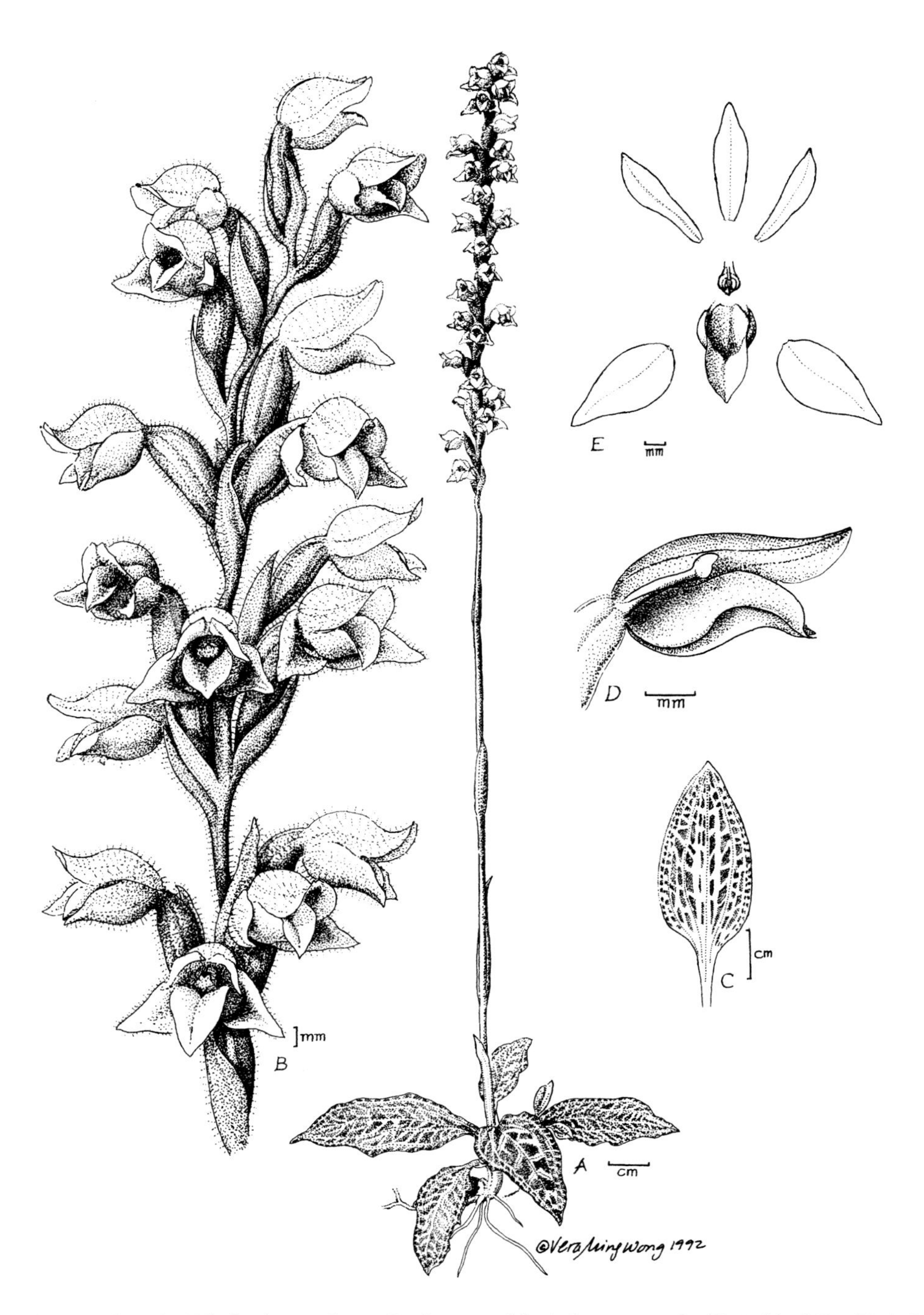

Goodyera tesselata ***A***—Whole plant in flower, ***B***—Portion of the inflorescence, ***C***—Typical leaf, ***D***—Typical flower, longitudinal section, ***E***—Typical flower, exploded view

The leaves are bluish green and have a faint reticulate pattern (photograph by Peter Dziuk).

Stems are typically 7–15 inches (18–36 cm) tall and flower between July 12 and August 10 (photograph by Richard Haug).

a driving force in plant evolution. In fact, it is widely accepted that *G. tesselata* itself arose through hybridization between *G. oblongifolia* and *G. repens* during the early post-Pleistocene (Kallunki 1976). The existence of stable populations of *G. tesselata* in Minnesota, which is hundreds of miles west of where *G. oblongifolia* occurs today, only highlights the effectiveness of hybridization as an engine of plant speciation (Kallunki 1981).

Allowing for some regional variation, *G. tesselata* strongly prefers a habitat of dry, sandy soil under native stands of pine trees, typically jack pine but also red pine. This holds true throughout most of the state, although in the northeastern counties you can expect to find it in a wider range of forest types and soil types.

According to accepted ecological principals, natural pine forests in Minnesota originate after a stand-replacing wildfire (MDNR 2003). The shallow rhizomes of *G. tesselata* would likely not survive a fire, but it is a mobile species, and it is easy to imagine it moving about in a patchwork of burned and unburned habitat, which is exactly what jack pine does.

Wildfire has been essentially eliminated as an ecological process in the pine ecosystems of most of Minnesota, replaced by clear-cutting for timber production. In the past, clear-cut jack pine was left to regenerate naturally, which seemed to suit *G. tesselata*. Unfortunately, cutover pine forests are rarely left to recover on their own anymore. They are being systematically converted to plantations, often in a heavy-handed fashion that eliminates the native understory and ground-layer plants. This does not bode well for *G. tesselata* and other sensitive forest plants.

There are usually fifteen to forty creamy white flowers, mostly on one side of the raceme (August 6).

The life history of *G. tesselata* is basically the same as described for *G. pubescens*, only accelerated. The rhizomes are much smaller, and the leaves are barely evergreen. The entire life cycle of a rhizome that arises as an offshoot takes perhaps only two to four years. Rhizomes originating from seeds may take longer to reach maturity, but not much longer. Either way, a rhizome produces flowers only once, then dies, leaving behind seeds and vegetative offshoots. This sequence may, to some extent, be synchronized within a population, leading to a mass die-off of an entire generation. Fortunately, the passing of one generation is marked by the beginning of another.

Genus *Liparis* Rich.
Twayblade orchids

The name *Liparis* is from the Greek word variously translated as "fat," "greasy," or "shining," in reference to the appearance of the leaves. There are about 250 species of *Liparis* distributed in tropical and temperate regions worldwide, with 3 species in the United States and 2 species in Minnesota (Magrath 2002).

Liparis is most closely related to *Malaxis;* both regenerate each spring from an annual pseudobulb produced at the base of the stem. The pseudobulb is an ovoid structure found just beneath the substrate, or sometimes partially exposed at the surface. It is enveloped in the base of the lowest foliage leaf and has a cluster of short, fibrous roots growing from the bottom. Each year, a new pseudobulb and a new set of roots are produced at the first internode of the stem directly above the pseudobulb of the previous year. In the spring, the old, spent pseudobulb can usually be seen still attached to the new, fresh one, but it will continue to fade as the season progresses.

L. liliifolia is self-incompatible, meaning it requires cross-pollination to produce viable seed (Whigham 2004). The insect that carries the pollinia from one flower to another has not been identified, although it has been reported that the flowers have been visited by flies of the family Sarcophagidae, the flesh flies (Catling and Catling 1991).

L. loeselii is an example of a rain-assisted auto-pollinated orchid. A single raindrop is all that is needed to transfer the pollinia from the rostellum onto the stigmatic surface (Catling 1980a).

A Key to the *Liparis* of Minnesota

1. Floral lip pale purple, 8–12 mm long, 6–9 mm wide; pedicel of fruiting capsule 1.1–1.8 cm long (pedicel and capsule together 2.3–3.6 cm long); leaves 2.5–9.5 cm wide (usually more than 4 cm), the blades 1.5–3× longer than wide; a plant of upland forests. .... ***L. liliifolia***

1. Floral lip yellowish green, 4–5.5 mm long, 2.2–3.5 mm wide; pedicel of fruiting capsule 0.3–0.7 cm long (pedicel and capsule together 1.1–2 cm long); leaves 1–5 cm wide (usually less than 4 cm), the blades 3–6× longer than wide; a plant of wetlands or occasionally uplands. .... ***L. loeselii***

Liparis liliifolia (L.) Rich. ex Lindl.
Lily-leaved twayblade; large-leaved twayblade

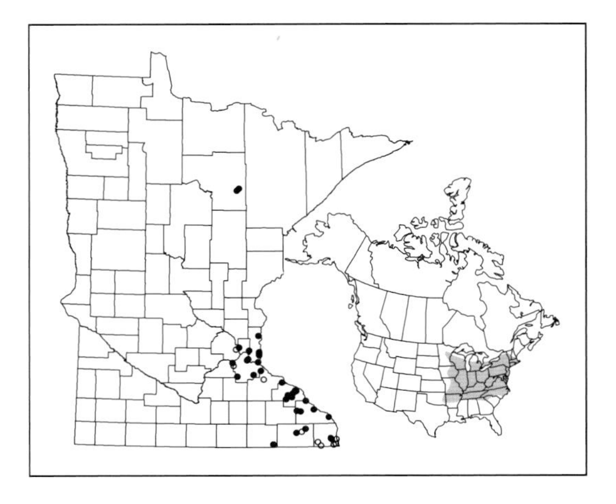

Plants 9–27 cm tall; **stem** angled or somewhat ridged in cross section, especially distally, leafless; **pseudobulb** ovoid, 1–3 cm long, shallowly buried; **roots** few, fibrous, 1–4 cm long. **Leaves** 2, basal, sheathing the pseudobulb and the lower portion of the stem, elliptic to elliptic-ovate, shiny and somewhat succulent, 5–16 cm long, 2.5–9.5 cm wide, the apex acute or obtuse. **Inflorescence** a terminal raceme, 4–14 cm long, with 6–24 flowers, each flower subtended by a slender bract about 2 mm long. **Flowers** somewhat conspicuous, although subtly colored; **ovary** and pedicel appearing confluent, together 8–14 mm long at anthesis, becoming an erect, winged or ribbed **capsule** 1.1–1.8 cm long; **sepals** linear, pale green or yellowish, 8–11.5 mm long; **petals** threadlike, purple, 8.5–12 mm long; **lip** purple, obovate, apiculate, 8–12 mm long, 6–9 mm wide. **Flowering** June 5–July 9, mostly the second and third weeks of June.

The seed capsules stand erect and have thin vertical ridges or ribs (July 20).

There are plants very similar to *Liparis liliifolia* in Japan and China (Magrath 2002), but nothing in North America has flowers like this plant. Visually, the flower is dominated by the broad, flat, purple lip. The petals and sepals are slender and inconspicuous. The seed capsule has several narrow, raised ribs or ridges that run lengthwise, and it sits erect at the top of a relatively long stalk. Only *L. loeselii* has similar capsules.

There is no mistaking this plant if flowers are present, but most plants are found without any flowers, just a pair of rather shiny succulent leaves. In that case, the only way to distinguish this plant from *L. loeselii* is the size and proportion of the leaves (see key on page 119), a distinction that is not always clear-cut. Habitats of the two species are normally quite different; *L. liliifolia* occurs in upland forests, and *L. loeselii* occurs in wetlands.

L. liliifolia is consistently found in forests with well-drained sandy or sandy loam soils. It is overwhelmingly associated with oaks, usually

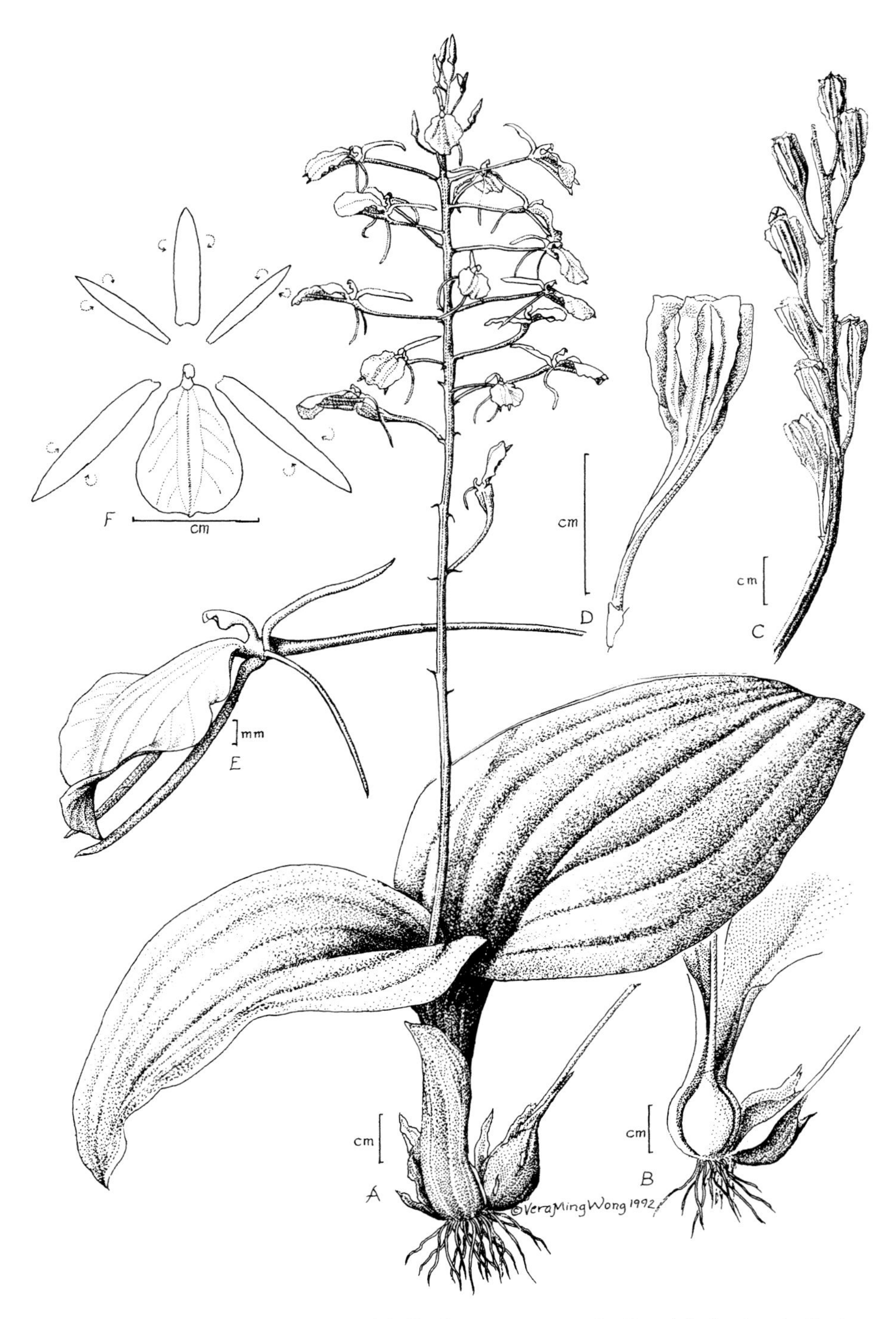

Liparis liliifolia ***A***—Whole plant with pseudobulb of previous season, ***B***—Pseudobulbs, longitudinal section, ***C***—Portion of stem in fruit (infructescence), ***D***—Single seed capsule, ***E***—Typical flower, ***F***—Typical flower, exploded view

You won't be confused by this orchid if you see it in flower; nothing else in Minnesota looks like it (photograph by Peter Dziuk).

The pseudobulb generates the roots and stem, then a replacement for itself (July 5).

some combination of northern pin oak, bur oak, or white oak. There will often be trembling aspen in the mix, and sometimes a few white pine in the vicinity. There are also a number of records from mature pine plantations, but I suspect this happens only where a plantation is established on good forest soils previously occupied by oak or aspen.

In Minnesota, forests of oak and aspen are considered fire-dependent. This means that without periodic ground fires, the oak and aspen trees would be slowly replaced by different species, such as shade-tolerant maples or basswood, in a process called forest succession. The implication is that all naturally occurring oak and aspen forests in Minnesota have a history of ground fires. It is unlikely that *L. liliifolia* itself is adapted to survive fire. In fact, the shallowly buried pseudobulb would probably be killed by even a "cool" ground fire. It seems more likely that it copes with fire by outmaneuvering it. For example, it might be burned out during a fire but later reestablish itself by seeds blown in from a nearby unburned patch of forest.

This is mostly academic now; wildfires in the oak–aspen ecosystems of Minnesota have been suppressed for perhaps a century and will likely never return, so irreversible forest succession is well underway. To forest succession add forest fragmentation and the invasion of the forest understory by the nonnative common buckthorn, which can quickly eliminate nearly everything else, and you have a very uncertain future for *L. liliifolia* in Minnesota.

In its favor, *L. liliifolia* is a rather mobile species. It appears to form small transient colonies that move about within a larger

The flower is a delicate structure dominated by the broad purple lip (July 3).

metapopulation. This ecological agility may help explain the seemingly incongruous occurrence of *L. liliifolia* in more than one tailings basin on the Iron Range in Itasca County. This is an example of long-range dispersion and is the only known case of *L. liliifolia* occurring beyond what is thought of as its "natural" range in Minnesota.

Liparis loeselii (L.) Rich.
Loesel's twayblade

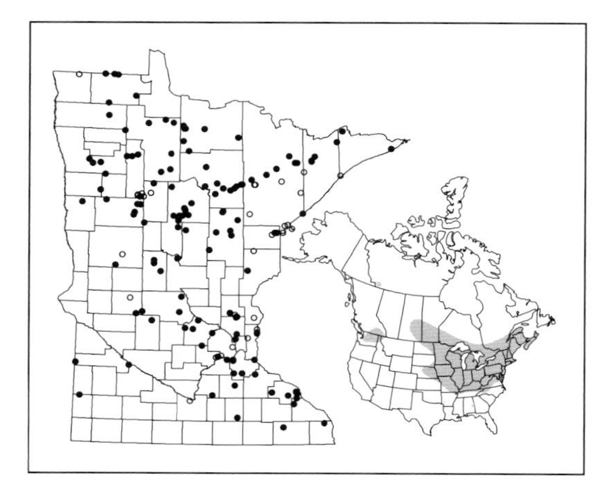

Plants 8–28 cm tall; **stem** angled or somewhat ridged in cross section, especially distally, leafless; **pseudobulb** ovoid, 1–2.5 cm long, superficial or shallowly buried; roots few, fibrous, 1–4 cm long. **Leaves** 2, basal, sheathing the pseudobulb and the lower portion of the stem, elliptic to elliptic-lanceolate, rather thick and fleshy, 4–17 cm long, 1–5 cm wide, the apex acute or obtuse. **Inflorescence** a terminal raceme 2.5–11 cm long, with 3–20 yellowish green flowers, each flower subtended by a slender bract about 2 mm long. **Flowers** yellowish green, somewhat inconspicuous; **ovary** and pedicel appearing confluent, together 4–10 mm long at anthesis, becoming an erect, winged or ribbed **capsule** 9–15 mm long; **sepals** oblong-lanceolate, 4.5–6 mm long; **petals** threadlike, 4.5–5.5 mm long; **lip** yellowish green, obovate to oblong, apiculate, 4–5.5 mm long, 2.2–3.5 mm wide. **Flowering** June 9–July 10, mostly the last 2 weeks of June.

The flowers are uniformly yellowish green, have an arching lip and thread-like petals (June 16).

The stem of a large *L. loeselii* can reach a height of about 11 inches (28 cm) and have as many as twenty flowers. But this orchid can also be incredibly small, only 3 or 4 inches tall with tiny leaves and just a few flowers, an exact miniature of the larger plants. These are probably young plants that have the potential to grow a little larger each year.

The flowers themselves are small and unremarkable: a pale yellowish green color, each with three narrow sepals, two tubular petals, and a peculiarly arching lip. Without the flowers there is no definitive characteristic that separates the two *Liparis* species, and they can be difficult to tell apart. Comparing the size and proportion of the leaves and the seed capsule usually works (see key on page 119).

Habitats of *L. loeselii* include a wide variety of wetlands and occasionally marginal uplands as well. Soils are either alkaline or weakly acidic and composed of peat, muck, sand, or wet loam. Sunlight is either direct or diffuse.

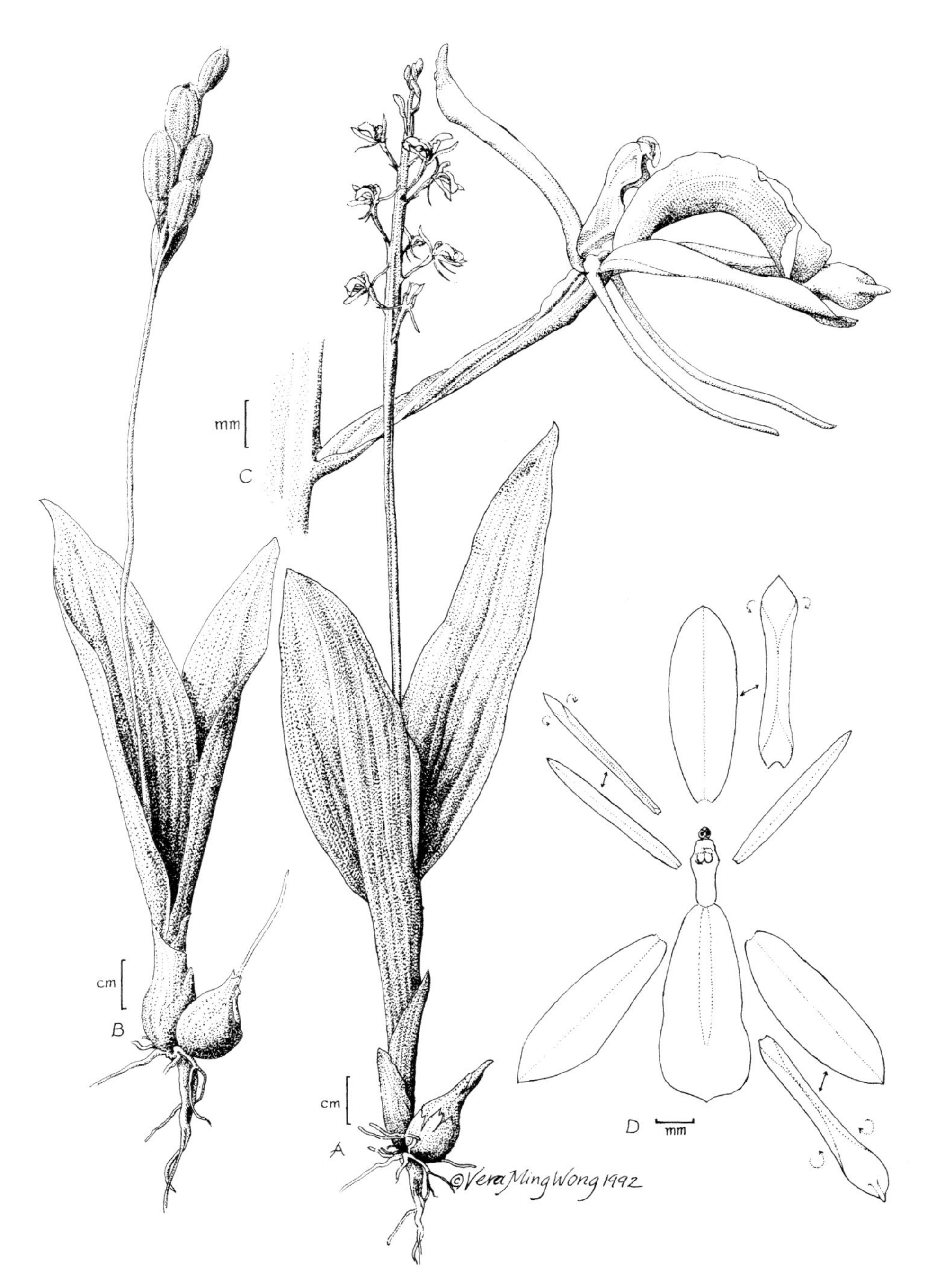

Liparis loeselii ***A***—Whole plant in flower, ***B***—Whole plant in fruit, ***C***—Typical flower, ***D***—Typical flower, exploded view

The pseudobulb is an annual structure that replaces itself every year (August 5, Clearwater County).

Each fruit is a winged or ribbed capsule that stands erect and holds thousands of seeds (July 21).

It can be said that *L. loeselii* occurs statewide, although habitats get rather sparse in prairie regions. It occurs predictably in prairie fens, but prairie fens are rare. It is found less predictably in wet prairies, prairie marshes, and sedge meadows.

In forested regions expect *L. loeselii* in seepage swamps, rich fens, floating sedge mats, open conifer swamps, shrub swamps, and sandy lakeshores. About 10–15 percent of the records are from what can be described as uplands, such as moist cliffs, mossy boulders, shrubby thickets, and pine forests. The upland occurrences may not be self-sustaining populations—perhaps just an adventurous plant exploring new terrain. It seems *L. loeselii* can pop up almost anywhere, usually perched on top of something rather than growing from it. Clearly, it doesn't take much to provide habitat for this tiny orchid.

Occasionally *L. loeselii* is found in neglected man-made habitats such as the margins of groundwater pools that develop at the bottom of abandoned gravel pits and in the drained and abandoned sediment basins used by the iron mining industry. These habitats were created by human activity, but in time they have come to support a stable community of mostly native species and become attractive to *L. loeselii*. However, do not expect to find this orchid in active industrial sites or urban settings.

It has been reported that seeds of *L. loeselii* are shed in autumn, germinate the following spring, and by August have produced their first foliage leaf and a small pseudobulb (Rasmussen 1995). Once a plant reaches that point, it will tend to get bigger in each successive year until it gets large enough to produce flowers. No one seems to know how long that takes, but it must happen rather quickly because plants don't live long. There are reports of European plants living for eight years (Jones 1998), although a study of American plants in Massachusetts found virtually no plants living more than five years (McMaster 2001). This is one example of accelerated population dynamics, not usually thought of as a hallmark of orchid populations.

Each flowering plant has two thick, fleshy leaves that attach at the base of the stem (photograph by Peter Dziuk).

Genus *Listera* R. Br.
Twayblades

The name *Listera* is in honor of Martin Lister (1638–1711), an English naturalist. This is a genus of about twenty-five species that occur in temperate and boreal habitats worldwide. There are eight species in the United States and three in Minnesota (Magrath and Coleman 2002). These are small orchids with a single pair of broad, opposite leaves that attach near the midpoint of the plant. The individual flowers are also quite small and have a two-lobed or forked lip.

Each year a single aerial stem and two to five slender roots are produced at the tip of a short, unbranched, fleshy rhizome. The rhizome will then grow 1 to 3 centimeters past that point, or node, and remain dormant until the next spring when it will produce a new stem and a new set of roots, creating a new node. Nodes from previous years will not produce stems again, although they will retain their roots and survive for perhaps two to four years.

The roots of *L. cordata* have been reported to sprout shoots along their length and at their tips in a remarkable feat of vegetative reproduction (Rasmussen 1986; Nieuwdorp 1972). I cannot discount this, but after examining the intact root systems of thirty-nine individual *L. cordata* plants, I am unable to confirm this. Clusters of plants growing only a few centimeters apart have been carefully excavated, and each one was found to have its own complete, independent root system. In fact, I have seen no evidence of any vegetative reproduction in this species. The belowground structures of *L. cordata* appear fundamentally the same as the two other *Listera* species that occur in Minnesota.

The pollination biology of *L. cordata* has been worked out in some detail. There isn't much known about the pollination biology of the two other Minnesota species, but the flower structure of all three species is similar, so they likely have a similar process.

The flowers of *L. cordata* are self-compatible but not self-pollinating. Therefore, pollination requires an insect and a very specific sequence of events (Ackerman and Mesler 1979). The foul odor emitted by the flowers attracts a variety of insects, most notably fungus gnats (Mesler et al. 1980). However, it is believed that any insect of the appropriate size and general structure can act as a pollinator (Catling and Catling 1991). When an insect feeds on the nectar of a newly opened flower, it will contact minute touch-sensitive trigger hairs at the tip of the rostellum, and a droplet of sticky, quick-drying liquid is shot from the rostellum onto the insect. Immediately afterward the margins of the rostellum reflex, thereby releasing the pollinia into the liquid (Ackerman and Mesler 1979). At about the same time, the broad, flap-like rostellum folds over the stigma to prevent self-pollination. The insect then flies away with the pollinia glued to its face. Approximately one day later, the rostellum retracts, and the stigma is exposed for pollination (Catling and Catling 1991).

A Key to the *Listera* of Minnesota

1. Lip 3–5 mm long, the apex cleft at least half the length of the lip resulting in 2 narrow, pointed lobes; column very short and inconspicuous, about 0.5 mm long. . . . . ***L. cordata***

1. Lip 7–12 mm long, the apex merely notched, or at the most cleft a third the length of the lip resulting in 2 broadly rounded lobes; column conspicuous, 2.5–3.5 mm long.

- **2.** Lip with broad basal auricles that clasp the column, the base nearly as broad as the apex, the apex notched one-fifth to one-third the length of the lip; pedicels and ovaries smooth, not glandular. . . . . ***L. auriculata***

- **2.** Lip without basal auricles although lateral "bumps" are present about one-fourth of the way up from the base, otherwise the lip tapers ± evenly from apex to base, the apex notched one-tenth to one-fifth of the length of the lip; pedicels and ovaries distinctly glandular. . . . . ***L. convallarioides***

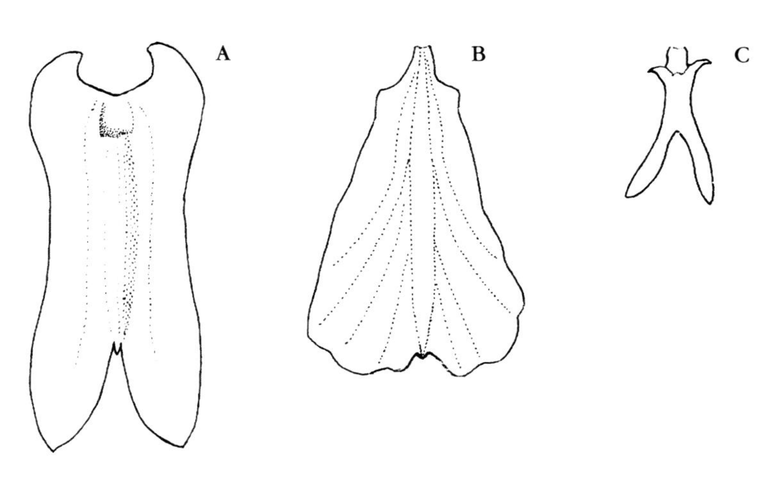

Comparison of floral lips of ***Listera*** spp. ***A***—*L. auriculata* (6× actual size), ***B***—*L. convallarioides* (4× actual size), ***C***—*L. cordata* (5× actual size)

Listera auriculata Wieg.

Auricled twayblade

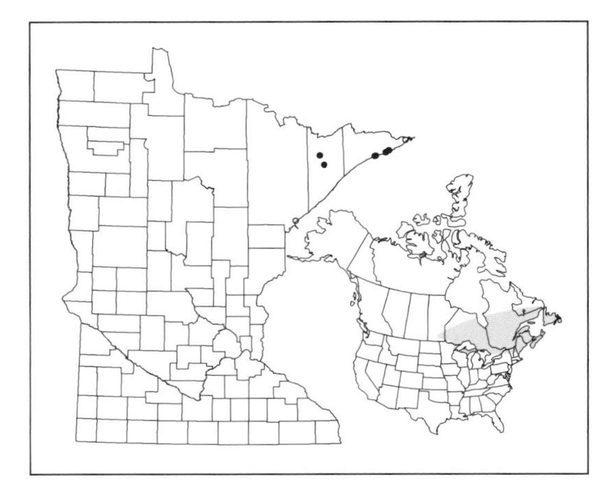

Plants 9–18 cm tall; **stem** glabrous; **rhizome** slender, unbranched, to 5 or more cm long, with internodes of 3–15 mm; **roots** few, fibrous, 2–6 cm long. **Leaves** 2, subopposite, sessile, ovate to elliptic, attached near the middle of the stem, 2.7–5 cm long, 2.1–3.6 cm wide. **Inflorescence** a terminal raceme with a glandular-hairy rachis, 4–7.5 cm long, with 8–16 pale green flowers, each flower subtended by a bract 2–7 mm long. **Flowers** small and inconspicuous; **pedicels** and **ovaries** glabrous; **dorsal sepal** elliptic to obovate, 3–3.5 mm long; **lateral sepals** elliptic to oblong, 3.2–4.5 mm long, distinctly falcate; **petals** linear to linear-oblong, 3–3.7 mm long, falcate; **lip** obovate to oblong or nearly rectangular, 7–10 mm long, 2–5 mm wide, apex cleft or notched approximately one-fifth to one-third the length of the lip, the base with auricles curving around and clasping the base of the column. **Capsules** spreading to ascending, about 8 mm long. **Flowering** June 15–July 25, mostly the last week in June and the first 2 weeks in July.

The fruits are small, globular capsules, which develop quickly after pollination (photograph by Michael Lee).

In Minnesota, *L. auriculata* is very rare and very difficult to find. In fact, it is thought to be rare throughout its geographic range, which is limited to a relatively small portion of eastern North America (Whiting and Catling 1977). If you think you've found this orchid (and before congratulating yourself) always look closely at the details of the flower to see if you might actually have *L. convallarioides*, which would be an even more exciting discovery. Perhaps the simplest way to tell the two apart is to look for a bristly covering of gland-tipped hairs on the ovary—*L. convallarioides* has it; *L. auriculata* does not.

There is one possible but unlikely complication: the two *Listera* species are known to hybridize when they come into close contact. The hybrid, named *L.* ×*veltmanii*, has an appearance almost exactly intermediate between its two parents, but it can be much taller than either one (Catling 1976).

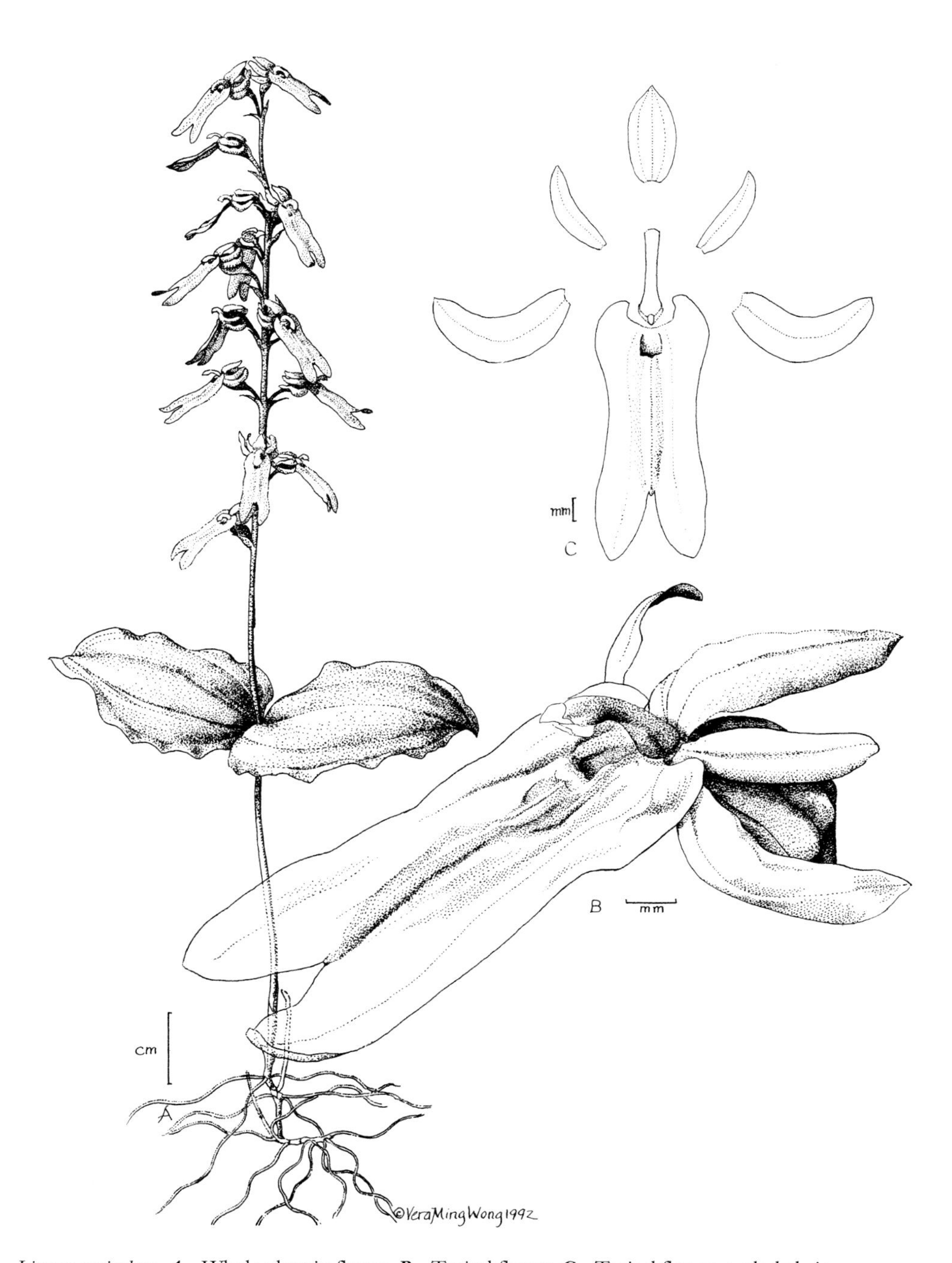

Listera auriculata ***A***—Whole plant in flower, ***B***—Typical flower, ***C***—Typical flower, exploded view

The hybrid will be found only where the two parents are growing in close proximity, which makes a hybrid very unlikely to occur in Minnesota.

The exact habitat of this orchid is rather difficult to characterize. The setting is in cool, moist, northern forests, usually under black ash, white spruce, balsam fir, or speckled alder, and, for whatever reason, often near the shore of Lake Superior. Within this setting, *L. auriculata* is typically localized in low-lying areas, perhaps favoring seasonally wet places along small streams or pond margins. These are not quite wetlands and certainly not swamps or bogs, but *L. auriculata* seems never far from water. The ground will often have patches of mosses, but not deep or continuous moss and not *Sphagnum* moss. Soils vary from poorly decomposed humus and loam to fine or coarse alluvial sediments such as silty sand or gravel. In all cases conditions are somewhat acidic.

Many of the habitats would seem to be at risk of flooding in the spring and ice-scouring in the winter. For this reason, it is possible that *L. auriculata* might not persist long in any one place. Instead it may rely on seeds carried on puffs of wind or perhaps on flowing water to reestablish itself at a nearby site. An example of this might be a site along Snake Creek (Lake County) discovered in 1985. There were about twelve plants under a canopy of black ash and American elm. They are known to have survived several years, but they did not survive a large tree falling on them in 1992. Another small population was found at the margin of a small shallow pond in 1991. Although the plants managed to endure flooding in 1994, they were apparently gone only a few years later.

A network of small transient populations, known as a metapopulation, seems a plausible explanation. A more detailed explanation would require careful monitoring of populations over a longer period of time, which would not be an easy task.

A single *L. auriculata* is silhouetted by the hand of botanist Lynden Gerdes (Lake County).

The entire plant will be no more than 7 inches (18 cm) tall and have eight to sixteen flowers and two leaves.

Listera convallarioides (Sw.) Elliot
Broad-leaved twayblade

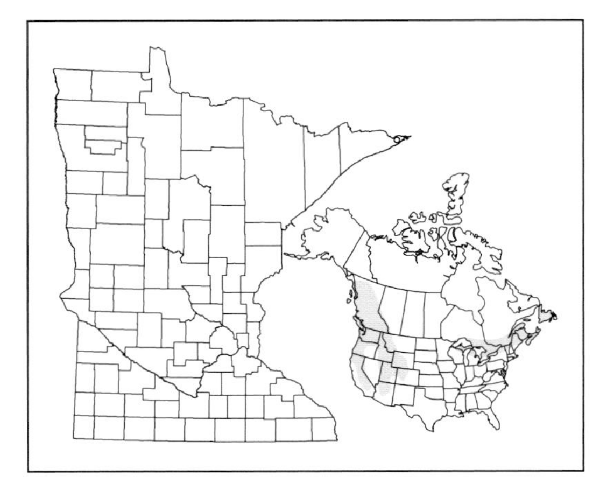

Plants 10–22 cm tall; **stem** glabrous; **rhizome** slender, unbranched, to 5 or more cm long, with at most 3–4 internodes in the range of 5–20 mm; **roots** few, fibrous to somewhat fleshy, from 2 to 12 or more cm long. **Leaves** 2, subopposite, sessile, broadly ovate to elliptic or nearly circular, attached near the middle of the stem, 2.5–5.7 cm long, 2.3–5.2 cm wide. **Inflorescence** a terminal raceme with a glandular-hairy rachis, 3.5–10 cm long, with 6–20 flowers, each flower subtended by a bract 3–5 mm long. **Flowers** small, yellowish green, inconspicuous; **pedicels** and **ovaries** glandular-hairy; **dorsal sepal** elliptic to lanceolate, 4.5–5 mm long; **lateral sepals** oblong to lanceolate, 4.5–5.5 mm long, distinctly falcate; **petals** linear, 4–5 mm long, falcate; **lip** narrowly triangular, 9–12 mm long, up to 6.5 mm wide, apex cleft or notched one-tenth to one-fifth the length of the lip, the base with lateral "bumps" rather than distinct auricles, otherwise tapering evenly to a narrow base. **Capsules** spreading to ascending, about 8 mm long. **Flowering** dates unknown in Minnesota; the single Minnesota specimen was collected in flower bud on July 5.

The lip of *L. convallarioides* is broad at the distal end and tapers to the base; compare to the flower of *L. auriculata*.

Positive identification of *L. convallarioides* will not be difficult, but in order to rule out the similar *L. auriculata* it will be necessary to examine the flower in detail. Take a close look at the shape of the lip (see comparison on page 129), and check the pedicels and ovaries for a dense covering of gland-tipped hairs, which are absent in *L. auriculata*.

L. convallarioides can cross with *L. auriculata* to produce a natural hybrid *L.* ×*veltmanii* (Catling 1976). Such a hybrid occurring in Minnesota is possible but very unlikely given the rarity of the two species. The two parents would have to be growing no farther apart than the distance a single fungus gnat (the likely pollinator) can fly.

Although *L. convallarioides* is known from a number of locations

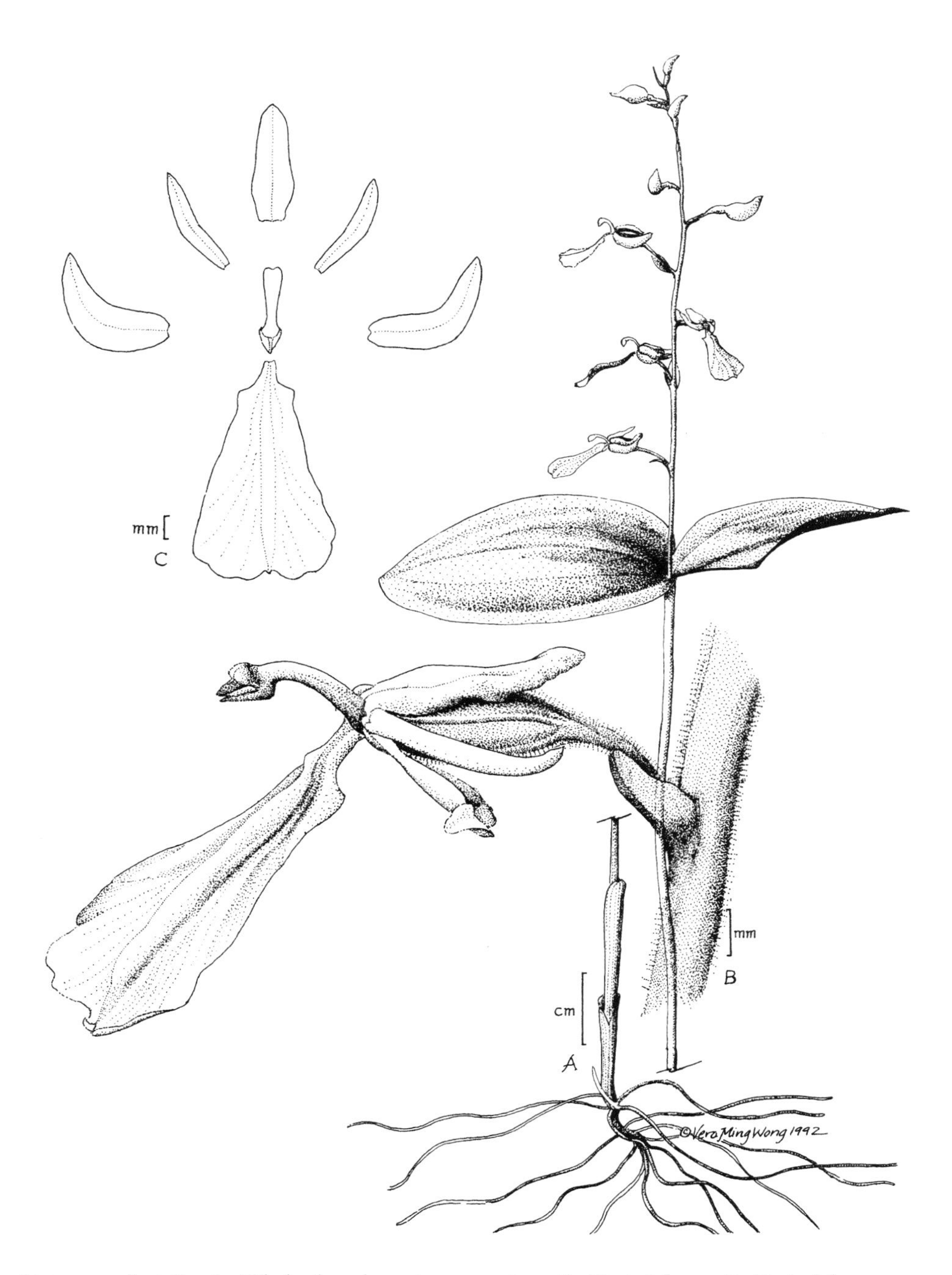

Listera convallarioides ***A***—Whole plant shown in two portions, ***B***—Typical flower, ***C***—Typical flower, exploded view

From left to right: Ned Huff, Carl Otto Rosendahl, Frederick King Butters (circa 1940)

on the Apostle Islands (Wisconsin) and Isle Royale (Michigan), there is only one documented record from Minnesota. It is a specimen in the University of Minnesota herbarium collected somewhere near Mineral Center in Cook County by C. O. Rosendahl and F. K. Butters on July 5, 1924. This was the occasion of Butters's first extensive collecting trip into Cook County. It was the first of many such trips, which would culminate in the publication of a landmark floristic study (Butters and Abbe 1953). On this particular trip the duo took their Model T Ford up the newly opened Highway 1 into Cook County—the first time the county had been accessible by car. They were almost certainly not searching for this species, and they apparently did not even recognize it when they found it. Luck, it seems, favors the intrepid.

It is not known if there was anything particularly unique about the forest where Rosendahl and Butters found *L. convallarioides*. It was described only as a "cedar-spruce-balsam forest," apparently referring to northern white cedar, black spruce, and balsam fir. These are common trees that dominate forested swamps in northeastern Minnesota, and the habitat was likely just that—a forested swamp. There would likely have been a carpet of *Sphagnum* moss overlaying wet peat, making the ground feel spongy or springy. Growing conditions would no doubt have been weakly acidic, cool, and shaded. In this situation, the roots of *L. convallarioides* would probably be in the moss and not in direct contact with the water table.

This same combination of tree species can also be found in moist upland forests that are not as wet as swamps. In that case, the soils would be damp but not wet and would feel firm underfoot. The soils would be high in organic matter, especially woody material in varying stages of decomposition, and there would probably be a lot of what is called "coarse woody debris"—the decomposing, moss-covered trunks and branches of fallen trees.

The habitat types, as I am interpreting them, are not particularly uncommon in northeastern Minnesota, but much of the region is not easily accessible and has not been thoroughly botanized, so there is a reasonably good chance that a population of *L. convallarioides* that was there in 1924 is still there waiting to be rediscovered. There's no reason someone can't get lucky again.

Notice the nonflowering plants of *L. convallarioides* clustered around the flowering plants (Bayfield, Wisconsin).

Listera cordata (L.) R. Br.
Heart-leaved twayblade

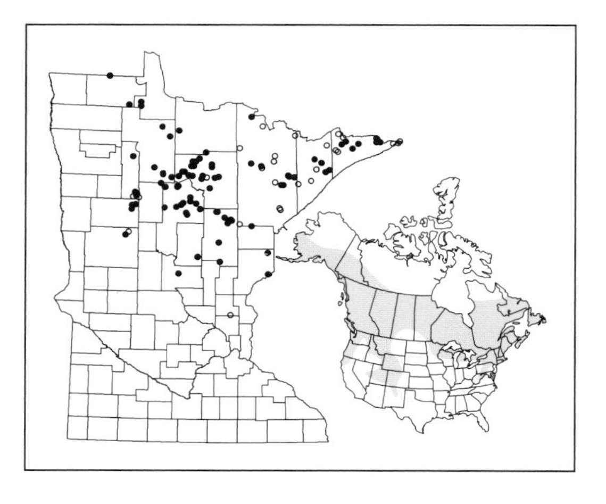

Plants 8–33 cm tall; **stem** glabrous; somewhat succulent; **rhizome** slender, unbranched, to about 5 cm long; **roots** few, fibrous, or somewhat fleshy, from 2–15+ cm long. **Leaves** 2, opposite, sessile, ovate-deltate, attached near the middle of the stem, 1–4 cm long, 0.8–3.3 cm wide. **Inflorescence** a terminal raceme with a glandular-hairy rachis, 2–13 cm long, with 6–21 flowers, each flower subtended by a minute bract. **Flowers** green, yellow-green, or reddish purple, minute, inconspicuous; **pedicels** and **ovaries** glabrous; **sepals** ovate-elliptic to oblong, 1.5–2.8 mm long; **petals** similar to the sepals but somewhat smaller; **lip** linear-oblong, 3–5 mm long, 1–2 mm wide, the apex cleft at least one-half the length of the lip, the base with a narrow tooth on each side. **Capsules** ascending, 2–4 mm long. **Flowering** May 25–July 5, pollination generally occurring by the third week of June, but the flowers persisting.

The flowers are minute and range in color from green to reddish purple.

This orchid has a circumpolar distribution, meaning it occurs in a wide band across North America as well as northern Asia, Europe, and Greenland. Plants with slightly larger leaves and flowers are found at high elevations in western North America and are sometimes recognized as var. *nephrophylla* (Magrath and Coleman 2002).

Although *L. cordata* is small and cryptically colored, it is not particularly difficult to find or to identify in northern Minnesota. The lasting visual image is provided by the paired leaves. They project horizontally from somewhere near the middle of the plant and seem peculiarly small in proportion to the entire plant, at least to some eyes. The deeply forked lip of the flower and the almost round ovaries are also features easily seen.

The habitat of *L. cordata* in Minnesota is overwhelmingly conifer swamps. This is one of the orchids you would have a good chance of seeing in nearly any well-developed conifer swamp north of the latitude of about Brainerd. Good habitats usually have a sparse to dense canopy of tamarack, black spruce, northern white cedar, or balsam fir. Expect the forest floor to have a nearly continuous cover of

Listera cordata ***A***—Whole plant shown in two portions, ***B***—Portion of the inflorescence, ***C***—Typical leaf, ***D***—Typical flower, exploded view

The leaves are said to be heart-shaped.

mosses, typically brown mosses and *Sphagnum* mosses.

Swamps do occur in the southern half of the state, but they are much rarer than in the north. They also tend to be smaller in the south and more isolated from other swamps. The only wetland conifer that remains common in the south is tamarack. Hardwood trees, such as black ash, red maple, and paper birch, assume more importance. Also, these southern Minnesota swamps tend to have fewer mosses and more sedges.

This tiny orchid is usually found rooted in the moist environment between the stems of the *Sphagnum* plants. The roots of *L. cordata* seem too frail or delicate to push through harder material, and they seem to need the constant supply of water that is wicked up through the closely packed stems of the *Sphagnum* plants. This is usually a reliable source of water, but if the *Sphagnum* dries out in drought years, the *L. cordata* will likely die.

Reproduction seems limited to seeds, which *L. cordata* produces in large numbers and with surprising efficiency. The number of *L. cordata* flowers that successfully produce seeds was reported in one study to be 61–78 percent (Ackerman and Mesler 1979). Most of

The vertical structure is the rhizome; the three lateral structures are the roots (June 8).

the terrestrial orchids mentioned in another study had fruit set of less than 50 percent (Mesler et al. 1980). The whole process happens very quickly: the lowermost flowers open first and are pollinated, reach maturity, and release seeds while the upper flowers are still courting pollinators (Stoutamire 1964).

It is not known how long it takes *L. cordata* to mature from seed. Artificially germinated *L. cordata* are still tiny protocorms with no chlorophyll at fifteen months (Stoutamire 1964). Vinogradova (1996) reports the first green leaf appears after two or three years of underground development. Once *L. cordata* appears aboveground, it will flower every year for an indefinite period. Since the root and rhizome system is perpetually self-renewing, an individual *L. cordata* never grows old.

This is one of Minnesota's smallest orchids (Beltrami County, May 28).

Genus *Malaxis* Solander ex Swartz
Adder's-mouth orchids

The name *Malaxis* is from the Greek word for "soft" or "delicate," perhaps in reference to the leaves. There are about 250 species of *Malaxis* worldwide; 10 species occur in the United States and 3 in Minnesota (Catling and Magrath 2002).

A taxonomic concept that would return two of our species (*M. monophyllos* var. *brachypoda* and *M. unifolia*) to the genus *Microstylis* has been recently published (Szlachetko and Margońska 2006) but is not followed here. More exhaustive study of this large and complex group of plants is needed.

Orchids of the genus *Malaxis* typically have inconspicuous greenish flowers with nectar readily accessible on the surface of the lip. This open flower design allows a variety of insects to assist in pollination, including small wasps, sawflies, gnats, and beetles. For some species of *Malaxis*, fungus gnats are especially important (Catling and Catling 1991).

The flowering stem of *Malaxis* arises from an annual pseudobulb that is enveloped in the base of a leaf at the lowest part of the stem. At some time during the growing season the portion of the stem just above the pseudobulb starts to swell and eventually becomes the pseudobulb for the next season (Kozhevnikova and Vinogradova 1999). This has the effect of elevating the plant a little more each year, which may explain why some plants often appear to be perched on top of their mossy surroundings rather than buried within it.

Roots, in the usual sense, are not apparent in *Malaxis* or are reduced to structures resembling short fine hairs that are easily missed. It is clear that *Malaxis* has no perennial structure; everything is renewed annually.

Malaxis possesses the smallest flowers of any Minnesota orchid, making it very difficult to see and measure critical details of floral morphology, especially in pressed specimens. For that reason floral characters are not emphasized in the key.

A Key to the *Malaxis* of Minnesota

1. Leaves 2–4 per stem, all clustered near the base of the stem, 1–3 cm long (generally less than 2.5 cm) and not more than 1 cm wide.
. . . . ***M. paludosa***

1. Leaf 1 per stem, appearing to be attached well above the base of the stem, 2.5–8 cm long and more than 1 cm wide.

2. Inflorescence usually more than 5 cm long (range of 4 to 11.5 cm) and less than 1 cm wide; flowers evenly spaced within the inflorescence; the longest pedicels no more than 3 mm long; floral lip with a narrow, pointed apex and dilated base.
. . . . . . ***M. monophyllos* var. *brachypoda***

2. Inflorescence usually less than 5 cm long (range of 1.5 to 6 cm) and at least 1 cm wide; flowers mostly crowded near the summit of the inflorescence with the lower ones more widely spaced; the longest pedicels (the lower ones) 3–8 mm long; floral lip with a wide, blunt, 3-toothed apex, not dilated at base.
. . . . ***M. unifolia***

Malaxis monophyllos (L.) Sw. var. *brachypoda* (Gray) Morris & Eames
White adder's-mouth

[*Malaxis brachypoda* (A. Gray) Fern.; *Microstylis monophyllos* (L.) Sw. subsp. *brachypoda* (A. Gray) Szlach. & Marg.]

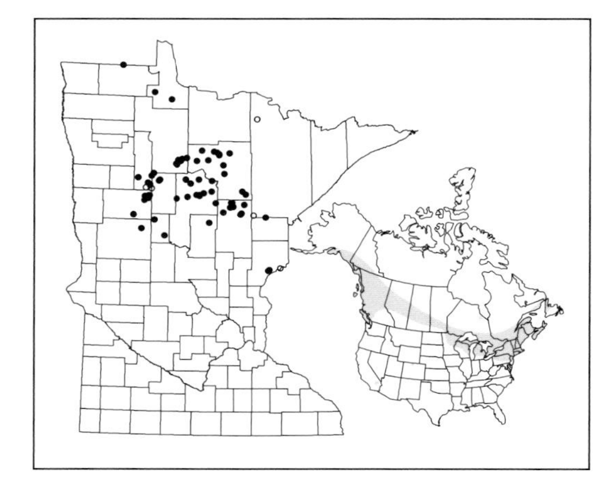

Plants 10–27 cm tall; **pseudobulb** ovoid to globular, 0.5–1.5 cm long, originating as a swelling at the base of the stem directly above the pseudobulb of the previous year; **roots** not apparent. **Leaf** 1, the petiole sheathing the lower portion of the stem with the blade appearing some distance above the base, blade elliptic, 2.7–8 cm long, 1.3–3.7 cm wide, the apex acute or obtuse. **Inflorescence** a slender terminal raceme, 4–11.5 cm long, with 12–35 flowers, each flower subtended by a lanceolate bract 1–2 mm long. **Flowers** resupinate, whitish or greenish white, minute, inconspicuous; **sepals** ovate-lanceolate to oblong-lanceolate, 1.7–2.5 mm long; **petals** linear to linear-lanceolate, reflexed, 1.5–2 mm long; **lip** somewhat triangular, contracted near the middle to produce a narrow, lanceolate tip, the base dilated to produce basal auricles that curve forward, 1.4–2 mm long, 1–1.7 mm wide at base. **Capsules** ascending, 3–5 mm long. **Flowering** June 20–July 25, primarily the last week of June and the first 2 weeks of July.

There is a single leaf that diverges from the stem some distance above the base (July 13, Clearwater County).

Malaxis monophyllos occurs across North America and Eurasia and seems to vary in only one significant characteristic: flowers of North American plants are resupinate (twisted 180 degrees) and are called var. *brachypoda;* flowers of Eurasian plants are not resupinate and are called var. *monophyllos* (Catling and Magrath 2002).

In the field, this plant is usually recognized by the single leaf and the relatively long, slender inflorescence of minute, evenly spaced, whitish flowers. The flowers themselves are uniquely structured with tiny pointed sepals radiating in a star pattern, but the flowers are so small the details are hard to see without a microscope.

The plant has only one leaf, which looks similar to the leaf of *M. unifolia*. In both species the leaf appears to be attached to the stem somewhere above the base. Actually, the leaf

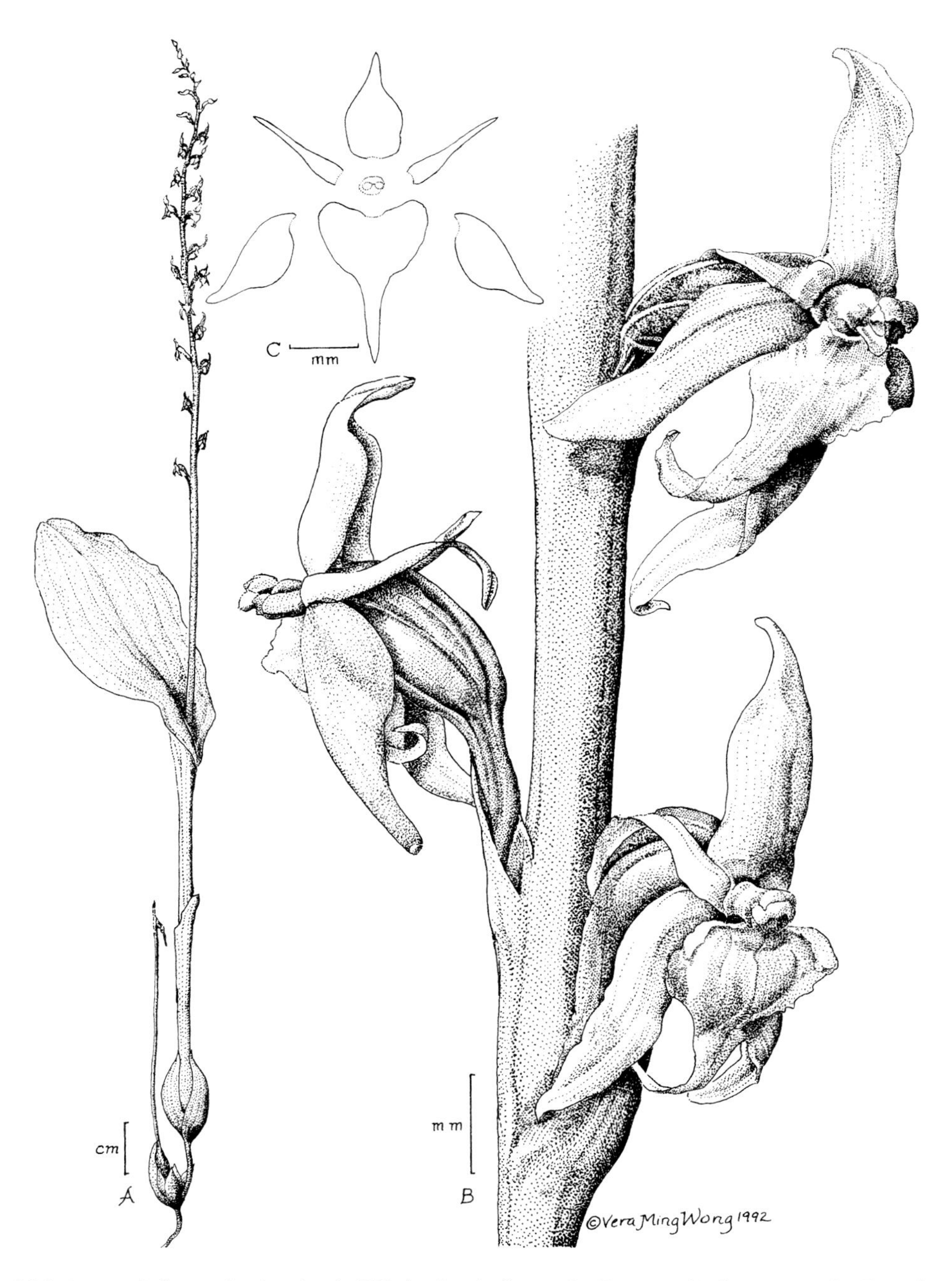

Malaxis monophyllos var. *brachypoda* ***A***—Whole plant in flower, ***B***—Portion of inflorescence, ***C***—Typical flower, exploded view

Look for a long, slender inflorescence with small, evenly spaced flowers (July 13, Clearwater County).

originates at the base of the stem, but the petiole sheaths the stem for some distance before the blade diverges.

This orchid is considerably less common than most other "bog" orchids and occurs in smaller numbers. Often only a few are found, or more often none, even in what might appear to be good habitat. Good habitat tends to be a conifer swamp, usually with a canopy of northern white cedar, black spruce, tamarack, or balsam fir. Occasionally black ash will be a significant component of the habitat. The immediate terrain is usually characterized by a subtly undulant topography of water-filled hollows a few feet across and slightly raised mounds of *Brachythecium* or *Sphagnum* moss, all set among a jumble of wind-thrown trees and tangled shrubs. This is a supermarket of microhabitats where orchids of a dozen species pick and choose the microhabitat of their choice, or perhaps it is the habitat that chooses the orchid.

Habitats of *M. monophyllos* var. *brachypoda* in Minnesota tend to be weakly acidic with a pH of perhaps 5.0 to 6.5. The fact that the water is not more acidic indicates an inflow of subsurface water that has been in contact with mineral soil somewhere not too distant. This gives the water a certain mineral richness that leads to a greater diversity of plant species, especially among the orchids. Within this setting, *M. monophyllos* var. *brachypoda* seems to occur in small micro-sites such as the edges of wet, mossy depressions where there is little immediate competition. It might be helpful to keep in mind that the moss is not a competitor of orchids. It is more like the growth medium of the orchid or a structural component of the habitat.

Suitable habitats seem widespread in the northern half of Minnesota, but something about habitats in the north-central counties must be different. Only in that region can *M. monophyllos* var. *brachypoda* be found with some regularity.

The flowers are white, but incredibly small and hard to see (July 9).

Malaxis paludosa (L.) Sw.
Bog adder's-mouth

[*Hammarbya paludosa* (L.) Kuntz]

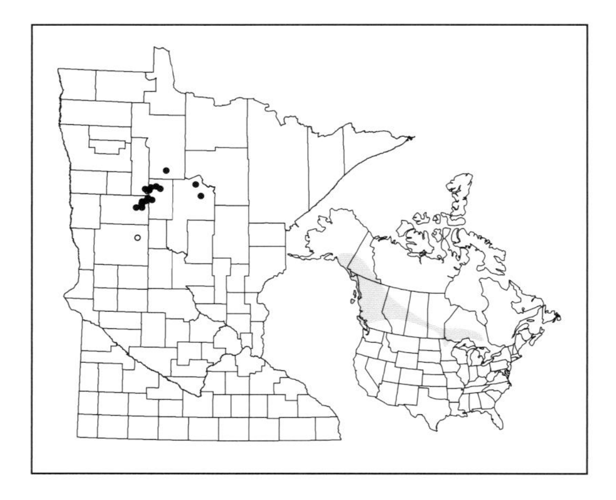

Plants 6–23 cm tall; **pseudobulb** globular, 4–7 mm long, originating as a swelling at the base of the stem some distance above the pseudobulb of the previous year; **roots** reduced to short fine hairs. **Leaves** 2–4, basal, sheathing the pseudobulb; the blade elliptic, 1–3 cm long, 0.3–1 cm wide; apex acute to obtuse, often with tiny foliar embryos at the tip. **Inflorescence** a terminal raceme 2.7–9 cm long, with 10–29 flowers, each flower subtended by a lanceolate bract 2–3 mm long. **Flowers** not resupinate, minute, yellowish green, inconspicuous; **sepals** ovate-lanceolate to elliptic, 2–3 mm long; **petals** ovate-lanceolate, 1–1.5 mm long; **lip** ovate, sometimes with a noticeable constriction above the middle producing a "nipple" at the apex, rarely with a second constriction below the first, resulting in a vague 3-lobed appearance, 1.7–1.9 mm long, about 0.8 mm wide. **Capsules** ascending, 3–4 mm long. **Flowering** July 10–August 29, primarily July 20–August 15.

The pseudobulb is tucked into the base of a leaf near the ground (August 4).

The identification of *M. paludosa* is rarely an issue. If you have found this plant, it is probably because you were looking for it, so you won't puzzle over its identity for long. But if in doubt, first locate the pseudobulb, a pea-sized swelling of the stem. This will narrow your choices to either a *Malaxis* or a *Liparis*. The small size of the flowers will eliminate *Liparis* and the key on page 143 will eliminate all the *Malaxis* except this one. Congratulations, you have found one of the rarest and most elusive plants in Minnesota.

The worldwide distribution of *M. paludosa* is considered circumboreal (Hultén 1958; Luer 1975), meaning it occurs throughout the boreal region in a more or less continuous circle around the Earth. But this is rather misleading; *M. paludosa* is actually infrequent in the main part of its range in north-central Eurasia, and it is extremely rare in North America (Zoladeski

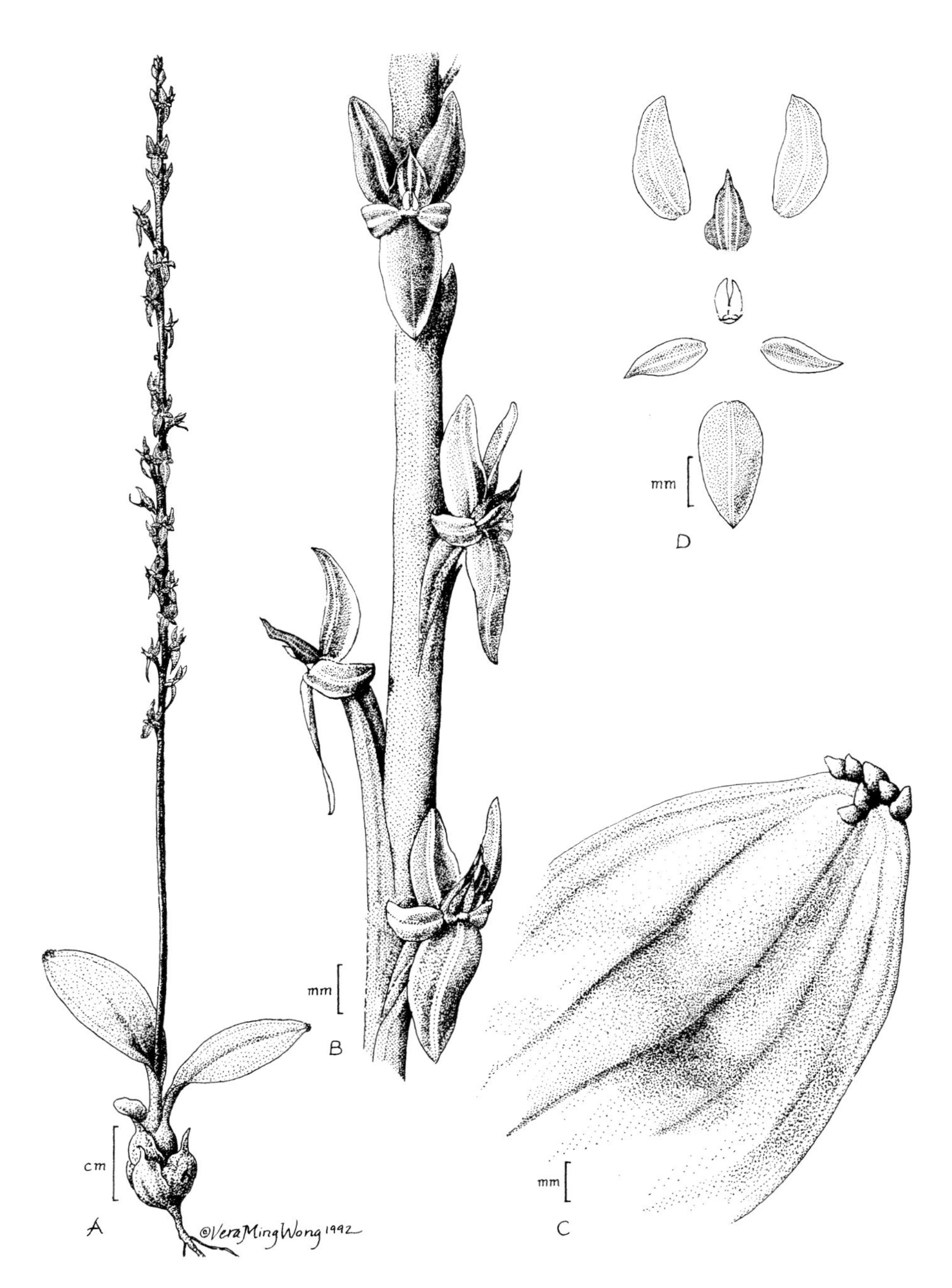

Malaxis paludosa ***A***—Whole plant in flower, ***B***—Portion of the inflorescence, ***C***—Leaf with foliar embryos at tip, ***D***—Typical flower, exploded view

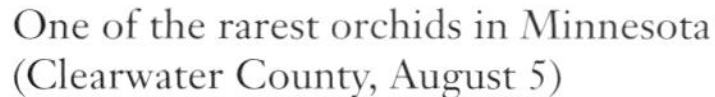

One of the rarest orchids in Minnesota (Clearwater County, August 5)

The petals and sepals are only about 0.06 inch (1.5 mm) long; flowers don't get much smaller than this (August 5).

1988). In fact, the discovery of this tiny orchid in North America dates back only to July 1904, when it was found by H. L. Lyon near New York Mills, Otter Tail County, Minnesota. Since then only a relative handful of plants have been found in North America, primarily in Alaska and Minnesota.

There is no obvious explanation as to why this tiny, seemingly frail orchid is found in a relatively small area in the northwestern part of the state and in so few other places. And yet it is clearly at home and quite well adapted to its environment. One population in Minnesota has been under observation since 1929 (confirmed as recently as 2010); that is at least eighty-one years at the same spot.

A curious feature of *M. paludosa* is its ability to create clusters of foliar embryos at the tips of some leaves (Dickie 1872). These appear to be simple embryo-like structures enclosed in a sterile jacket of cells. But the "embryos" do not arise from sexual reproduction; they arise directly from leaf tissue. Development of the tiny embryos after they become independent of the leaf has not been studied, but it appears that each embryo develops the same way a seedling does (Taylor 1967).

It should be added that *M. paludosa* does produce true seedlings in the typical way, through cross-pollination of its tiny flowers, which are dwarfed by any insect pollinator larger than a fungus gnat (Reeves and Reeves 1984).

The typical habitat of *M. paludosa* in Minnesota is classified as a rich conifer swamp or rich spruce swamp (MDNR 2003). Visually, you would see a carpet of *Pleurozium* and *Sphagnum* mosses under a canopy of black spruce with occasional northern white cedar, tamarack, or balsam fir. Typically the shrub layer is fairly open with only minor amounts of alder-leaved buckthorn, red-osier dogwood, speckled alder, or bog birch. The forest floor will have fine-leaved sedges, such as *Carex leptalea* or *Carex disperma*, and scattered ferns and insectivorous plants such as sundews and purple pitcher plants. *M. paludosa* will likely be found in semishaded areas "perched" on low moss hummocks, appearing as if not anchored at all (Rowe 2007).

Typical habitat of *Malaxis paludosa* in Minnesota (Clearwater County)

Malaxis unifolia Michx.
Green adder's-mouth

[*Microstylis unifolia* (Michx.) Britton, Stern. & Pogg.]

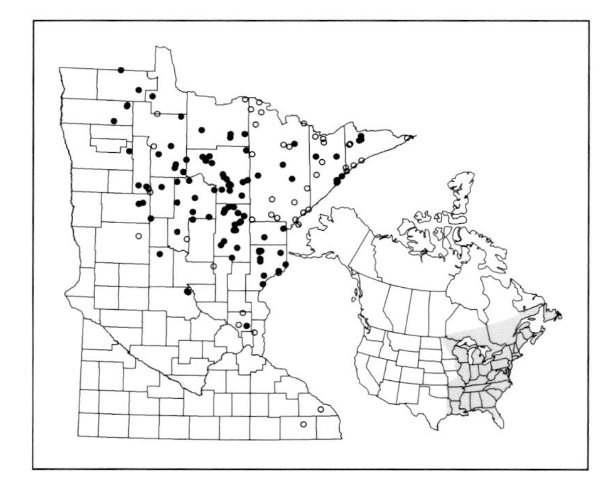

Plants 9–35 cm tall; **pseudobulb** globular, 0.5–1.5 cm long, developing from the side of the pseudobulb of the previous year or from a swelling on the stem above it; **roots** few, fibrous, 0.5–2 cm long. **Leaf** 1, the petiole sheathing the lower part of the stem with the blade appearing near the middle of the stem, the blade ovate to nearly elliptic, 2.5–7.5 cm long, 1.3–4 cm wide. **Inflorescence** a condensed terminal raceme 1.5–6 (8) cm long, with 25–95 flowers mostly crowded near the summit with the lower ones more widely spaced, each flower subtended by a subulate to triangular bract 0.5–2 mm long. **Flowers** resupinate, minute, green, inconspicuous; **sepals** linear-oblong to elliptic, about 1.5 mm long; **petals** linear, recurved, about 1.5 mm long; **lip** about 2 mm long and 1.5 mm wide, generally rectangular in outline, with 3 teeth at the apex, the middle tooth much smaller than the lateral teeth, the base with rounded or pointed auricles. **Capsules** spreading to slightly drooping, 4–5 mm long. **Flowering** July 1–August 10, peaking during the second or third week in July.

Each year a new pseudobulb is produced directly above the previous one, which will soon disappear (August 5).

The individual flowers of *M. unifolia* are too small to reveal any structural detail without a microscope or at least a hand lens, but in aggregate the flowers have a unique appearance and are easily remembered. The lower flowers are widely spaced and seem to sit awkwardly at the ends of unnecessarily long stalks. Progressing upward, the flowers become more closely spaced and the stalks get shorter until everything is condensed into a flat-topped cluster. It seems as if the cluster should open and expand as the plant grows, but it never does.

The tightly packed flowers at the top of the inflorescence don't make obvious sense. Few of them will ever set seed. Perhaps the flowers function more as a single compound flower, using their collective presence to entice more pollinators.

This plant is relatively common in northern Minnesota, but it is extremely rare in southern Minnesota. In fact, there are only two authentic records from far southern Minnesota. One is from

Malaxis unifolia ***A***—Whole plant in flower, ***B***—Inflorescence, ***C***—Flower, fully open, ***D***—Flower, partially open, ***E***—Typical flower, exploded view

This black spruce swamp in Clearwater County supports a healthy population of *M. unifolia*.

Winona County, dated 1890, and the other is from Fillmore County, dated 1892. The latter record is a voucher specimen collected by H. Hooslef and bears the note: "This is the only specimen I have found here." Not very hopeful, but *M. unifolia* probably still exists somewhere in southern Minnesota, although it will take luck or hard work to find it again.

In northern Minnesota, *M. unifolia* occurs in a variety of habitats. The most common habitat, by a small margin, is conifer swamps, usually in the shade of northern white cedar, black spruce, or speckled alder. It is usually rooted in living *Sphagnum* moss or in the underlying organic material that is in varying stages of decomposition. Within the whole range of peatland types, these habitats tend to be toward the "rich" end of the nutrient scale. The pH of such a habitat would likely indicate a weakly acidic environment. Exposure ranges from full sunlight to full shade.

Perhaps paradoxically, it is not at all unusual to find *M. unifolia* in dry upland habitats, typically in sandy

Individual flowers are too small to reveal much detail, but the way they cluster at the top is distinctive (August 5).

Platanthera aquilonis ***A***—whole plant in flower, ***B***—Portion of inflorescence, ***C***—Typical flower, exploded view

Notice the yellowish lip of the flower, and notice the mosquito—it is a potential pollinator (July 9).

the stigma and are almost parallel to each other, with the tips more widely separated than in *P. aquilonis*.

The position of the anther sacs may seem like a trivial difference, but it has profound implications. It is known that *P. aquilonis* is facultatively autogamous (Wallace 2006), meaning that unless a pollinator, probably a mosquito in this case, visits the flower and removes the pollinia from the anther sacs as soon as it opens, the flower will pollinate itself (Catling and Catling 1991). This happens when the caudicle bends forward and downward, causing the pollinia to fall out of the anther sacs and onto the stigma (Sheviak 2001).

Among the orchids, *P. aquilonis* is rather common in Minnesota and occurs essentially statewide in a variety of wetland habitats. Conditions range from acidic to alkaline, sunny to shady, loamy to peaty.

Habitats in the prairie region include fens, wet prairies, and sedge meadows. Prairie fens are permanently saturated with calcareous groundwater, often with deposits of marl or tufa in shallow pools. The pH is typically in the range of 7.0 of 8.5, well into the alkaline end of the scale. The soil is peat, but of a type derived from the decomposed remains of sedges rather than mosses. In fact, mosses are sparse in prairie fens, and *Sphagnum* moss is absent.

Wet prairies and sedge meadows are different from fens in that they sometimes become dry at the surface during the summer, so peat does not accumulate. The soil is generally loam derived from glacial till, although there may be a thin layer of organic material on the surface.

Habitats of *P. aquilonis* in the forested region are similar to those in the prairie region in most regards. They are continually wet or moist, but they tend to be more shaded and more acidic, although not strongly acidic. These conditions are found in forested swamps, in shrub swamps, on mossy lakeshores, and along river margins. Good habitat is often found along habitat edges and in ecotones where an upland meets a lowland.

Plants will occasionally reach 30 inches (75 cm) in height and have as many as forty flowers (photograph by Peter Dziuk).

Platanthera clavellata (Michx.) Luer

Small green wood-orchid; club-spur orchid

[*Gymnadeniopsis clavellata* (Michx.) Rydb.; *Habenaria clavellata* (Michx.) Sprengel]

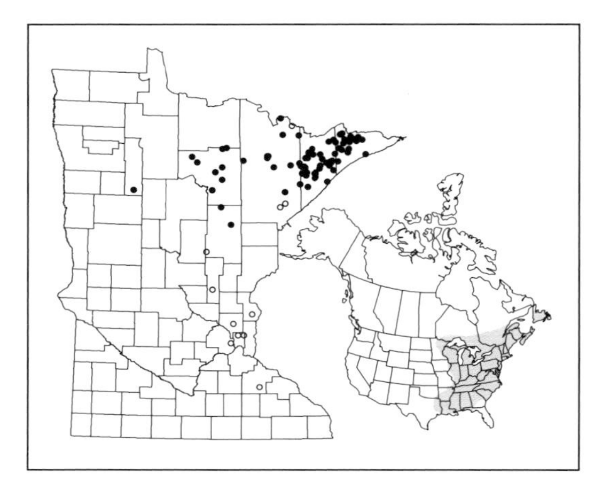

Plants 15–42 cm tall; **stem** erect, arising from the midpoint of a somewhat thickened horizontal **tuber** 3–10 cm long; **roots** 2 per tuber, slender, fleshy, growing laterally for a distance of 10 or more cm. Principal **leaf** 1, attached somewhat below the middle of the stem; obovate to oblanceolate or oblong; 5–14 cm long, 1–3 cm wide, an additional 1–3 vestigial bract-like leaves usually present above the principal leaf. **Inflorescence** a short, dense, terminal raceme, 1.5–5 cm long, with 5–20 flowers, each flower subtended by a lanceolate bract up to 1.1 cm long. **Flowers** imperfectly resupinate, each twisted into a ± horizontal position, greenish yellow or greenish white; **sepals** ovate, 2–4.5 mm long; **petals** similar to the sepals; **lip** oblong, shallowly toothed at apex, 2.5–5.5 mm long, 1.5–3 mm wide; **spur** club-shaped (clavate), 9–11 mm long. **Capsules** ascending, 6–10 mm long. **Flowering** July 10–August 10, peaking the last 2 weeks of July.

Notice that each flower is turned sideways, a characteristic of the species (photograph by Peter Dziuk).

The flowers of *P. clavellata* are usually a subtle greenish white and seem to blend into the background, although sometimes they are more white than green and may catch the eye. In any case, it takes only a moment to recognize this orchid. The first thing you notice is that the flowers appear tightly packed in a dense cluster at the top of a rather naked-looking stem, and the flowers look strangely askew. Each flower is twisted slightly off vertical one way or the other with the spur pointing sideways.

The strange "askewness" of the flower and the awkward tilting of the spur begs the question of pollination—is this flower pollinated by some strange sideways-flying insect? There is undoubtedly a story here, but only part of it is known. To the best of my knowledge, no one has caught an insect in the act of pollinating this plant, but the orchid has been caught in the act of pollinating itself (Catling

Platanthera clavellata ***A***—Whole plant in flower, ***B***—Inflorescence, ***C***—Portion of the inflorescence, ***D***—Typical flower, exploded view

Normally, *P. clavellata* has only one leaf, and it is attached somewhere below the middle of the stem.

The annual replacement tuber can be seen coming off the left side of the stem (July 23).

1983, 1984). The mechanism and the forces involved have not been fully described, but somehow the pollen mass breaks up and falls out of the anther sacs directly onto the stigmatic arms where auto-pollination occurs (Catling and Catling 1991).

P. clavellata has been found in most forested regions of the state, although it has not been found in southern Minnesota for several decades and not at all in the far northwestern counties. Most of the recent records have come from the central part of the Arrowhead Region. There may be more *P. clavellata* there than elsewhere, but more likely botanists have just gotten pretty good at finding it there. It should be noted that this is not a common orchid anywhere in Minnesota. Finding it requires a fair amount of luck or a lot of practice.

One good place to look is a floating *Sphagnum* mat surrounding open water in a peat-filled basin. This sort of habitat is usually dominated by fine-leaved sedges with patches of knee-high ericaceous shrubs, all within a matrix of thick, fluffy moss. Ecologists call these habitats fens. Trees, when present, are likely to be sparse and stunted black spruce, or sometimes tamarack, northern white cedar, or balsam fir.

A floating mat is not essential for *P. clavellata*. It can also be found in fens that develop on a flat, level plain where there is no open water. This type of fen might look similar to floating mats, but the peat sits on soil. Since it does not float on water, the surface is spongy but not bouncy, and there is no chance of breaking through. If there is an inlet and outlet for water to flow through a fen of this type, the water will tend to be richer in minerals and less acidic, in which case it may qualify as a rich fen. If the water comes primarily from precipitation rather than inflow, it will be lower in mineral nutrients and more acidic and called a poor fen.

Spotting *P. clavellata* in its habitat is not hard; finding the right habitat is another matter (July 29, Lake County).

Platanthera dilatata (Pursh) Lindl. ex Beck. var. *dilatata*
Tall white bog-orchid

[*Habenaria dilatata* (Pursh) Hook.; *Limnorchis dilatata* (Pursh) Rydb.]

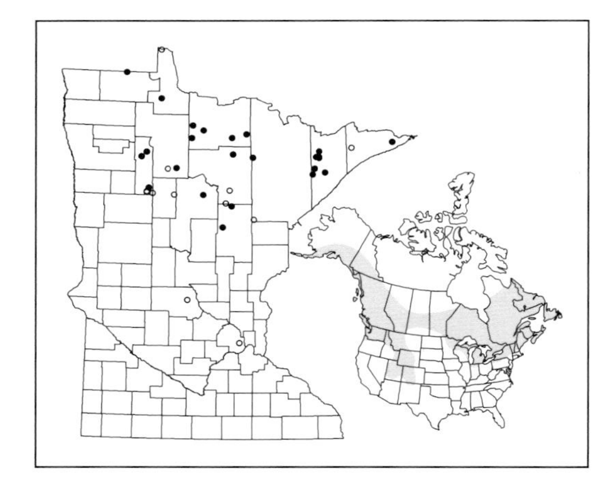

Plants 36–75 cm tall; **stem** leafy throughout or at least the lower two-thirds; **tuber** vertical, slender, tapering, 4–18 cm long; **roots** 2 per tuber, slender, fleshy, growing laterally for a distance of 20 or more cm. **Leaves** 3–6, scattered along the stem, lanceolate to linear or narrowly elliptic, to 20 cm long and 2 cm wide, gradually decreasing in size upward until they grade into the bracts. **Inflorescence** a terminal raceme, 5–23 cm long, with 10–60 flowers, each flower subtended by a lanceolate bract 0.7–2.7 cm long. **Flowers** white, fragrant, conspicuous; **dorsal sepal** ovate-elliptic, 3.3–7.3 mm long; **lateral sepals** ovate to lanceolate or narrowly elliptic, 4–9 mm long; **petals** similar in size and general shape to the sepals but somewhat hooked (falcate) and converging with the dorsal sepal to form a vague hood over the column; **lip** linear-lanceolate, abruptly dilated at base, 5–8 mm long, 1–3.3 mm wide, spur 4.5–8 mm long. **Capsules** erect to ascending, 7–13 mm long. **Flowering** July 1–August 7, mostly the last 2 weeks in July.

The flowers are pure white and intensely fragrant (August 5, Clearwater County).

There are three varieties of *P. dilatata* var. *dilatata* in North America, each differing in the length of the spur. The spur is the structure that produces nectar and in that way influences pollination (Sheviak 2002b). Minnesota populations appear to be relatively uniform and fall easily into var. *dilatata*, which is the variety with an intermediate-length spur.

Morphologically, *P. dilatata* var. *dilatata* is very similar to the other two bog-orchids in Minnesota, the green-flowered *P. aquilonis* and *P. huronensis*. The most obvious difference is the brilliantly white and intensely fragrant flowers—unmistakable in the field. As dried herbarium specimens, the white flowers will eventually fade to a pale yellowish brown color and are often misidentified as *P. huronensis*. In that case, the shape of the floral lip may be the best characteristic for separating the two. The base of the lip of *dilatata* var. *dilatata* is, as

Platanthera dilatata var. *dilatata* ***A***—Whole plant in flower, ***B***—Portion of the inflorescence, ***C***—typical flower, ***D***—Typical flower, exploded view

P. dilatata var. *dilatata* is a tall, slender orchid that can reach 30 inches (75 cm) in height (August 5, Clearwater County).

the name suggests, strongly dilated, sometimes nearly circular in outline. The lip of *P. huronensis* has straight sides or at most only a slight bulge.

Each of the three bog-orchids has a slightly different range of habitats, those of *P. dilatata* var. *dilatata* being the most restrictive. On occasion all three orchids can be found growing at the same site. But to accommodate *P. dilatata* var. *dilatata* the site will need to be some sort of very wet conifer swamp or rich fen, and habitat conditions will need to be stable on a scale of decades, perhaps centuries. Only peatlands with intact and stable hydrologic systems are suitable for *P. dilatata* var. *dilatata*. In this regard, *P. dilatata* var. *dilatata* is perhaps a good indicator of a stable climax community.

Notice the base of each lip is dilated; that's the source of the name *dilatata* (August 5).

Conifer swamps that support *P. dilatata* var. *dilatata* tend to have a thin or patchy canopy of black spruce, tamarack, or northern white cedar. Expect there to be scattered, knee-high ericaceous shrubs such as Labrador tea and bog laurel, a few ferns, wispy clumps of fine-leaved sedges, and an assortment of perhaps eight to ten orchid species. These habitats will have a lush carpet of moss, primarily moss in the genus *Sphagnum*. Shallow depressions or "bog holes" will typically have a few inches of standing water, the top of the water table. The source of the water is often hidden springs or seeps that deliver the water from an underground aquifer. Since the water comes from a relatively stable and reliable source, the habitat will be little affected by drought or flooding and have a slightly acidic pH in the range of 5.0 to 6.5.

There are also records of *P. dilatata* var. *dilatata* from similar but nonforested peatlands called fens. There is actually a range of fen types where *P. dilatata* var. *dilatata* might be found. Some are water tracks in large peatland complexes; others are floating mats at the edge of small lakes or ponds. There are such things as prairie fens, also called calcareous fens, but in Minnesota *P. dilatata* var. *dilatata* has not been found in prairie fens—or any prairie habitat for that matter. The reason is probably because prairie fens are alkaline rather than acidic.

Platanthera flava (L.) Lindl. var. *herbiola* (R. Br.) Luer
Tubercled rein-orchid

[*Habenaria flava* (L.) R. Br. var. *herbiola* (R. Br.) Ames & Correll]

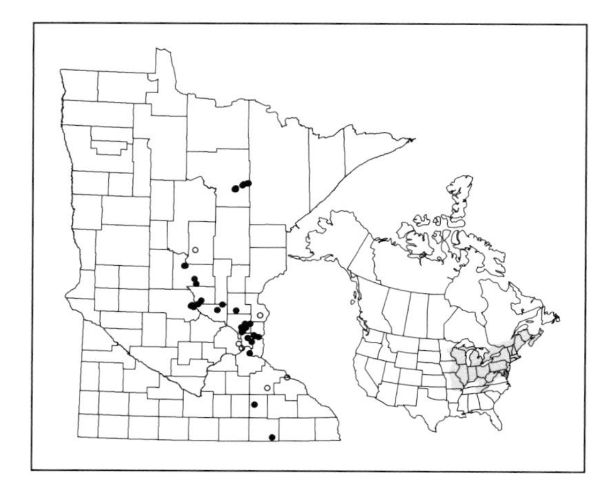

Plants (10) 17–55 cm tall; **stem** leafy throughout or predominantly in the middle portion, arising from the midpoint of a somewhat thickened horizontal **tuber** 5–15 cm long; **roots** 2–6 per tuber, slender, fleshy, growing laterally for up to about 12 cm. **Leaves** 2–5; lanceolate to ovate-lanceolate or elliptic to oblong; to 18 cm long and 5 cm wide, gradually decreasing in size upward until they grade into the bracts. **Inflorescence** a terminal raceme, 5–14 cm long, with 14–53 flowers, each flower subtended and often exceeded by a lanceolate bract 0.8–2.7 cm long. **Flowers** greenish or yellowish green, fragrant; **sepals** ovate, 2–3.2 mm long; **petals** similar to the sepals; **lip** oblong, 2.7–3.8 mm long, 1.3–3.3 mm wide, with a tooth-like projection on each side near the base and a single prominent tubercle rising vertically from near the base of the lip, the apex scalloped or shallowly toothed; spur 4.5–5.5 mm long. **Capsules** ascending, 7–10 mm long. **Flowering** June 20–July 15, mostly the last week of June and the first week of July.

Each flower has a knobby tubercle near the base of the lip (photograph by Peter Dziuk).

Platanthera flava is a plant of eastern North America. It has distinct northern and southern varieties that are distinguished by the shape of the lip, length of the bracts, and density of the inflorescence (Sheviak 2002b). Only the northern variety, var. *herbiola*, as described above, occurs in Minnesota.

Confirmation of *P. flava* var. *herbiola* is simple; just look for the tubercle that gives this orchid its name. It is a small but very noticeable knob rising from the top of the lip just inside the flower. It can be seen on every flower, even withered flowers. The purpose or function of the tubercle is unknown, but it likely plays a role in pollination, which is reportedly accomplished by a variety of insects ranging from mosquitoes to butterflies (Stoutamire 1971; Luer 1975).

Platanthera flava var. *herbiola* ***A***—Whole plant in flower, ***B***—Portion of the inflorescence, ***C***—Typical flowers, ***D***—Typical flower, exploded view

There is another peculiarity concerning *P. flava* var. *herbiola* that has not been adequately explained. Contrary to most species of *Platanthera*, this one is commonly found growing in dense patches with as many as two hundred stems per square meter. The obvious interpretation is that this plant is somehow spreading underground and is sending up shoots from an interconnected system of roots or rhizomes (Sheviak 2002b). Although this explanation may contain some truth, I have carefully excavated such clumps and found each stem attached to a separate and independent root-tuber system, with no evidence of underground spreading. Clearly there is more going on here than meets the eye.

The stem arises from the center of the slender tuber, which is the diagonal structure in front of the smaller roots (July 16).

The normal habitat of *P. flava* var. *herbiola* is moist or wet meadows, prairies, or sunny swales in savannas and woodlands. It also occurs at the margins of shallow marshy lakes, especially where there is a community of low-growing native grasses or sedges. Habitats tend to be oriented along some transitional edge, but that varies from site to site.

Soils are generally moist acidic sand with a thin layer of organic material or duff on the surface and sometimes a clay layer below the surface. Groundwater is usually at or near the surface. Sunlight is either direct for most of the day or lightly filtered through trees or shrubs; *P. flava* var. *herbiola* will slowly disappear if its habitat becomes completely shaded.

Wet meadow habitat on the Anoka Sand Plain (Anoka County)

The best habitats are probably on the broad, sandy glacial outwash plain known as the Anoka Sand Plain just north of the Twin Cities. Fire and drought were important factors influencing the vegetation of the Sand Plain. It has been observed several times that dormant-season fires in the spring can result in a flush of *P. flava* var. *herbiola* appearing aboveground. This sort of a response is very rare among orchids, even prairie orchids.

With one notable exception, the habitats of *P. flava* var. *herbiola* can be considered high-quality remnants of native habitats that have somehow survived being drained, plowed, or invaded by nonnative plant species, especially reed canary grass and smooth brome. The exception is the drained tailings basins on the Iron Range in Itasca County where *P. flava* var. *herbiola* has recently made an unexpected appearance.

Stems can be up to about 22 inches (55 cm) tall and produce flowers from about June 20 through the middle of July (photograph by Peter Dziuk).

Platanthera hookeri (Torr. ex Gray) Lindl.
Hooker's orchid

[*Habenaria hookeri* Torr. ex Gray]

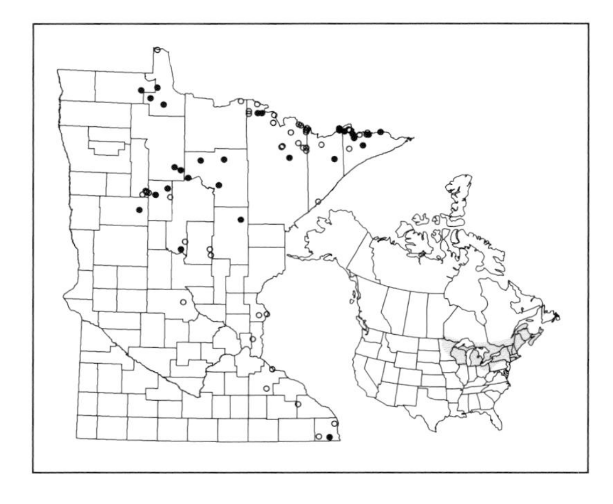

Plants 15–45 cm tall; **stem** leafless and bractless; **tuber** vertical, tapering, 5–15 cm long; **roots** 2 per tuber, thick, fleshy, growing horizontally for a distance of 2–10 cm. **Leaves** 2, basal, elliptic to orbicular, widely spreading or lying ± flat on the ground, 5.5–15 cm long, 4–10.5 cm wide. **Inflorescence** a terminal raceme, 6–23 cm long, with 6–27 flowers, each flower subtended by a lanceolate bract 1.1–2.1 cm long. **Flowers** relatively large but made inconspicuous by their yellowish green color; **dorsal sepal** ovate, 6–10 mm long, converging with the petals and arching the lip; **lateral sepals** narrowly oblong, reflexed, 7.5–11 mm long; **petals** linear-lanceolate, hooked (falcate), 5–7.5 mm long; **lip** lanceolate, 7.5–13 mm long, 1.6–5 mm wide, often more whitish than the rest of the flower; **spur** 1.2–2 cm long, a uniform width or often narrowing near the tip. **Capsules** erect or ascending, 11–18 mm long. **Flowering** June 3–July 6, mostly the last 2 weeks of June.

Viewed from the side, each flower looks something like a gaping mouth or pinching fingers (Hubbard County).

There are two orchids that need to be considered here: *P. hookeri* and *P. orbiculata*. They are very different orchids but share one unmistakable feature: both species have a pair of large, round, fleshy leaves that lie more or less flat on the ground. There is no easy way to tell the two orchids apart on the basis of the leaves alone, and it is common to find just the leaves. Individual plants don't flower regularly, but the leaves do come up every year.

When looking at the flower of *P. hookeri*, you see that the dorsal sepal and petals curve over the top of the flower and the lip curves upward from beneath, almost completing a circle. When viewed from the side, the flower looks something like a gaping mouth or pinching fingers. Meanwhile, the lateral sepals are reflexed

Platanthera hookeri ***A***—Whole plant in flower, ***B***—Inflorescence, ***C***—Typical flower, ***D***—Typical flower, exploded view

straight back like wings. The whole flower is green or greenish, although the lip may be somewhat whiter than the rest of the flower.

The brown vertical structure is the current tuber, the small white structure next to it is its replacement for next year (June 20).

P. hookeri is not a common plant in Minnesota, and it never occurs in large numbers. Often just five to ten plants are found, rarely more. Individual plants have been reported to reappear each year for up to twenty-eight years, and speculatively for forty years, qualifying it as long-lived (Reddoch and Reddoch 1997). But as is the case with all *Platanthera*, this one never truly grows old. It completely renews itself each year, so there is no intrinsic limit to how long an individual can continue to reappear at the same spot—it is entirely dependent on events in its environment.

The environment also influences the percentage of plants that flower each year. It has been reported that cool wet weather in June and July of one year will result in a greater percentage of plants flowering the following year (Reddoch and Reddoch 1997).

It seems *P. hookeri* could be found in any part of the state that provides substantial tracts of good undisturbed forest habitat. Yet, for reasons that are not obvious, most of the records are from the Border Lakes region in the northeast. This may reflect the distribution of botanists rather than the distribution of *P. hookeri*, or there could be a more ecological basis.

About 90 percent of the records come from upland forests of one type or another. In northern Minnesota it is usually found in dry sandy soil under pines but also in somewhat moist soil under a mix of trees such as trembling aspen, paper birch, white spruce, or balsam fir. In southern Minnesota it appears to prefer forested north-facing slopes dominated by oaks.

The remaining 10 percent of occurrences have been found in mossy conifer swamps where *P. hookeri* has been found growing in association with *Sphagnum* mosses, feather mosses, and black spruce trees. As in upland habitats, swamp habitats are well shaded with an acidic substrate. Swamp occurrences are perhaps not typical for this species, but they have been documented.

Note the two fleshy basal leaves and the smooth stem (Hubbard County).

Platanthera huronensis (Nutt.) Lindl.
Tall green bog-orchid

[*P. hyperborea* (L.) Lindl. var. *huronensis* (Nutt.) Luer; *P.* ×*media* (Rydb.); *Limnorchis huronensis* (Nutt.) Rydb.]

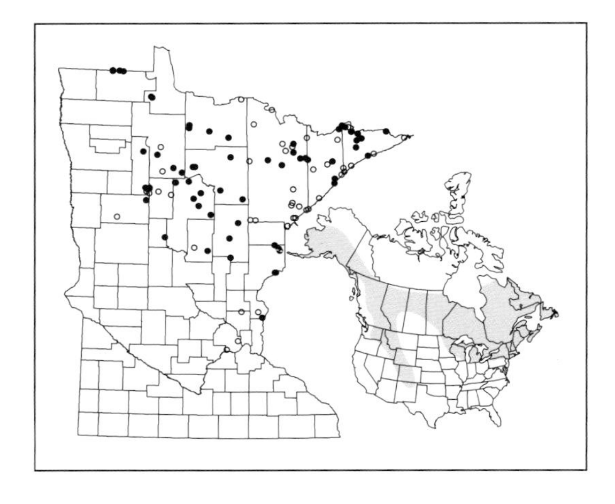

Plants 25–105 cm tall; **stem** leafy throughout or just the lower half or two-thirds; **tuber** slender, vertical, tapering, 8–22 cm long; **roots** 2–4 per tuber, fleshy, growing horizontally for 20 or more cm. **Leaves** 2–7; oblong, narrowly obovate, narrowly elliptic or linear; to 30 cm long and 6 cm wide, gradually decreasing in size upward until they grade into the bracts. **Inflorescence** a dense terminal raceme, 5–35 cm long, with 10–60 flowers, each flower subtended by a lanceolate bract 1–4 cm long. **Flowers** whitish green, fragrant, inconspicuous singly but often conspicuous in aggregate; lateral **sepals** spreading to slightly reflexed, about as long as the petals; **petals** ovate to lance-falcate, 3–5 mm long; **lip** lanceolate to nearly linear, often whiter than the rest of the flower, 4.5–7 mm long, 1.5–3 mm wide, slightly to markedly dilated at base; **spur** cylindric, 4.5–7 mm long. **Capsules** erect to ascending, 9–17 mm long. **Flowering** June 20–August 5, mostly the first 2 weeks of July.

The central structure is the tuber with the replacement tuber just starting; the other structures are roots (July 9).

There are several useful characteristics to distinguish *P. huronensis* from the similar *P. aquilonis*. First, the flowers are noticeably fragrant and the lip tends to be whitish green rather than yellowish. Actually, the lip is often whiter than the rest of the flower. The spur is usually about as long as the lip and it tends to hang downward, curving forward only at the tip. Also, the spur is usually a slender cylinder shape rather than a thicker club shape. And in most cases, the lip and spur of *P. huronensis* are measurably larger than those of *P. aquilonis*, with fewer than 10 percent of specimens showing any overlap (see key on page 158).

At a distance, the two species usually look too much alike to tell apart, even for a specialist. However, occasionally, *P. huronensis* (a tetraploid) will produce extremely robust specimens that may reach waist-high and have a thick, dense inflorescence. Apparently, *P. aquilonis* (a diploid) never takes such a form.

Platanthera huronensis ***A***—Whole plant in two parts, ***B***—Portion of the inflorescence, ***C***—Typical flower, exploded view

The flowers of *P. huronensis* tend to be whitish green, and compared to *P. aquilonis* the spur is long and slender (July 13, Clearwater County).

For more conclusive identification, a specialist would use 10× magnification to examine the position of the two anther sacs at the tip of the column, which is the primary reproductive structure at the center of the flower. The anther sacs of *P. aquilonis* are low in relation to the stigma, and they are wide apart at their bases but close to each other at their tips. In *P. huronensis* the anther sacs are held higher and are nearly parallel to each other. The position of the anther sacs is of critical importance to pollination biology. It seems that *P. huronensis* relies on small insects, mostly mosquitoes, to cross-pollinate, while *P. aquilonis* is known to auto-pollinate (Sheviak 2002b).

When comparing the habitats of *P. huronensis* and *P. aquilonis*, there are obvious similarities but also subtle differences. Both species occur in wetlands, although neither occurs where there is standing water. The habitat differences seem to reflect the chemical nature of the habitat. In general, habitats of *P. aquilonis* have a pH range of 5.0 to 8.5 (acidic to alkaline), and *P. huronensis* 5.0 to 6.5 (strictly acidic).

Perhaps the most common habitat of *P. huronensis* is rich swamp forests, usually under conifers such as northern white cedar, tamarack, or black spruce, with a complement of fine-leaved sedges, *Sphagnum* mosses, and small ericaceous shrubs. There may also be hardwood trees, particularly black ash, or large shrubs such as speckled alder. It is also possible to find *P. huronensis* on wave-splashed bouldery or rocky lakeshores and on gravel bars in streams. In most cases, *P. huronensis* will be in shade, or at least partial shade. Sometimes it is found growing in full sunlight, but rarely far from trees. The soil in these habitats is most often peat, less often wet loam, sand, or gravel.

There are at least a dozen plants here, each with its own root/tuber system (August 5, Clearwater County).

Platanthera lacera (Michx.) G. Don
Ragged fringed orchid

[*Habenaria lacera* (Michx.) R. Br.; *Blephariglottis lacera* (Michx.) Farw.]

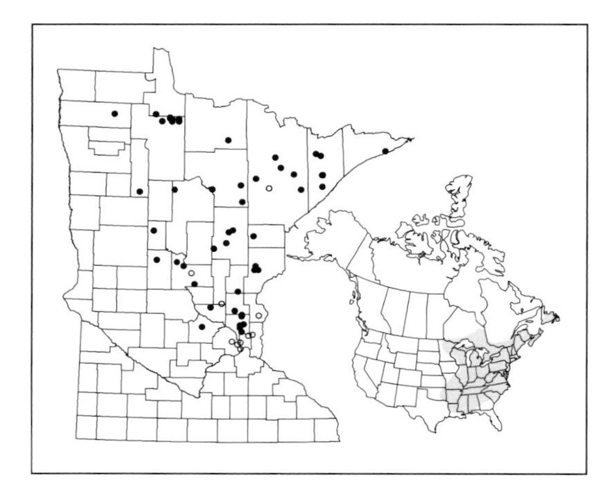

Plants 20–77 cm tall; **stem** leafy throughout or just the lower half or two-thirds; **tuber** slender, vertical, tapering, 4–8 cm long; **roots** 2 per tuber, slender, fleshy, growing laterally for 2–6 cm. **Leaves** 2–7, the lower ones lanceolate to narrowly elliptic, 5–14 cm long and 1–3.5 cm wide, decreasing in size upward until they grade into the bracts. **Inflorescence** a terminal raceme, 4–25 cm long, with 15–60 flowers, each flower subtended by a lanceolate bract 0.7–2.5 cm long. **Flowers** whitish or greenish white, sometimes showy and conspicuous, more often not; **sepals** ovate to suborbicular, 3–7 cm long, the dorsal somewhat smaller than the lateral; **petals** linear-oblong, 2.8–6 mm long; **lip** 7–13 mm long, 8–18 mm wide, divided into 3 major segments: the lateral segments incised more than halfway to the base producing a deep fringe of threadlike divisions, the middle segment incised less deeply or merely toothed; **spur** 1.1–2 cm long. **Capsules** erect, 8–13 mm long. **Flowering** June 20–August 10, peaking about the third week of July.

You can see the long vertical tuber and the small white nascent replacement tuber; the horizontal structures are roots (July 29).

The general appearance of *P. lacera* can be quite variable; no two individuals seem to look exactly alike. The flower color varies from creamy white to greenish white, and the size varies from knee-high to ankle-high. The flowers themselves are sometimes small and few in number, and the fringed segments of the lip can be so slender they practically disappear.

When it comes to the identification of *P. lacera*, the greatest source of confusion is the occasional white-flowered variant of *P. psycodes*, which normally has purple flowers. Any uncertainty can usually be settled by comparing the shape of the petals and the length of the spur, the petals of *P. lacera* being quite narrow and the spur comparatively short. Also,

Platanthera lacera ***A***—Whole plant in flower, ***B***—Portion of flowering stem, ***C***—Typical flower, ***D***—Typical flower, exploded view

Note the deeply fringed lip and the bonnet formed by the petals and sepals (July 15, Anoka County).

the flowers of *P. lacera* are never as white as a white-flowered *P. psycodes*. Complicating the issue is a rare hybrid between *P. lacera* and *P. psycodes* named *P. ×andrewsii*. Flowers of the hybrid are various shades of purple green and have a form intermediate between the two parents (Catling and Catling 1994).

The whole plant is 8–30 inches (20--77 cm) tall, usually shorter than the surrounding grasses and sedges (July 29).

Another similar orchid is *P. praeclara*, which is a very rare species confined to prairie habitats. It always has white flowers like *P. lacera*, but every aspect of the flower is so much larger, and the shape of the petals so consistently different, there should be no confusion.

Most records of P. *lacera* in the southern half of the state are from the Anoka Sand Plain, a broad, flat landscape just north of the Twin Cities. Sand Plain habitats of *P. lacera* tend to be wet meadows, sedge meadows, grassy swales, and the edge of marshes. These habitats are often brushy with willows, dogwoods, and alders. Large trees will probably be absent or in scattered groves. The soils are usually sandy, although there may be a thin layer of organic material on the surface, or perhaps just leaf litter. The water table is typically at or near the surface most of the year, allowing the soil to remain moist except in drought years.

Habitats in the northern half of the state are at least superficially different from those on the Anoka Sand Plain. The substrate is typically peat instead of sand. The peat may be two to three feet deep and is likely covered by a carpet of *Sphagnum* moss. The whole system would typically be sustained by groundwater that rarely drops much below the top of the peat and gives the ground a spongy feel. These habitats are often called fens and typically develop within large peatland complexes. Usually these habitats have no trees, but occasionally *P. lacera* is found under a sparse tree cover or in openings between trees, usually tamarack, northern white cedar, or black spruce. Any shrubs in the vicinity would likely be knee-high ericads, such as leatherleaf or Labrador tea. It should be noted that *P. lacera* has on occasion turned up in highly altered habitats such as abandoned tailings basins on the Iron Range.

Platanthera obtusata (Banks ex Pursh) Lindl. subsp. *obtusata*
Bluntleaved rein-orchid

[*Habenaria obtusata* (Banks ex Pursh) Rich.]

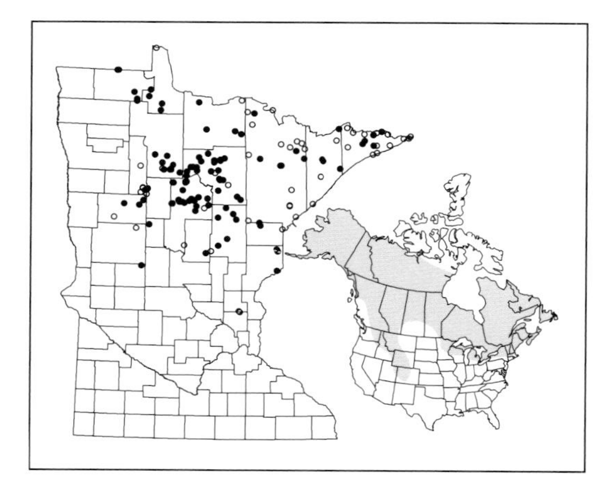

Plants 6–28 cm long; **stem** leafless and usually bractless above the base; **tuber** slender, vertical, tapering, 2–10 cm long; **roots** 0 or up to 3 per tuber, slender, fleshy, growing laterally 1–5 cm. **Leaf** 1, basal, obovate, 4–15 cm long, 1.5–4.4 cm wide, apex rounded or blunt. **Inflorescence** a terminal raceme, 2–11 cm long, with 4–18 flowers, each flower subtended by a lanceolate bract 0.4–1.7 cm long. **Flower** inconspicuous, whitish or greenish white; **dorsal sepal** broadly ovate-orbicular, 2–4 mm long; **lateral sepals** ovate-lanceolate, 2.7–5 mm long; **petals** broadly lanceolate, dilated below the middle, 2.2–4.2 mm long; **lip** narrowly lanceolate, ± dilated at base, 3.5–6 mm long, 0.3–0.8 mm wide, **spur** 4.5–7 mm long, tapering to a pointed tip. **Capsules** erect or ascending, 5–8 mm long. **Flowering** June 20–August 1, mostly the last week in June and the first 3 weeks in July.

The pale vertical structure is the replacement tuber; it is the only structure that will survive the winter (July 8).

The "subsp. *obtusata*" in the Latin name of this orchid is used to distinguish it from the rare Eurasian subsp. *oligantha*. It differs from our plant by having smaller flowers, a wider floral lip, and a dense, few-flowered inflorescence (Sheviak 2002b).

No single characteristic defines this plant, yet it is rarely misidentified. There is a rather ordinary-looking leaf that comes from the base of the stem, which is easily overlooked until the moss in which it grows is parted and the connection is seen. The flowers are a shade of white, but not the sort of radiant white that draws attention.

If you spend an hour in a conifer swamp and see only one orchid, it will probably be this one, although it will probably not be the one you were hoping to find. Your disappointment can be forgiven; this is not a particularly impressive orchid. It seems to possess nothing new among the species of *Platanthera*, and the features it has

Platanthera obtusata subsp. *obtusata* ***A***—Whole plant in flower, ***B***—Portion of the flowering stem (inflorescence), ***C***—Typical flower, ***D***—Typical flower, exploded view

The flower has a narrow lip that tapers to a point (July 13, Clearwater County).

taken from the other *Platanthera* have been downsized and made simpler—a single leaf, a stem barely ankle-high, few if any roots, plain white flowers—a minimalist orchid if ever there was one. But whatever this orchid possesses seems to work; this is often the most abundant orchid in its habitat. And it has found a use for mosquitoes! It has designed small packets of pollen for them to carry from one plant to another, which they do in exchange for only a small reward of nectar. This may prove, once and for all, that orchids are indeed smarter than humans.

This is not the only orchid that uses mosquitoes as pollinators, but the flower of *P. obtusata* subsp. *obtusata* seems to have been designed specifically with mosquitoes in mind. To reach the nectar, a mosquito must enter through the front of the flower, which triggers the pollinia to spring forward and cement themselves to the mosquito's head; it won't work with a creature smaller or larger than a standard mosquito (Stoutamire 1968; Thien and Utech 1970). The mosquito then has no choice but to transport its cargo to the next flower it visits where it delivers its load to the waiting stigma, thereby completing the transaction. Perhaps not surprisingly, *P. obtusata* subsp. *obtusata* seems to be most abundant where mosquitoes are the thickest, and the flowers appear at the time of year when mosquitoes seem the hungriest.

The typical habitat of *P. obtusata* subsp. *obtusata* in Minnesota is a conifer swamp where it grows in the shade of any or all of the coniferous wetland trees, particularly northern white cedar, black spruce, tamarack, and balsam fir. It is perhaps more tolerant of shade than other swamp orchids. In fact, it is never far from the shade of mature trees. It would be quite unexpected to find *P. obtusata* subsp. *obtusata* on floating mats or open fens. And it does not often venture out of native habitats onto ditch banks, sediment basins, gravel pits, or other human-created habitats where you sometimes find other orchids.

The custom of *P. obtusata* subsp. *obtusata* is to loosely anchor itself in moss or firm, moist peat, usually at the base of a large swamp tree or where moss mounds over tree roots or decaying logs. These sites are fairly rich in terms of mineral nutrients and have a pH in the weakly acidic range.

Each plant produces a single leaf that attaches near the base of the stem (July 8).

Platanthera orbiculata (Pursh) Lindl.
Lesser roundleaved orchid

[*Habenaria orbiculata* (Pursh) Torr.]

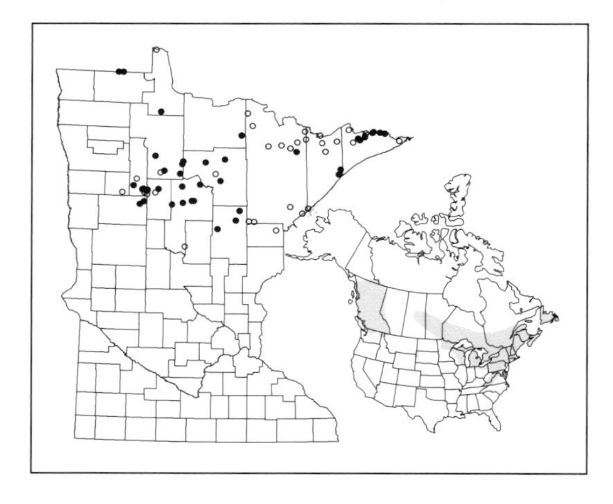

Plants 20–60 cm long; **stem** leafless above the base, 1–6 bracts; **tuber** slender or rather stout, vertical, tapering, 3–12 cm long; **roots** 1–4 per tuber, slender, fleshy, 2–10 cm long. **Leaves** 2, basal, broadly elliptic to orbicular, widely spreading or ± lying flat on the ground, 6–19 cm long, 4–16 cm wide. **Inflorescence** a terminal raceme, 5–25 cm long, with 6–33 flowers, each flower subtended by a lanceolate bract 0.6–1.6 cm long. **Flowers** large and conspicuous, white to greenish white; **dorsal sepal** orbicular to depressed-orbicular or broadly ovate, 3.5–6 mm long, **lateral sepals** irregularly ovate, 7–10 mm long; **petals** narrowly ovate, 5.5–7.2 mm long; **lip** entire, linear or lance-linear, with a blunt or rounded tip, 9–15 mm long and about 2 mm wide, **spur** 2–2.7 cm long, slightly thickened at the tip. **Capsules** erect, 12–16 mm long. **Flowering** July 10–August 15, mostly the third and fourth week in July.

The flowers are pollinated by large hawk moths that are active in the evening (photograph by Otto Gockman).

Platanthera orbiculata is too often and unnecessarily confused with *P. hookeri*. The two orchids are not at all alike except for one obvious feature: both have a pair of large, round, fleshy leaves that appear to be pressed flat on the ground. This can be a problem because most of these plants do not produce flowers in any given year, just leaves, and without flowers it can be difficult to tell the two species apart. With luck you might find dried stalks from the previous year. They should still have remnants of bracts, which are just small pointed leaves 1–2 cm long. This will tell you it is *P. orbiculata* and not *P. hookeri*. The two species might be growing in the same area, although not likely in the same habitat and almost certainly not mixed together.

Some guidebooks describe a similar orchid with a common name something like greater roundleaved orchid or large round leaf orchid. It will have the Latin name *P. macrophylla*. Regardless of what you might read, it does not occur in Minnesota.

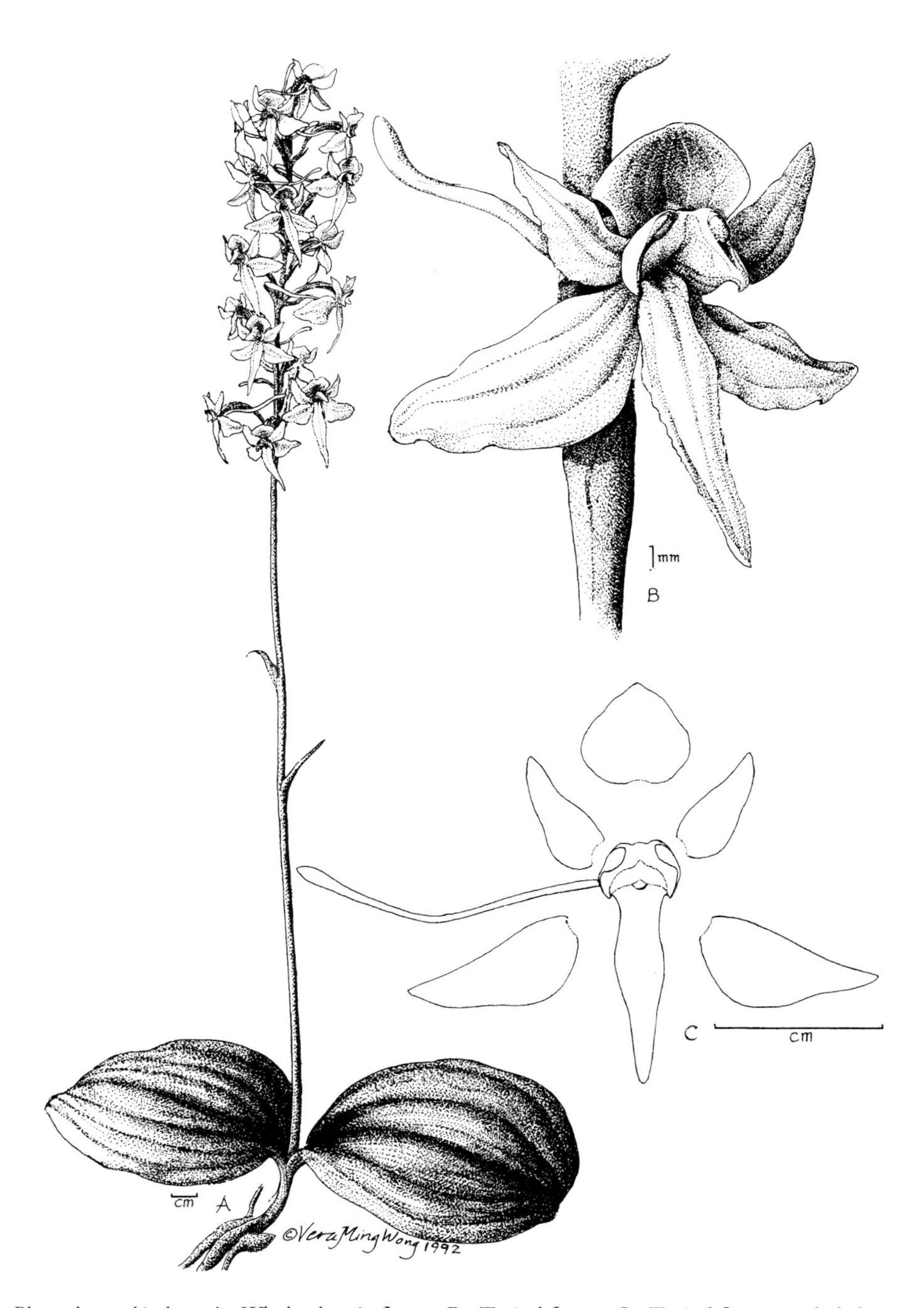

Platanthera orbiculata ***A***—Whole plant in flower, ***B***—Typical flower, ***C***—Typical flower, exploded view

There are two large fleshy leaves at the base and one to six small pointed bracts on the stem (Clearwater County).

When you find *P. orbiculata*, it will not be in large numbers, usually just a few scattered plants. This makes it seem rather ephemeral or transitory, although one study came to the conclusion that individuals can reappear in the same spot for fifteen to twenty or more years (Reddoch and Reddoch 1997).

In the north-central counties, *P. orbiculata* is found primarily in forested swamps of the type ecologists call forested rich peatlands (MDNR 2003). These are rather dense forests dominated by wetland conifers such as northern white cedar, balsam fir, black spruce, and less often tamarack. Walking is often made difficult by the accumulation of decades or perhaps centuries of downed and tangled tree trunks half buried in wet, peaty muck, all overlain with a carpet of living *Sphagnum* mosses and brown mosses.

The mosses may form slightly raised mounds called hummocks, which is where *P. orbiculata* will likely be found. In fact, the tuber and roots of *P. orbiculata* may be entirely within the living moss—they may not even reach the wet black peat. The groundwater is typically near the top of the peat and is wicked upward to the orchid roots by the closely packed stems of the living moss. The water, in this case, has a pH between about 5.5 and 6.5—nominally acidic but not strongly acidic.

Expect habitats in the northeastern counties to be somewhat different than those in the north-central counties. They are more likely to be mesic upland forests rather than swamps. And the rooting zone may be moist loamy soil derived from noncalcareous till rather than peat. The canopy may be composed of hardwood trees, such as trembling aspen, paper birch, and yellow birch. Conifers may be nearby, particularly white spruce and northern white cedar. Although habitats do vary, it is safe to consider *P. orbiculata* a forest species, at least in Minnesota. Do not expect to find it in open fens, floating mats, or sedge meadows.

The flowers of *P. orbiculata* are large and ghostly white (July 22, Clearwater County).

Platanthera praeclara Shev. & Bowles
Western prairie fringed orchid

[*Habenaria leucophaea* (Nutt.) Gray var. *praeclara* (Shev. & Bowles) Cronq.; *Blephariglottis praeclara* (Shev. & Bowles) Baumb. & Lueckel]

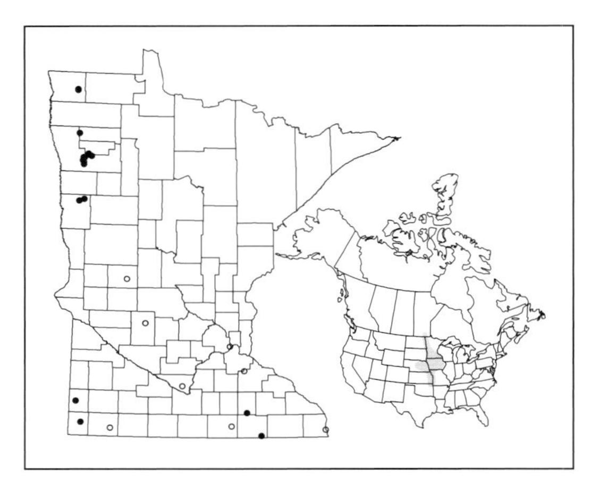

Plants 40–88 cm tall; **stem** leafy throughout; **tuber** slender, vertical, tapering, 5–8 cm long; **roots** few to several, fleshy, slender, 3–10 cm long. **Leaves** 5–10, the lower and middle ones lanceolate to ovate-lanceolate, acute, 9–16 cm long, 1.5–3.5 cm wide, gradually decreasing in size upward until they grade into the bracts. **Inflorescence** a terminal raceme, 5–15 cm long, with 4–33 flowers, each flower subtended by a lanceolate bract 2–6.5 cm long. **Flowers** white, large, and conspicuous; **sepals** ovate to suborbicular, the lateral ones obliquely asymmetric, 9–14 mm long; **petals** fan-shaped (flabelliform) with the apical margin shallowly and irregularly toothed, 1–1.7 cm long; **lip** 1.7–3.2 long, 2–3.8 cm wide, divided into 3 major fan-shaped segments, the lateral segments incised more than halfway to the base, the middle segment usually incised less deeply, **spur** curved, 3–6 cm long. **Capsules** erect, 2–3 cm long. **Flowering** July 1–July 29, usually peaking before July 20.

You can see the opening to the nectar tube (spur) at the center of the flower.

P. praeclara is a distinctive and spectacular orchid. It would be difficult to confuse it with anything else in Minnesota. In 1986 it was split off from *P. leucophaea*, which turns out to be a somewhat smaller species that occurs to the east and south of Minnesota (Sheviak and Bowles 1986).

Historically, *P. praeclara* occurred throughout the prairie region of Minnesota and much of the Midwest. Today, it survives only in remnant habitats with no significant history of agriculture, cattle grazing, or herbicide use. In fact, viable populations are now largely restricted to the Red River Valley and Aspen Parkland.

From a global perspective, this is Minnesota's rarest orchid. It is

Platanthera praeclara ***A***—Whole plant in flower, ***B***—Inflorescence, ***C***—Typical flower, ***D***—Typical flower, exploded view

A plant can stand as high as 35 inches (88 cm), raising it above the surrounding prairie vegetation.

officially listed as endangered in Minnesota, threatened in the United States, and endangered in Canada. Because it is so rare, an extraordinary effort has been made to keep a count of all known plants across its range. Because nonflowering plants can be very hard to find in prairies, only flowering plants have been consistently counted. They seem to have reached a peak in the early 1990s when almost 52,000 were counted. Nearly all the plants were in three metapopulations (population clusters) in the Red River Valley section of the Prairie Parkland Province (MDNR 2005b). This breaks down, roughly, as 23,000 in the Vita Prairies (Manitoba, Canada); about 15,000 in Minnesota (mostly in interbeach habitats in Polk County); and about 13,000 in the Sheyenne Delta of North Dakota. There are also small numbers scattered in isolated remnant habitats in Iowa, Nebraska, Missouri, Kansas, and southern Minnesota.

The replacement tuber stands as an exact replica to the left of the current tuber (July 21).

The count in 2009 was only 2,723. The numbers seem to have rebounded in 2010, although an analysis has not yet been completed. The cause of the decline has not been determined. Since the 1990s the numbers in Minnesota have plummeted. It may portend a long-term trend or perhaps it is just the low point of a cycle.

It is known that drought kills plants, especially the young and the weak, which suffer high mortality during abnormally dry springs (MDNR, unpublished data). It is also believed that plants in low depressions can be killed by standing water during the growing season. And flowering-age plants are very susceptible to fire. A burn after the plants appear aboveground in early May can severely damage a population, and the damage can take several years to heal (Willson et al. 2006).

Flowers are pollinated exclusively by night-flying sphinx moths (Westwood and Borkowsky 2004; Sheviak and Bowles 1986). Seeds mature by autumn and are dispersed by early winter. Some of the seeds may germinate the following spring, and a few may wait another year. It is not known how many years pass between germination and when a seedling first appears aboveground, but once the first green leaf is produced it takes, on average, another six years before the first flowers are produced (MDNR, unpublished data). Mortality is high during this juvenile stage, but flowering-age plants are quite long-lived, at least twenty-five years in one case (MDNR, unpublished data).

Platanthera psycodes (L.) Lindl.
Small purple fringed orchid

[*Habenaria psycodes* (L.) Spreng.; *Blephariglottis psycodes* (L.) Rydb.]

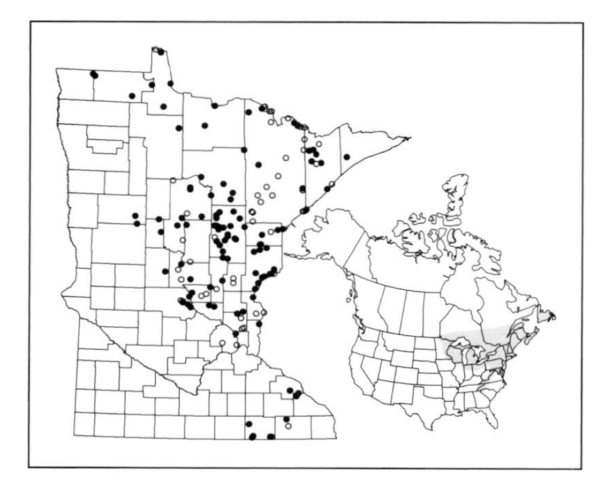

Plants 44–100 cm long; **stem** leafy throughout or predominantly the lower two-thirds; **tuber** slender, vertical, tapering, 3–8 cm long; **roots** 4–10, slender, fleshy, growing to a length of 3–8 cm. **Leaves** 4–12, the lower and medial leaves elliptic to narrowly elliptic or oblong-elliptic, 10–17 cm long, 2–7 cm wide, gradually or abruptly decreasing in size upward until they grade into the bracts. **Inflorescence** a dense terminal raceme, 4–22 cm long, with 20–125 flowers, each flower subtended by a lance-linear bract 1–3.5 cm long. **Flowers** purplish, fragrant, conspicuous; **sepals** ovate to broadly elliptic or oblong, 4–6.5 mm long; **petals** obovate to spatulate, with shallowly and irregularly toothed margins, 4–8 mm long; **lip** 6–12 mm long, 7–14 mm wide, divided into 3 major fan-shaped (flabelliform) segments, each segment incised less than halfway to the base resulting in a relatively shallow fringe, **spur** curved, 1.7–2.3 cm long. **Capsules** erect, 7–12 mm long. **Flowering** July 3–August 20, mostly the last 2 weeks in July.

This is the only fringed orchid with purple flowers in Minnesota (July 28, Pine County).

P. psycodes is as distinctive in life as it is in photographs. It is rarely confused with any other species in Minnesota. The tall stature of the plant and the purple flowers are conclusive. There is a similar species, the greater purple fringed orchid (*P. grandiflora*) that grows farther east, but not in Minnesota.

Be prepared to look past flower color. There is a rare white-flowered form of this species named *P. psycodes f. albiflora*. It differs only in having white flowers instead of purple. It might bring to mind *P. lacera* or *P. praeclara*, but all other species can be ruled out by carefully comparing the fine details of the flowers, particularly the length of the spur and the shape of the petals.

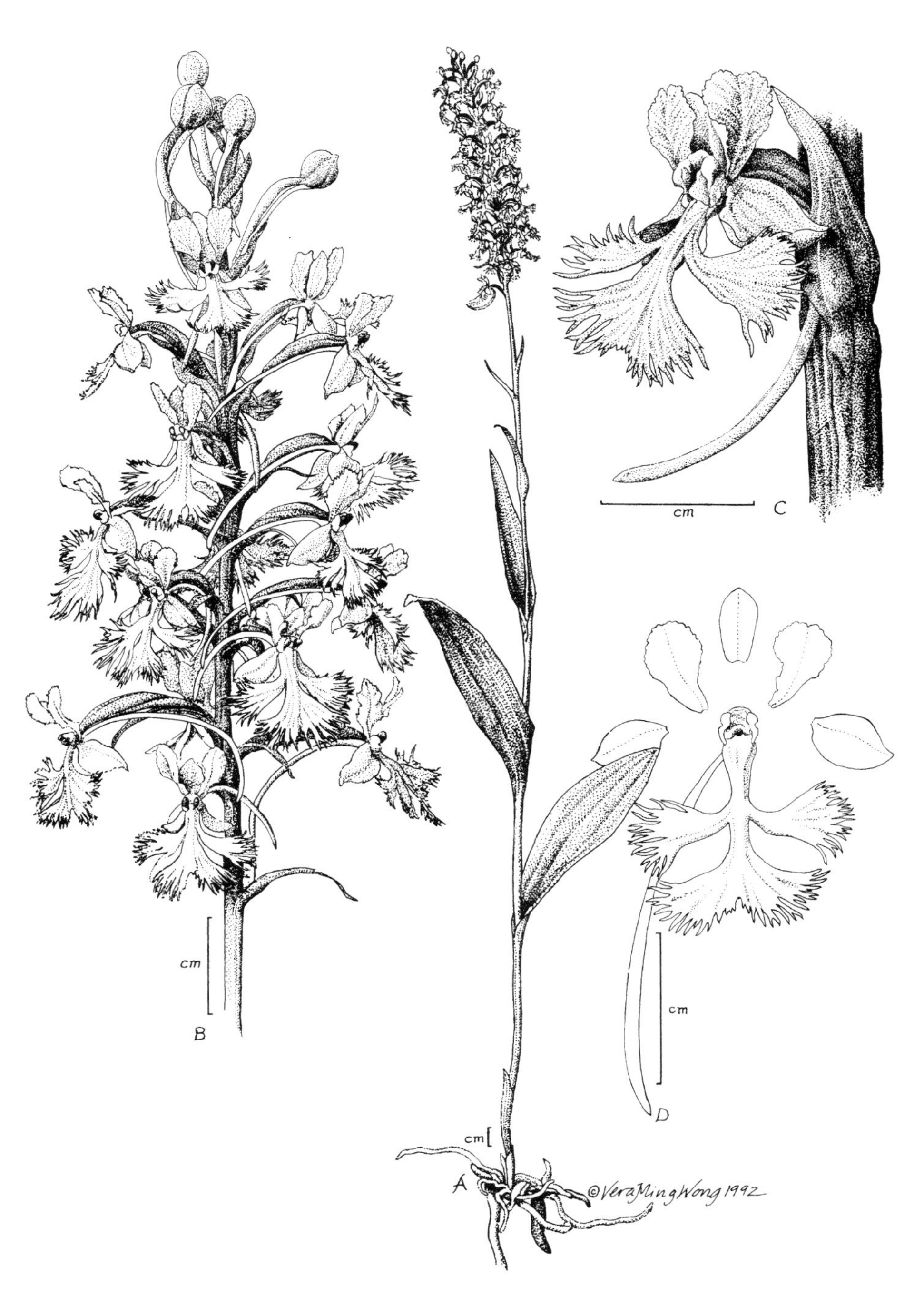

Platanthera psycodes ***A***—Whole plant in flower, ***B***—Inflorescence, ***C***—Typical flower, ***D***—Typical flower, exploded view

P. psycodes is a tall, slender orchid usually found in the open with grasses and sedges (July 28, Pine County).

There is a wild hybrid between *P. psycodes* and *P. lacera* named *P. ×andrewsii*. The flowers of such a hybrid would be some shade of purple-green, and the fringe of the lip would be more deeply divided than that of pure *P. psycodes* (Catling and Catling 1994). The hybrid has not been documented in Minnesota, but it is probably out there somewhere where the ranges and habitats of the two species overlap.

There is no doubt that *P. psycodes* is a wetland plant, but don't look for it in bogs or conifer swamps or cattail marshes; it won't be on floating mats or in anything that people call fens. Those places are too wet and too "peaty." The best habitats for *P. psycodes* are wet only during the spring and after heavy rainfalls; the rest of the time they are only moist. The soil will always feel firm underfoot—not bouncy or springy. The soils range from sandy and sandy loam to silty or clayey. There may be a thin layer of organic material on the surface but not any significant amount of peat. The pH will typically be weakly acidic or about neutral. You might find these conditions in low brushy thickets under alder, willows, or dogwood, or in wet meadows or sedge meadows. Good habitat can also be found under a thin or moderate canopy of deciduous trees, particularly black ash or aspen, especially on a low river terrace where there might be groundwater seeps or where there might be heavy clay soil that holds moisture well.

In some parts of the state, mostly the northeast, *P. psycodes* has been found on gently sloping sandy beaches—not in the bare wave-washed zone, but in the zone of perennial vegetation that sometimes develops farther back from the water. This is the transition zone where wetland grades into upland. These habitats are usually in full sun or partial shade of shrubs or overhanging tree branches.

Another habitat that is too common to ignore is roadside ditches, but not just any ditch. Only shallow, moist ditches with level bottoms that are well vegetated with native species, and only where road crews don't regularly mow or spray herbicides. Wherever you find this orchid, even on a roadside, you feel you are in good orchid habitat.

The lip of each flower is divided into three segments; each segment has a fringed margin.

Genus *Pogonia* Juss.

The name *Pogonia* is from the Greek word meaning "bearded," in reference to the bristles on the upper surface of the floral lip. Two of the three species occur in East Asia and the other in North America (Sheviak and Catling 2002a).

Pogonia is one of three Minnesota orchid genera that have pink flowers with a conspicuous crest of short fleshy bristles on the lip. The other two genera are *Arethusa* and *Calopogon*. According to Thien and Marcks (1972), the bristles of all three genera exhibit strong absorption of ultraviolet light. This is the wavelength of light that insect pollinators typically sense most strongly. In this case, the pollinator is likely to be a medium to large bee such as a queen or worker of the genus *Bombus* (Thien and Marcks 1972).

Any bee that is attracted to the flower of a *Pogonia* will probably land directly on the bristles. It will then crawl toward the back of the flower where the column and lip form a narrow tube containing a small quantity of nectar. The bee, upon withdrawing from the flower, brushes against the fringed anther where it picks up pollen, which adheres to its head (Thien and Marcks, 1972). Any bee that arrives with pollen already on its head from a previous flower will encounter the stigma first and deposit pollen when it pushes its way into the flower.

Pogonia ophioglossoides

Pogonia ophioglossoides (L.) Ker Gawler
Rose pogonia

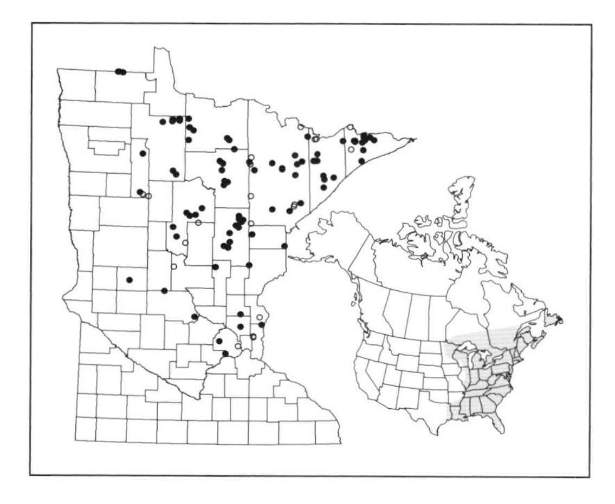

Plants 15–45 cm tall; **rhizome** vertical, slender, unbranched, with internodes of 1–4 cm (rarely more than 3–4 internodes are present); **roots** 2 per node, slender, fleshy, spreading laterally for distances of 20 or more cm, producing shoots adventitiously. **Leaf** 1, attached at about the middle of the stem, sessile, elliptic to oblong, 3–12 cm long, 0.6–2.1 cm wide. **Inflorescence** 1 flower (occasionally 2) subtended by leaflike bract 1.2–5 cm long. **Flower** pink to purple, conspicuous; **sepals** elliptic, wide-spreading, 1.3–2.4 cm long; **petals** broadly elliptic, 1.3–2.3 cm long; **lip** pinkish with purple veins, narrowly oblong-spatulate, widest near the apex and ± tapering to the base, 1.4–2.1 cm long, 5–10 mm wide, conspicuously bearded with a crest of short, fleshy yellow-white bristles rising vertically from the upper surface, apical margin shallowly fringed. **Capsules** erect, 15–25 mm long. **Flowering** June 20–July 30, mostly the second and third weeks of July.

The petals and sepals close loosely around the shaggy-looking lip.

The flower of *Pogonia* is conspicuously pink, although not the intense radiant pink of *Arethusa* or *Calopogon*. Another difference is the flower points forward with the petals and sepals loosely closed around the shaggy-looking lip. You don't get a good sense of the flower until you kneel down and look at it head-on the way a bee does.

Clearly, the flower of *Pogonia* is the attention-getter, but the underground structures are both simple and elegant. The roots of *Pogonia* serve the customary role of all orchid roots of capturing and "digesting" fungal hyphae, but they also do something that is quite extraordinary. A bud appears some distance back from the growing tip of the root. The bud contains a leaf primordium, and will become, in essence, the first leaf of a new plant (Holm 1900; Carlson 1938).

The bud grows upward as a leaf petiole until it reaches the surface, then it produces a single green leaf blade. By the end of the first year, a node will have developed on the petiole 1 to 4 centimeters above the base, and everything above the node will die back in preparation

Pogonia ophioglossoides ***A***—Whole plant in flower, ***B***—Typical flower, ***C***—Typical flower, exploded view

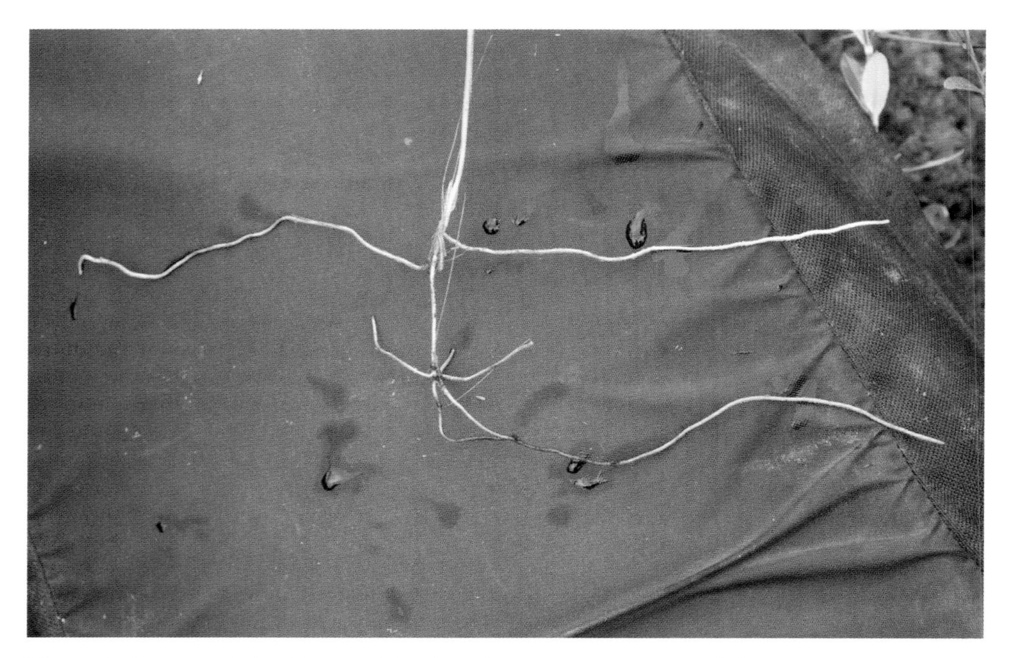
The vertical structure is the rhizome; the horizontal structures are the roots (July 16).

The flower appears in midsummer, usually the second or third week of July.

for winter. The following spring, growth will begin from the dormant node, which will produce another green leaf and this time a pair of roots that spread laterally in opposite directions. About this time, the connection with the parent plant is broken. The offspring will continue the process of producing a single leaf and an additional node each year for perhaps three to five years until the new plant has accumulated enough stored nutrients to produce a flowering stem rather than just a single leaf.

This is a process of true vegetative reproduction, an accomplishment credited to many orchids but achieved by few. Actually, the ability to sprout new plants from the roots of an existing plant is quite rare among all plants, not just orchids.

The most common place to find *Pogonia* is on floating vegetation mats that sometimes develop around ponds or along the margins of slow-moving streams. You will know you are in good habitat when you are standing in a thick, fluffy carpet of *Sphagnum* moss that moves in undulating waves as you walk on it. There may be a thin layer of floating peat beneath the moss, although floating mats often have little peat. They might be just deep mats of floating *Sphagnum* loosely held together by the roots of scattered knee-high shrubs and perhaps the rhizomes of sedges. This makes walking treacherous, a calculated risk at best. There's always the danger of breaking through, especially when approaching the thin edge of the mat where *Pogonia* is most likely to be found.

The risk-averse orchid seeker will be glad to hear that *Pogonia* also occurs in more "grounded" peatlands that are not directly associated with open water. In these situations, the peat will be buoyant enough to quake when you walk on it, but it is supported by solid ground so you won't fall through. In some cases these habitats are called water tracks. These are unique places where a broad stretch of water slowly seeps through a peatland like a flowing river. This keeps the peat continually saturated and supplied with mineral cations carried from some not-too-distant upland.

A floating vegetation mat at the edge of a small pond in Aitkin County

Genus *Spiranthes* Rich.
Ladies'-tresses orchids

The name *Spiranthes* is from the Greek words meaning "coiled flowers," in apparent reference to the spiraled arrangement of the flowers.

The genus has undergone many taxonomic changes, and as now construed it contains forty-five species (Sheviak and Brown 2002). Representatives of *Spiranthes* are found in North America, South America, Eurasia, and Australia, with twenty-three species in the United States and five in Minnesota.

Spiranthes have no corm, bulb, or obvious rhizome belowground. The stem appears to arise directly from the top of a cluster of rather stout, fleshy roots. The roots seem to function as food storage organs much as a tuber might; hence they are often called tuberous roots. The sequence of growth is not entirely clear, but among Minnesota species it appears that each root continues to grow for perhaps two years and then begins to fade and shrivel. By fall of its third year, the old root is replaced by a new root produced at the base of the stem above the old root. There is a constant turnover of roots with each plant having between two and seven functional roots at any given time. Species of *Spiranthes* in general tend to mature quickly from seed but don't live long, rarely as long as ten years (Ames 1921; Anderson 1991; Antlfinger and Wendel 1997).

Long-tongued bees, such as bumblebees, probe flowers for the nectar secreted in the base of the flower. In the process they pick up pollinia on their eyes or mouthparts and transfer them to other flowers (Catling and Catling 1991; Catling 1983). It is clear that *S. lacera* and *S. romanzoffiana* are sexual species and require this transfer of pollinia. It seems, however, that *S. casei* var. *casei*, *S. cernua*, and at least in some instances *S. magnicamporum*, can produce viable seed without pollination (Catling 1983). This happens through the asexual process of agamospermy, a rare process among North American orchids.

This sets the stage for understanding the nature of *S. cernua*, which is facultatively agamospermic, meaning it can produce viable seeds both sexually and asexually. Even stranger, there can be a mix of both types of seeds in a single seed capsule (Sheviak and Brown 2002).

Furthermore, *S. cernua* has been identified as a polyploid, facultatively apomictic compilospecies (Sheviak 1991). In practical terms, this means *S. cernua* is a variable species with a complex hybrid origin. Gene flow from related species has created a variety of recognizable forms that can be perpetuated in pure lines through asexual reproduction. But since *S. cernua* can also reproduce sexually, the genes from related species can be recombined in novel ways. All this obscures the boundaries of what botanists call *S. cernua*.

Fortunately for Minnesota-based orchid enthusiasts, the *S. cernua* we see in Minnesota is relatively consistent in form and can almost always be told from the two related species that occur here, *S. magnicamporum* and *S. casei* var. *casei*. Still, it pays to be skeptical when trying to identify anything that looks like *S. cernua*, and don't be in a hurry. Check all the plants in a population; it is possible that you may have more than one species. Characteristics of the flowers are important, but also pay close attention to the shape and condition of the leaves.

Spiranthes magnicamporum

A Key to the *Spiranthes* of Minnesota

1. Flowers (perianth) 3.5–6.2 mm long; leaves 1.8–5 cm long, proportionately broad; inflorescence consisting of flowers arranged in a single vertical column that has a gradual spiral twist.

2. Spikes loosely flowered, the ratio of spike length in millimeters to flower number is equal to or greater than 2.3; inflorescence with gland-tipped hairs; basal leaves present when the flowers are at their peak. . . . . ***S. lacera* var. *lacera***

2. Spikes densely flowered, the ratio of spike length in millimeters to flower number is less than 2.3; entire plant essentially glabrous; basal leaves withering before the flowers reach their peak. . . . . ***S. lacera* var. *gracilis***

1. Flowers (perianth) 5.5–12 mm long; leaves 5–28 cm long, proportionately narrow; inflorescence consisting of 1 or more vertical columns in a ± tight spiral twist.

3. Sepals converging with the petals to form a "hood" that ± arches over the column; lip strongly constricted near the middle, appearing fiddle-shaped (pandurate) when flattened; inflorescence with sparse hairs 0.1–0.2 mm long. . . . . ***S. romanzoffiana***

3. Sepals and petals separate, not forming an obvious hood; lip not constricted or only slightly constricted near the middle, not fiddle-shaped; inflorescence with dense hairs 0.2–0.4 mm long.

4. Leaves present when the flowers are at their peak; lip constricted slightly near the middle; bracts on middle and upper portion of stem not generally overlapping; lateral sepals ± appressed.

5. Flowers (perianth) 8–12 mm long, ± pure white, arranged in two or more spiraled columns; leaves uniformly slender in proportion, usually less than 1 cm wide. . . . . ***S. cernua***

5. Flowers (perianth) 5.5–8 mm long, creamy white or yellowish white, arranged in a single spiraled column; leaves variable in proportion, the lower leaves obviously shorter and broader than the upper leaves and often more than 1 cm wide. . . . . ***S. casei* var. *casei***

4. Leaves withering before the flowers reach their peak; lip not constricted; bracts on middle and upper portion of stem generally overlapping; lateral sepals curved and spreading, often arching over the top of the flower. . . . . ***S. magnicamporum***

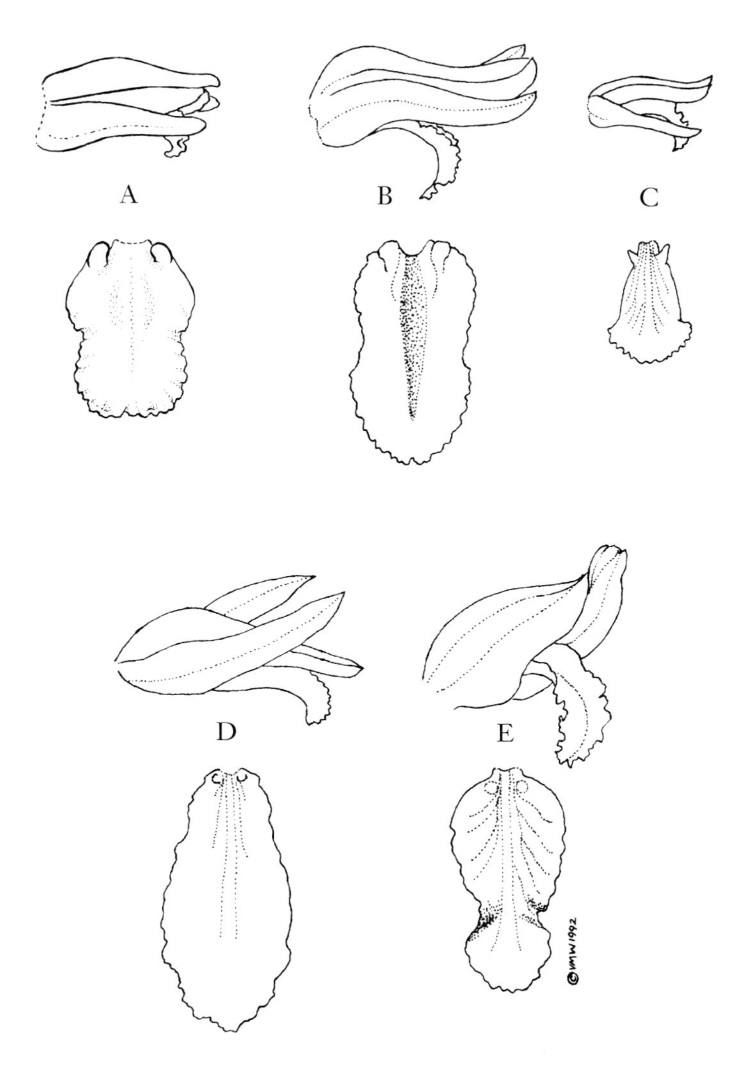

Flowers and floral lips of *Spiranthes* ***A***—*S. casei*, ***B***—*S. cernua*, ***C***—*S. lacera* (both varieties), ***D***—*S. magnicamporum*, ***E***—*S. romanzoffiana* (all shown approximately 3.5× actual size)

Spiranthes casei Catling & Cruise var. *casei*
Case's ladies'-tresses

[*S.* ×*intermedia* auct. non Ames]

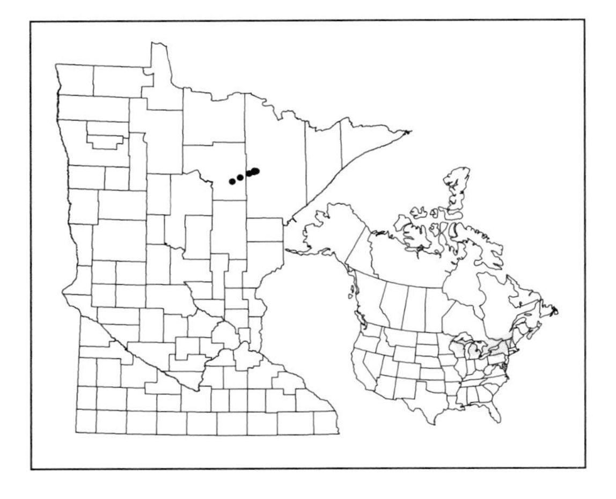

Plants 14–38 cm tall; **stem** arising from a descending cluster of 2–7 fleshy tuberous roots. **Leaves** 2–5, clustered on the lower portion of the stem, the lowermost ovate-lanceolate, 5–10 cm long, 1–2 cm wide, withering at anthesis; the middle leaves persisting through anthesis, linear-lanceolate to oblanceolate, 10–20 cm long and 0.5–1 cm wide, the uppermost decreasing in size until they grade into the bracts. **Inflorescence** a terminal spike, 5–12 cm long, with 14–35 flowers arranged in a single vertical column spiraled 3–6 times; each flower subtended by an ovate-lanceolate bract 7–15 (20) mm long. **Flowers** ivory to yellowish white, strongly nodding, perianth 5.5–8 mm long; **sepals** creamy white to greenish white, lanceolate, obtuse, 5–7 mm long, lateral sepals appressed; **petals** similar to sepals; **lip** ovate to ovate-oblong, often darker centrally, 5–7.5 mm long, 3–5 mm wide, margins thin, delicately crisped, apex truncate, basal calli incurved, prominent. **Capsules** ascending to erect, 5–8 mm long. **Flowering** August 20–September 15, perhaps peaking the first week in September.

The lowermost leaves of *S. casei* var. *casei* are wider than those of *S. cernua* (September 2).

The seemingly superfluous appellation "var. *casei*" is necessary to distinguish Minnesota plants from var. *novaescotiae* Catling, which is a smaller variety restricted to southern Nova Scotia (Sheviak and Brown 2002).

Compared to *S. cernua*, the lower leaves of *S. casei* var. *casei* are noticeably shorter and broader, but they may be gone by the time the flowers appear. The flowers are measurably smaller and appear more "closed" than those of *S. cernua*, meaning the sepals and petals don't flare out as much and they are not pure white like *S. cernua;* they are creamy white or yellowish white. Also, the spike of *S. casei* var. *casei* is a single vertical column of flowers in a gentle spiral. The spike of *S. cernua* has two or

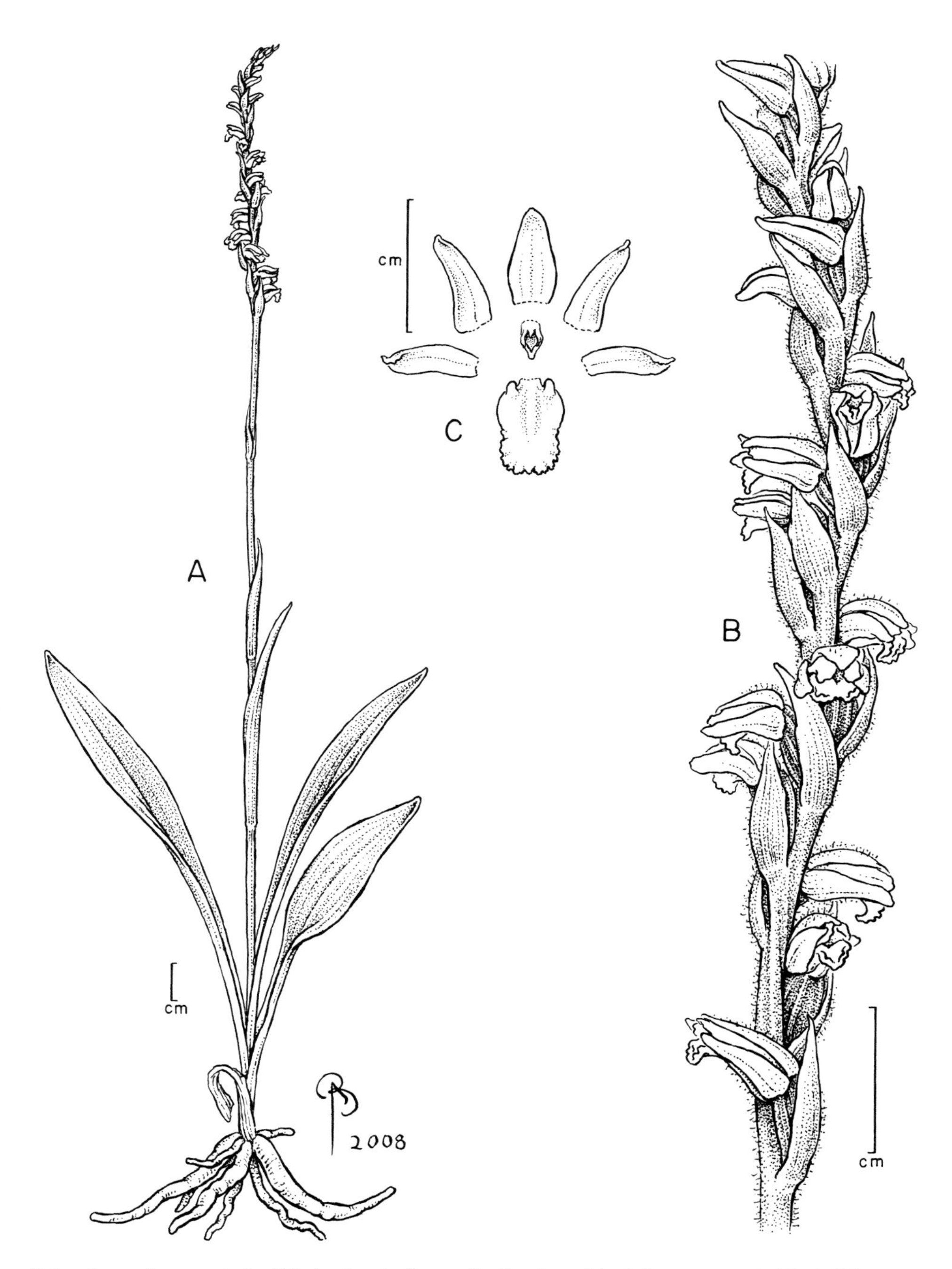

Spiranthes casei var. *casei* ***A***—Whole plant in flower, ***B***—Portion of the inflorescence, ***C***—Typical flower, exploded view

Spiranthes casei var. *casei* is most like *S. cernua*, but the flowers are slightly smaller and the sepals and petals don't flare out as much (August 27, St. Louis County).

more vertical columns twisted into a tight spiral. Be aware that *S. cernua* and *S. casei* var. *casei* may occur mixed together in the same habitat.

S. casei var. *casei* was not recognized as a distinct species until 1974, when it was separated from the *S. cernua* complex (Catling and Cruise 1974). It was not known to occur in Minnesota until 2000 when it was discovered near Hibbing by Rolf Dahle and Audrey Engels. Rolf and Audrey went on to find it at six distinct locations, all within about twenty-five miles of each other.

Curiously, all six known locations of *S. casei* var. *casei* are in drained tailings basins on the Iron Range in Itasca and St. Louis Counties; it has been found nowhere else in Minnesota. The basins are typically hundreds of acres in size and were created to dispose of the mineral residue, called tailings, of iron ore and taconite mining. The tailings are carried to the basins in a slurry of water. Over a period of years the basins become filled with water and the tailings settle out to the bottom. Then the water is drained, leaving a basin filled with a fine-textured reddish "soil."

Audrey Engels and Rolf Dahle where they first found *S. casei* in Minnesota (September 2009)

In time, the basins are colonized by common plants from adjacent habitats. After a period of perhaps twenty or thirty years, a young forest will typically develop with scattered stands of trembling aspen, balsam poplar, paper birch, and speckled alder. There will also be a variety of grasses, sedges, and forbs, mostly native forest species or early successional generalists, as well as several species of nonnative weeds. At some point in this process of reforestation, the habitat becomes very attractive to *S. casei* var. *casei* and a variety of other native orchid species.

Where the first *S. casei* var. *casei* came from is not known, most likely somewhere beyond the borders of Minnesota. How the first *S. casei* var. *casei* arrived in Minnesota is easier to imagine. It almost certainly arrived as a single wind-borne seed, which is how orchids generally disperse from one area to another. But the surprising aspect is how quickly it happened and how consistently it was repeated from one basin to another. This is not a fluke—it happened at least five times over the past thirty to forty years.

In many important ecological aspects, the tailings basins on the Iron Range, in spite of their human origin, closely resemble the natural habitats where *S. casei* var. *casei* is found elsewhere; perhaps we should not be too surprised that *S. casei* var. *casei* found them.

Stems can attain a height of about 15 inches (38 cm) and produce flowers in late August or early September (St. Louis County).

Spiranthes cernua (L.) Rich.
Nodding ladies'-tresses

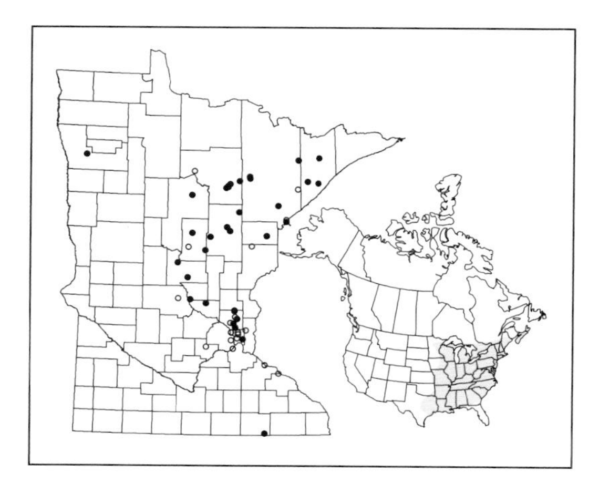

Plants 10–40 cm tall; **stem** arising from a spreading or descending cluster of 2–5 fleshy tuberous roots 2–7 cm long. **Leaves** primarily basal, generally present at anthesis, linear to narrowly oblanceolate, 6–28 cm long, 0.4–1.4 cm wide, stem leaves reduced to bladeless bracts, the upper ones generally not overlapping. **Inflorescence** a terminal spike, 3–11 cm long, with 9–35 flowers densely packed in 2 or more vertical columns spirally twisted on the stem, each flower subtended by an ovate-acuminate bract 7–17 mm long. **Flowers** white to creamy or ivory, nodding or occasionally ascending, perianth 8–12 mm long; **sepals** ± appressed, lanceolate, 5.5–11 mm long; **petals** similar to sepals; **lip** ovate to oblong, 5.5–11 mm long, 3–6 mm wide, slightly constricted near the middle, the portion above the constriction recurved and with a ragged wavy margin. **Capsules** ascending to erect, 4–8 mm long. **Flowering** August 10–September 20, peaking in the last week of August or the first week of September.

The stem and leaves come from a cluster of fleshy, tuberous roots (September 2).

It seems most orchids from southern and western Minnesota that are identified as *S. cernua* are actually *S. magnicamporum*, a species that was split off from *S. cernua* in 1973 (Sheviak 1973). True *S. cernua* is actually a rare plant outside the Anoka Sand Plain. Outdated field guides and plant manuals only confuse the situation.

The ideal flower of *S. cernua* is pure white and scentless. The floral lip, if laid flat, can be seen to have a slight constriction near the middle. The lateral sepals lie parallel to the rest of the flower, mostly straight but with the tips incurved. The leaves remain healthy and green throughout anthesis, which peaks around the first of September.

The flowers of *S. magnicamporum* are similar to those of *S. cernua*, but they are intensely fragrant and the lip lacks any constriction. The lateral sepals spread outward and upward from the base and often arch above the rest of the flower. The leaves are gone before the flowers appear, which on average is a week later than *S. cernua*. The presence or absence of leaves is a fairly consistent and reliable

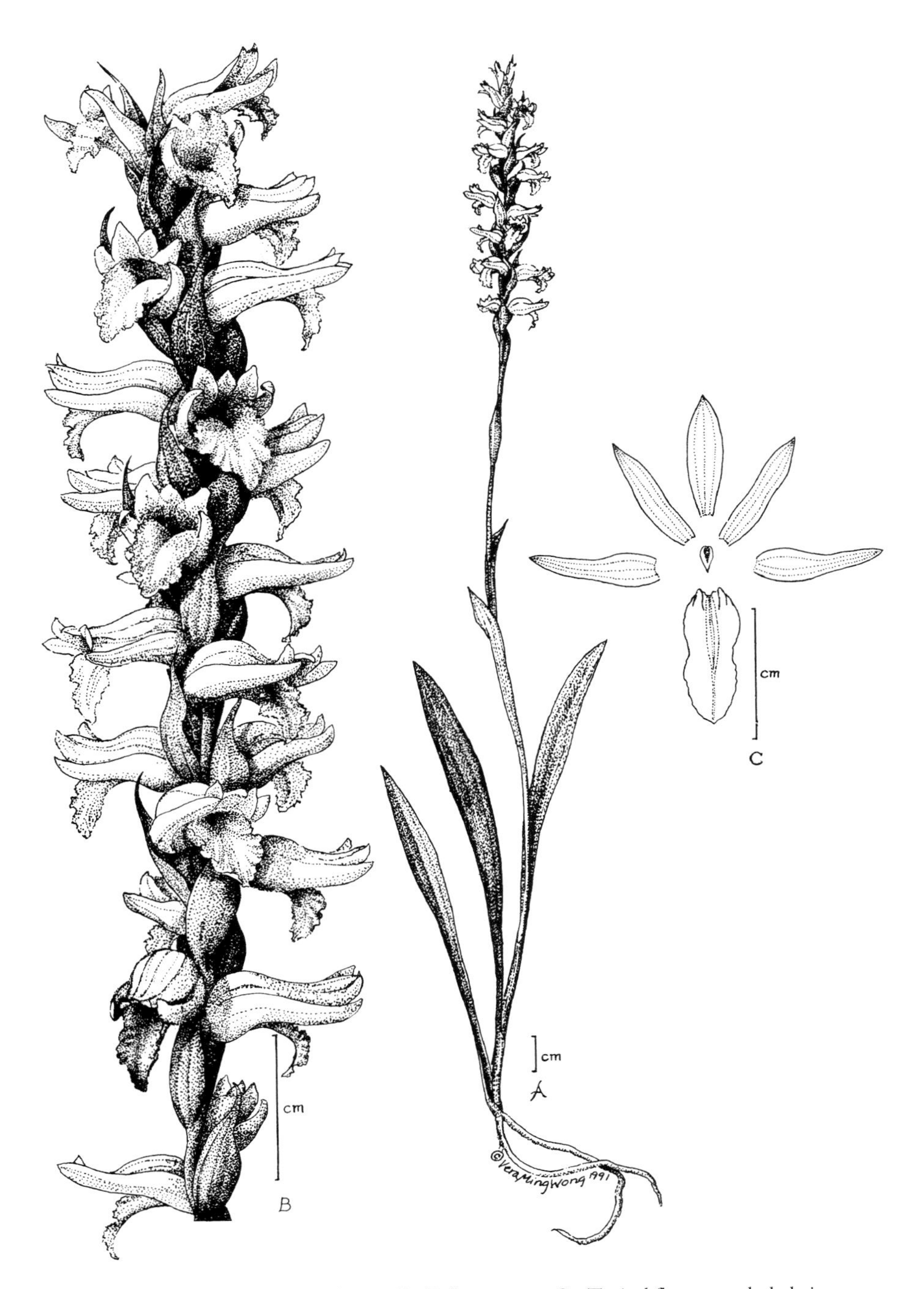

Spiranthes cernua ***A***—Whole plant in flower, ***B***—Inflorescence, ***C***—Typical flower, exploded view

The zone between the water and the trees supports hundreds of *S. cernua* (September 2, St. Louis County).

feature and should be the first thing you look for. Also, the habitats and geographic ranges of the two species are different—they rarely, if ever, occur together.

Identifying specimens from northeastern Minnesota requires a different caution. In the northeast it is *S. casei* var. *casei* not *S. magnicamporum* that is the look-alike to be considered, and *S. casei* var. *casei* may be found growing with *S. cernua*.

S. cernua is found in a variety of habitats in Minnesota, most often in seasonal wetlands. These are places where the soils might be wet in the spring or after heavy rain, but only moist or even dry by the end of the summer. The soil is typically sand or sandy loam or a thin layer of peaty material over sand; the recurring theme appears to be moist sand.

Often *S. cernua* is found at the margins of wet meadows or marshes. It will usually be away from the shade of trees although it might be found among scattered willow or dogwood shrubs. It is also found in sparse vegetation adjacent to ponds and lakes. These are not wave-lapped beaches but rather the level or gently sloping region back from the water in a transition zone characterized by more stable vegetation. The ponds are often quite small and shallow and develop on nearly level terrain, with water levels rising and falling with the local water table. Similar habitats are sometimes found at the bottoms of sandy ditches and abandoned gravel pits, as well as drained sediment basins that are in the process of revegetating. These newly created habitats usually have the largest populations, sometimes hundreds of individuals, but conditions change quickly, and the plants may disappear before long.

The best naturally occurring habitats are probably on the Anoka Sand Plain in east-central Minnesota. This is a broad, sandy outwash plain with level to gently rolling terrain. The native vegetation has now been largely replaced with agricultural and urban development, but it still provides remnant examples of excellent habitat.

S. cernua needs direct sunlight and moist soil (September 2, St. Louis County).

Spiranthes lacera (Raf.) Raf. var. *gracilis* (Bigelow) Luer
Southern slender ladies-tresses

[*S. gracilis* (Bigelow) Beck]

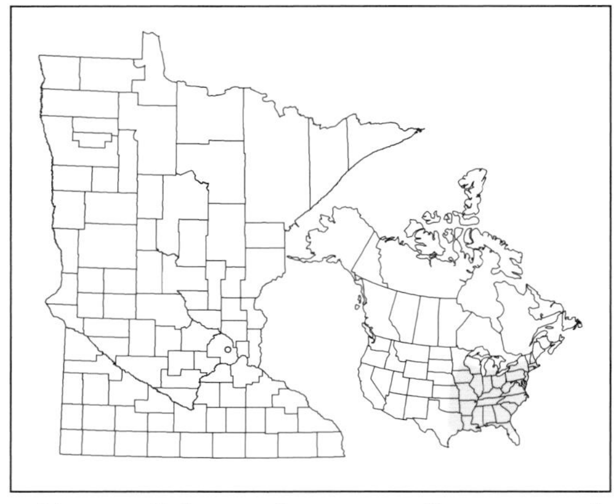

Plants 15–65 cm tall; **stem** arising from a descending cluster of 2–6 fleshy tuberous roots. **Leaves** basal, although usually withering before the flowers reach their peak, obovate, 2–5 cm long, 1–2 cm wide. **Inflorescence** with flowers loosely to tightly arranged in a single vertical column spirally twisted on the stem or sometimes second; the ratio of spike length (in millimeters) to flower number is less than 2.3; mostly without a distinct space between the lowest flowers; glabrous; each flower subtended by a lanceolate bract. **Flowers** white, small, inconspicuous at a distance; **sepals** lanceolate to lance-linear, about 5 mm long; **petals** linear to oblanceolate, about 5 mm long; **lip** oblong, 4–7.5 mm long, apex rounded and dilated; central portion green with clearly defined, broad, crisp white apron. **Flowering** dates unknown for Minnesota, expected to be in August and probably later than *S. lacera* var. *lacera*.

Spiranthes lacera var. *gracilis* from a site in Indiana (photograph by Michael Homoya)

Spiranthes lacera is divided into two varieties. They look very much alike, but if you carefully apply the key on page 212, you can expect nearly all specimens to fall neatly into one variety or the other. First, notice that the flowers of var. *gracilis* are more closely spaced than those of var. *lacera*, with an average of one or more flowers per 2.3 millimeters of inflorescence. This number is arrived at by dividing the length of the spike measured in millimeters by the total number of flowers. If the result is less than 2.3, then the specimen has passed one test for var. *gracilis*. Next, look for hairs on the stem and spike—var. *gracilis* will have essentially none. Also, the leaves will be gone by the time the flowers are at their peak, and the flowers are reported to peak later in the season than those of var. *lacera*.

Be aware that var. *gracilis* is very rare in Minnesota; in fact it may no longer exist in the state. If it is still here, it is likely to be in meadows, prairies, or grassy habitats in the southern third of the state.

Botanists in other states find var. *gracilis* in prairie hay meadows and report that it might be especially evident in September after mowing. It might also be

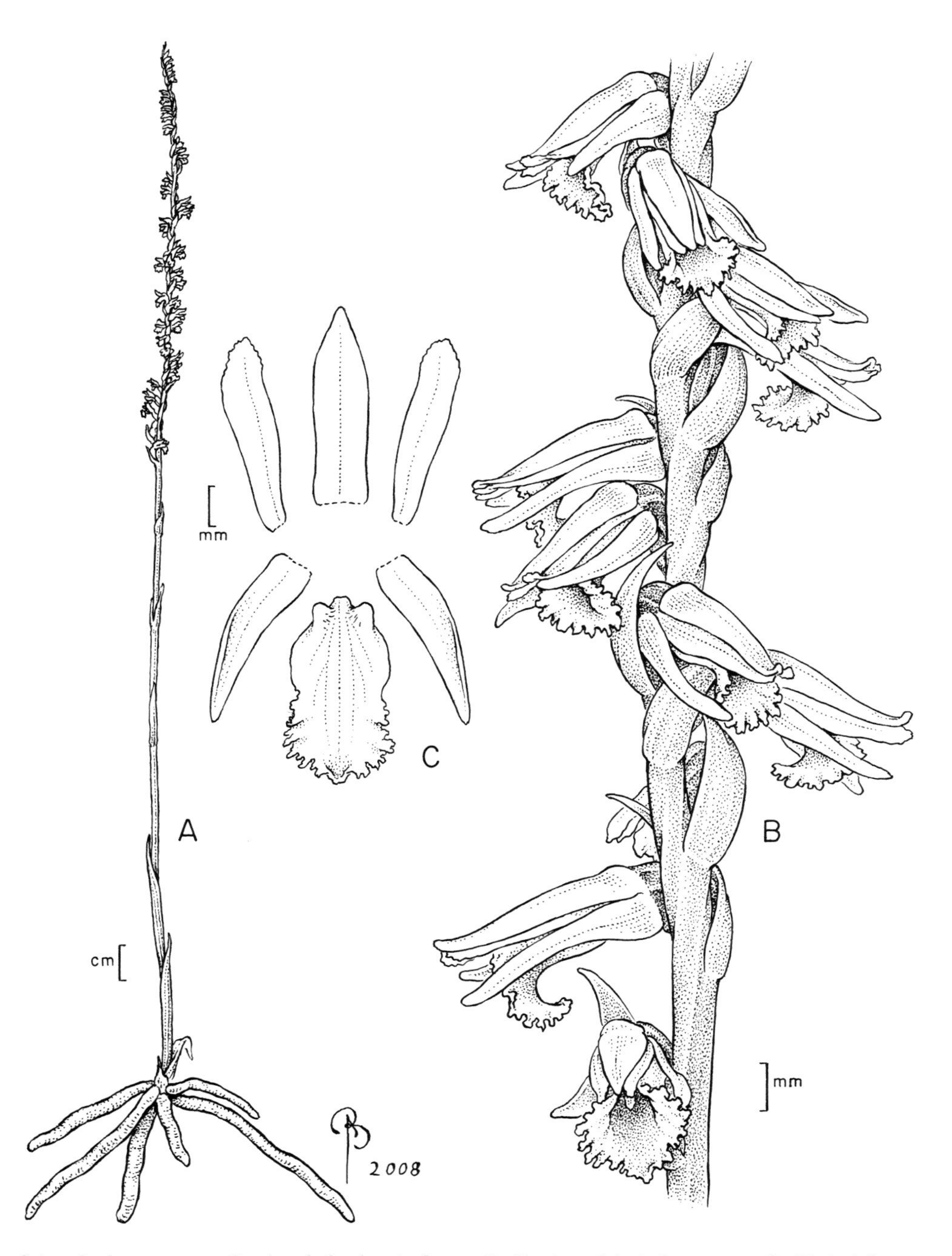

Spiranthes lacera var. *gracilis* ***A***—whole plant in flower, ***B***—Portion of the inflorescence, ***C***—Typical flower, exploded view

Aiton's 1889 herbarium specimen (MIN 92815) from Hennepin County. Photograph courtesy of the J. F. Bell Museum of Natural History, University of Minnesota.

found in previously grazed prairies as long as the prairie hasn't been grazed so heavily that all the native prairie species have been beaten out, leaving only exotic pasture grasses. It is thought that var. *gracilis* flowers more abundantly in mowed areas and after prairie fires (Charles Sheviak, personal communication, 2009).

Much of this is supposition. All that is actually known about this orchid in Minnesota comes from two specimens on deposit in the University of Minnesota herbarium. Both are dated August 1889 and bear the location "Hennepin County." One says "meadow" and the other says "peat meadow," but it seems likely that they were both collected at the same time and place. The label of one specimen bears the name George B. Aiton, a prominent scholar and educator of his day. The other specimen has the label of John H. Sandberg, an amateur botanist whose private herbarium would subsequently be acquired by the University of Minnesota and mark the establishment of the first public research herbarium in the state.

The significance of the specimens was not understood until the taxonomy of the species reached some level of stability. Although the identification of the specimens, confirmed by Charles Sheviak in 2008, is reasonably certain, the taxonomic relationship of the two varieties continues to be debated. In spite of lingering uncertainties, it is my opinion that this variety did, and perhaps still does, occur in prairies in southern Minnesota. It is known to occur on the Iowa side of the Iowa–Minnesota border (in Winneshiek County) and nearby Wisconsin (Grant County), and someday it may be found again in Minnesota.

Closely spaced flowers in a single spiraling column are a characteristic of *S. lacera* var. *gracilis* (Indiana; photograph by Lee Casebere).

Spiranthes lacera (Raf.) Raf. var. *lacera*
Northern slender ladies'-tresses

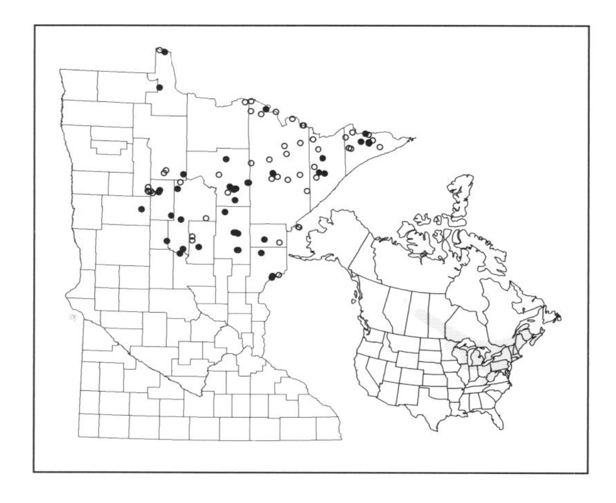

Plants 15–45 cm tall; **stem** arising from a descending cluster of 2–6 fleshy tuberous roots 1.5–6 cm long. **Leaves** basal, normally present at anthesis, ovate-elliptic or obovate, 1.8–5 cm long, 0.7–2 cm wide. **Inflorescence** 2.5–15 cm long, consisting of 7–45 flowers arranged in a single vertical column, the ratio of spike length (in millimeters) to flower number is equal to or greater than 2.3, the column of flowers spirally twisted on the stem or occasionally secund, often with a distinct space between the lowest flowers; sparsely hairy-glandular; each flower is subtended by an ovate-acuminate bract 3.5–8.5 mm long. **Flowers** inconspicuous at a distance, white, perianth 3.5–6.2 mm long; **sepals** lanceolate to linear, 3.5–6.2 mm long; **petals** similar to sepals; **lip** oblong, 4–6 mm long, 1.5–2.8 mm wide, with a ragged wavy margin on the apical portion, central portion green to yellowish green, with narrow, crisp white apron clearly defined. **Capsules** ascending, 4–7 mm long. **Flowering** July 15–August 20, usually peaking the last week of July or the first few days of August.

The leaves are basal and persist all summer (photograph by Erika Rowe).

Currently, there are thought to be two distinct varieties of *S. lacera* in eastern North America (Sheviak and Brown 2002; Catling 1980b), var. *lacera* and var. *gracilis*. Although there is considerable overlap in their geographic ranges, they are often thought of as a northern variety and a southern variety. Apparently both varieties occur in Minnesota. There is little doubt that var. *lacera* is the common variety occurring in forests in northern Minnesota. There is, however, some mystery surrounding var. *gracilis*. It is believed to occur in grasslands in the southern part of the state. The two varieties look similar but can be reliably told apart using the key on page 212.

S. lacera var. *lacera* is a very slender, delicate plant with a single column of tiny white flowers arranged in a gentle spiral. It does not stand out from its background and does not advertise its presence with bright or flamboyant colors (although the bees that pollinate it

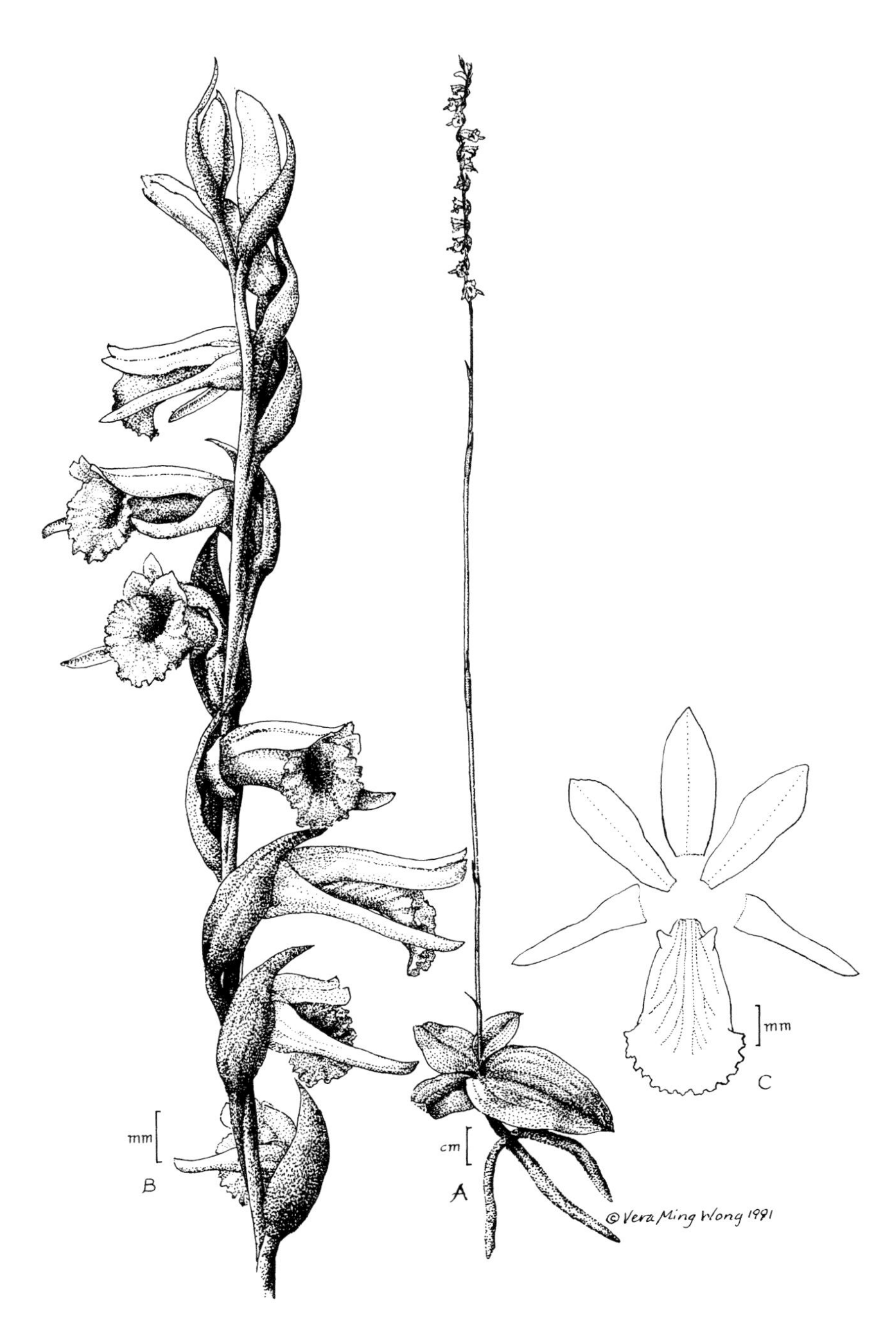

Spiranthes lacera var. *lacera* ***A***—Whole plant in flower, ***B***—Portion of the inflorescence, ***C***—Typical flower, exploded view

The intermingled root systems of two separate plants (August 16)

may have a different perspective on the matter). When you first notice it, you may wonder how many times you have walked past it without seeing it.

Without fail, the habitats of *S. lacera* var. *lacera* are high and dry; this is not a wetland plant. In Minnesota, it is strongly associated with jack pine that grow in dry sandy or rocky soil. The soil is often no more than coarsely crumbled rock or wind-blown sand that came to rest in some rocky crevice. The soil may have very little organic material or structure and little capacity to hold water. Other plants in this habitat often turn brown and die back early in a dry year, but this orchid manages to stay green longer than most. The flowers may not last as long in a dry year, but they seem to last long enough to be pollinated and produce thousands of seeds.

Similar habitats can be found in moss or lichen mats that grow amid stunted trees on high ridges, as well as on cliffs and bedrock outcrops. When these habitats get caught in forest fires, they often burn down to bare rock. I have no explanation, but after only a few years some of these burned areas host huge populations of *S. lacera* var. *lacera*. Numbers easily reach into the thousands.

It is not a stretch to say that all orchids posses a certain amount of mobility. Admittedly, a rooted orchid does not move about much. Orchid seeds, on the other hand, are not so constrained. They go wherever the wind takes them, and the wind sometimes takes the seeds of *S. lacera* var. *lacera* to unexpected places. In fact, it is not unusual to see an odd plant appear in an abandoned mine site, a drained sediment basin, or a sandy or gravelly embankment. I would not expect to come back after ten years and find the plant still there, since these are not optimal habitats, but that does not diminish the significance of the event. During its brief stay it will probably send its progeny on another wind-borne voyage to scout for new territory.

The flowers of *S. lacera* var. *lacera* are small and delicate, no more than a quarter of an inch (6.2 mm) long (photograph by Erika Rowe).

Spiranthes magnicamporum Schev.
Great Plains ladies'-tresses

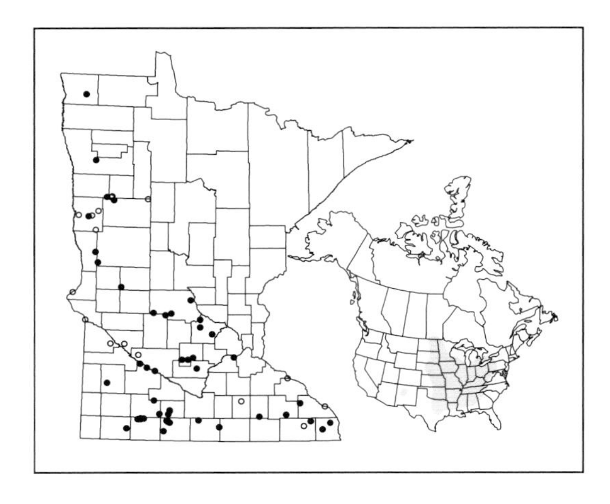

Plants 15–45 cm tall; **stem** arising from a descending cluster of 2–5 fleshy tuberous roots 3–11 cm long and 3–6 mm thick. **Leaves** linear-lanceolate to oblanceolate, essentially basal, up to 14 cm long and 1.2 cm wide, withering about 2 weeks before the flowers appear; cauline leaves reduced to 4–6 bladeless bracts, the upper ones usually overlapping. **Inflorescence** a terminal spike, 4–15 cm long, with 13–48 flowers densely packed in 2 or more vertical columns, the columns gently spiraled on the stem, each flower subtended by an ovate-acuminate bract 7–23 mm long. **Flowers** fragrant, white to ivory, nodding, perianth 8–12 mm long; **lateral sepals** curved and spreading, often arching above the flower, lanceolate, 7–11 mm long; **petals** similar to sepals; **lip** oblong-obovate, 7–11 mm long, 3.5–6 mm wide, not constricted near the middle, appearing to taper or curve evenly to the base, the upper portion with a ragged wavy margin. **Capsules** ascending, 4–9 mm long. **Flowering** August 20–September 24, mostly the first 2 weeks of September.

The flowers are pollinated primarily by bumblebees (August 24).

S. magnicamporum is chronically misidentified as *S. cernua*, and for good reason—the two species look very much alike. The flowers of both species are about the same size and color, and both appear to be "nodding" when viewed from the side. Similarities aside, there is a difference in the shape of the lip that can be seen if it is removed from the flower and laid flat. But before dissecting a flower, look for the leaves at the base of the stem. If the leaves are still green and fresh when the flowers are open, then you likely have *S. cernua;* if they are withered or gone entirely, then you probably have *S. magnicamporum*. Even after the leaves of *S. magnicamporum* have withered, the stem and flowers remain fresh and active. The early loss of the leaves is normal for this species, even in wet years. Also, when you examine a fresh flower, notice that the lateral sepals of *S. magnicamporum* adopt a position different from those of *S. cernua*. They tend to rise up and over the top of the flower instead of going

Spiranthes magnicamporum ***A***—Whole plant in flower, ***B***—Portion of the inflorescence, ***C***—Typical flower, exploded view

The thick, fleshy, belowground parts are often called tuberous roots (August 24).

straight forward. A more obvious difference is the strong fragrance of *S. magnicamporum*, which is absent from *S. cernua*.

A side-by-side comparison of the two species would be revealing, but it is not likely since the two species rarely if ever occur together; the habitats are actually quite different, and the phenologies are offset somewhat—the peak of *S. cernua* is about a week earlier than the peak of *S. magnicamporum*.

The habitats of *S. cernua* are seasonal wetlands on acidic sand in sparsely vegetated communities of early successional plants. These habitats often develop at the margins of ponds and marshes, and primarily in a wooded matrix in the eastern part of the state.

S. magnicamporum, on the other hand, is a true prairie plant. It is typically found in mesic and wet-mesic prairies, most often in calcareous glacial till. These are true prairies where there is a dense sod and a well-established community of what might be called late successional native prairie species. Most of the records from the southeastern counties are a little different. They are from dry bluff prairies, in rocky or gravelly soil on steep south- and west-facing slopes.

Many surviving populations of *S. magnicamporum* seem to be in railroad prairies, probably because that's where most of the surviving prairies are. These are the long, linear strips of prairie that have survived on the unused right-of-way between the train tracks and the adjacent road or farm field. Unfortunately, time is taking a toll on these prairie strips. The effects of ecological isolation, herbicide drift from adjacent agricultural land, and the relentless waves of invasive plant species have robbed most of these habitats of their biological complexity. The native prairie grasses are being replaced by monotypic stands of European pasture grasses like smooth brome grass, quack grass, or reed canary grass. When this happens, *S. magnicamporum* is one of the first species to disappear.

The habitat is a gravelly, rocky bluff prairie in Fillmore County (August 24).

Spiranthes romanzoffiana Cham.
Hooded ladies'-tresses

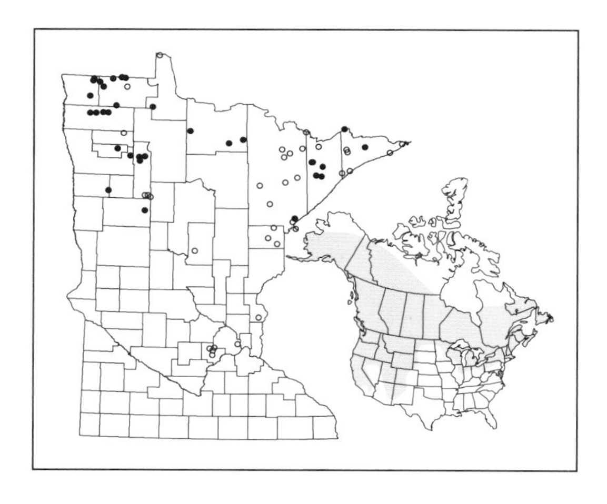

Plants 13–46 cm tall; **stem** arising from a descending or spreading cluster of 2–6 fleshy, tuberous roots 1.5–5 cm long and 2–7 mm thick. **Leaves** present during anthesis, linear to narrowly lanceolate or oblanceolate, the lower leaves 5–24 cm long and 2.5–9 mm wide, the middle and upper leaves becoming progressively smaller. **Inflorescence** a terminal spike, 2.5–13 cm long, with 11–45 flowers in 2 or more vertical columns that are ± spirally twisted on the stem; each flower subtended by an ovate-acuminate bract 8–20 mm long. **Flowers** white to ivory, ascending, perianth 6.5–11.5 mm long; **sepals** and **petals** converging to form a hood that ± arches over the lip, the tip of the hood curving upward; **lip** 6–11.5 mm long, 3–4.5 mm wide, strongly constricted above the middle to produce a fiddle-shaped (pandurate) outline when flattened, the portion above (distal to) the constriction reflexed and with a ragged wavy or nearly entire margin. **Capsules** ascending, 5–9 mm long. **Flowering** July 17–August 26, mostly the last week in July and the first week in August.

The petals and sepals merge over the top of the flower forming the "hood" that gives this orchid its common name.

At first glance, *S. romanzoffiana* looks much like *S. cernua* or *S. magnicamporum*, but there are a number of simple ways to identify this plant. First, learn to recognize the "hood" that gives this orchid its common name. It is formed by the sepals and petals converging over the top of the flower. Also, the lip seems to dangle downward from about the middle of the flower. If the lip is removed from the flower and laid flat, you will notice the middle is constricted, which gives the whole lip the shape of a fiddle. And the flowers of *S. romanzoffiana* tend to be creamy white rather than the pure white of *S. cernua* and *S. magnicamporum*.

Although this is not a common orchid in our region, it can be found across much of northern Minnesota. The most recent records are from the northwest, primarily in the Aspen Parkland ecological section (MDNR 2005b).

Habitats of *S. romanzoffiana* in the Aspen Parklands include sedge-dominated fens, mostly of the type called calcareous fens, rich fens,

Spiranthes romanzoffiana ***A***—Whole plant in flower, ***B***—Inflorescence, ***C***—Typical flower, exploded view

Flowering usually peaks during the last week in July or the first week in August (photograph by Scott Milburn).

or spring fens. These habitats are fed by mineral-rich groundwater so they are permanently wet, even in years of low precipitation. In other words, these are not seasonal or ephemeral wetlands. These are stable, full-functioning plant communities with intact hydrologic systems. The soil is soft, spongy peat with a pH in the range of weakly acidic to distinctly alkaline. The pH may measure as high as 8.0, in which case the peat will likely be derived from decomposing sedges rather than *Sphagnum* moss. In fact, *Sphagnum* is usually an indicator of acidic conditions, so it may be replaced by brown mosses that can tolerate the high pH. Trees will generally be absent or there may be scattered groves of tamarack. These habitats are at the edge of the prairie so wildfires were probably common prior to human settlement.

Other suitable habitats in the northwest include sedge meadows and wet prairies where the soil tends to be more loamy than peaty. These non-fen wetlands are likely to have more sedges and fewer mosses but otherwise would appear similar.

In the northeast—deeper into the forested region of Minnesota—the habitats of *S. romanzoffiana* tend to become more acidic and nutrient-poor. They are still called fens, but poor fens rather than rich fens, or they may fall into the category of swamps. They also tend to be forested rather than open, and *Sphagnum* moss becomes a more frequent groundcover. In this setting *S. romanzoffiana* tends to be in sunny or partially shaded openings or edges.

Records from southern Minnesota all date to the nineteenth century and include a specimen collected near Linn Lake in Chisago County in 1892, a number of specimens from somewhere in Minneapolis between 1878 and 1890, and a cluster of records from the vicinity of Waconia in Carver County collected in 1881. All the records from southern Minnesota are believed to be from tamarack swamps, which likely do not exist anymore.

The flowers tend to be cream colored rather than pure white (photograph by Otto Gockman).

Phenology of Minnesota Orchids

Species Name	May	June	July	August	September	October
Amerorchis rotundifolia (round-leaved orchid)						
Aplectrum hyemale (putty-root)						
Arethusa bulbosa (dragon's-mouth)						
Calopogon oklahomensis (Oklahoma grass-pink)						
Calopogon tuberosus var. *tuberosus* (tuberous grass-pink)						
Calypso bulbosa var. *americana* (fairy-slipper)						
Coeloglossum viride (long-bracted orchid)						
Corallorhiza maculata var. *maculata* (spotted coral-root)						
Corallorhiza maculata var. *occidentalis* (western spotted coral-root)						
Corallorhiza odontorhiza var. *odontorhiza* (autumn coral-root)						
Corallorhiza striata var. *striata* (striped coral-root)						
Corallorhiza trifida (early coral-root)						
Cypripedium acaule (stemless lady's-slipper)						
Cypripedium arietinum (ram's-head lady's-slipper)						
Cypripedium candidum (small white lady's-slipper)						
Cypripedium parviflorum var. *makasin* (northern small yellow lady's-slipper)						
Cypripedium parviflorum var. *pubescens* (large yellow lady's-slipper)						
Cypripedium reginae (showy lady's-slipper)						
Epipactis helleborine (broad-leaved helleborine)						
Galearis spectabilis (showy orchis)						
Goodyera pubescens (downy rattlesnake-plantain)						
Goodyera repens (lesser rattlesnake-plantain)						
Goodyera tesselata (tesselated rattlesnake-plantain)						
Liparis liliifolia (lily-leaved twayblade)						
Liparis loeselii (Loesel's twayblade)						

Species Name	May	June	July	August	September	October
Listera auriculata (auricled twayblade)						
Listera convallarioides (broad-leaved twayblade)			*dates unknown*			
Listera cordata (heart-leaved twayblade)						
Malaxis monophyllos var. *brachypoda* (white adder's-mouth)						
Malaxis paludosa (bog adder's-mouth)						
Malaxis unifolia (green adder's-mouth)						
Platanthera aquilonis (northern green bog-orchid)						
Platanthera clavellata (small green wood-orchid)						
Platanthera dilatata var. *dilatata* (tall white bog-orchid)						
Platanthera flava var. *herbiola* (tubercled rein-orchid)						
Platanthera hookeri (Hooker's orchid)						
Platanthera huronensis (tall green bog-orchid)						
Platanthera lacera (ragged fringed orchid)						
Platanthera obtusata subsp. *obtusata* (bluntleaved rein-orchid)						
Platanthera orbiculata (lesser roundleaved orchid)						
Platanthera praeclara (western prairie fringed orchid)						
Platanthera psycodes (small purple fringed orchid)						
Pogonia ophioglossoides (rose pogonia)						
Spiranthes casei var. *casei* (Case's ladies'-tresses)						
Spiranthes cernua (nodding ladies'-tresses)						
Spiranthes lacera var. *gracilis* (southern slender ladies'-tresses)			*dates unknown*			
Spiranthes lacera var. *lacera* (northern slender ladies'-tresses)						
Spiranthes magnicamporum (Great Plains ladies'-tresses)						
Spiranthes romanzoffiana (hooded ladies'-tresses)						

Glossary

acidic having a pH less than 7.0
acuminate contracted to a narrow point; the sides of the angle concave
acute tapering evenly to a point; the sides straight or somewhat convex and forming an angle less than 90 degrees
adventitious a structure or organ developing in an unusual or abnormal location, such as a stem originating from a root
aerial existing or growing in the air rather than in the ground or water
agamospermy the formation of seeds without fertilization; a type of asexual reproduction in which the progeny are genetically identical to the parent
alder-leaved buckthorn *Rhamnus alnifolia;* a multistemmed deciduous shrub in the buckthorn family (Rhamnaceae); a common native shrub in wet, primarily forested habitats in much of Minnesota, reaching a maximum height of about 1 meter
alkaline having a pH greater than 7.0
allopolyploid having two or more complete sets of chromosomes derived from different species
allozyme an allelic enzyme detected through protein electrophoresis, often used in genetic research such as hybrid identification and estimation of genetic variation
alluvial of or relating to a stream or river
American elm *Ulmus americana;* a broad-leaved deciduous tree in the elm family (Ulmaceae); a formerly common native tree in mesic forests throughout Minnesota, especially in the central and southern counties, reaching a maximum height of about 37 meters
anther the portion of the stamen that contains the pollen or pollinia
anther sac a pocket-shaped cavity in the anther containing pollen
anthesis the period of time when the flower is fully developed and functional
apiculate ending abruptly in a short, pointed tip
apomixis a form of asexual reproduction in which viable seeds are produced without fertilization, the resulting progeny being genetically identical to the parent plant
appressed lying close and flat against a surface
ascending growing obliquely upward
auricle an ear-shaped appendage or lobe
auto-pollination automatic self-pollination
autogamous self-pollination; pollination of a flower by its own pollen
balsam fir *Abies balsamea;* a needle-leaved evergreen tree in the pine family (Pinaceae); a common native tree in late successional forests in northern Minnesota, reaching a maximum height of about 26 meters and age of 200 years
balsam poplar *Populus balsamifera;* a broad-leaved deciduous tree in the willow family (Salicaceae); a fairly common native tree in early successional forests throughout the northern half of Minnesota, reaching a maximum height of about 25 meters and age of 200 years
basal positioned at or arising from the base of a structure or organ
basswood *Tilia americana;* a broad-leaved deciduous tree in the linden family (Tiliaceae); a common native tree in mesic forests throughout Minnesota, reaching a maximum height of about 35 meters
bearberry *Arctostaphylos uva-ursi;* a low-growing, broad-leaved evergreen shrub in the heath family (Ericaceae); a common shrub in dry, sandy pine forests and on exposed bedrock in central and northern Minnesota
big bluestem *Andropogon gerardii;* a tall, perennial, clump-forming member of the grass family (Poaceae); a common and often dominant native grass in prairies throughout Minnesota
Big Woods an ecological subsection in south-central Minnesota that coincides with a large block of deciduous forest present at the time of Euro-American settlement

bitternut hickory *Carya cordiformis;* a broad-leaved deciduous tree in the walnut family (Juglandaceae); a common native tree in late successional mesic forests in southeastern Minnesota, reaching a maximum height of about 34 meters

bladderworts *Utricularia* spp.; a genus of aquatic insectivorous plants in the family Lentibulariaceae

blade the expanded portion of a leaf

black ash *Fraxinus nigra;* a broad-leaved deciduous tree in the olive family (Oleaceae); a common native tree in swamps and moist forests throughout the forested region of Minnesota, reaching a maximum height of about 33 meters

black cherry *Prunus serotina;* a broad-leaved deciduous tree in the rose family (Rosaceae); a common native tree in upland forests of central and southern Minnesota, reaching a maximum height of about 30 meters and an age of 200 years or more

black spruce *Picea mariana;* a needle-leaved evergreen tree in the pine family (Pinaceae); a common native tree in swamps and bogs in northern Minnesota, reaching a maximum height of about 25 meters and age of 250 years or more

blue-bead lily *Clintonia borealis;* a common forest herb in the lily family (Liliaceae)

bog a plant community or habitat type occurring on deep, saturated peat and isolated from the influence of groundwater; characteristically acidic and nutrient-poor

bog birch *Betula pumila;* a broad-leaved deciduous shrub in the birch family (Betulaceae); a common multistemmed shrub in shallow wetlands throughout most of Minnesota, reaching a maximum height of about 3.4 meters

bog laurel *Kalmia polifolia;* a broad-leaved evergreen shrub in the heath family (Ericaceae); a common native inhabitant of bogs and swamps in northern Minnesota, reaching a height of about 70 centimeters

boreal of or relating to the north. Used in an ecological context to describe the climatic region between the temperate (to the south) and the arctic (to the north)

bracken fern *Pteridium aquilinum;* a common and widespread fern of the family Dennstaedtiaceae; noted for large, highly divided leaves and the ability to spread underground

bract a modified or reduced leaf, typically at the base of a flower or on a stem

buckthorn *see* common buckthorn

bur oak *Quercus macrocarpa;* a broad-leaved deciduous tree in the beech family (Fagaceae); a common native tree in savannas, woodlands, and early successional forests throughout most of Minnesota, especially in the southeast and central counties, reaching a maximum height of about 34 meters and age of 400 years or more

calcareous soil or water containing calcium (in the form of calcium carbonate)

callus (pl. calli) an isolated thickening of tissue, especially a stiff protuberance on the lip of an orchid

capsule a dry, dehiscent fruit derived from a compound ovary of two or more carpels

cattail *Typha* spp.; any of a number of large, perennial plants in the family Typhaceae; two species, *T. angustifolia* and *T. latifolia*, are common and often dominant in wetlands throughout most of Minnesota

caudicle the structure within the flower of an orchid to which the pollinia are attached

cauline on or of the stem, as leaves arising from the stem

chromosome a threadlike strand of DNA in the nucleus of a cell that carries the genes and functions in the transmission of hereditary information

circumboreal occurring throughout the boreal region in a more or less continuous ring around the earth

circumneutral referring to a pH value around neutral; sometimes codified as pH 5.5 to 7.5

circumpolar occurring throughout the Arctic region in a more or less continuous ring around the North Pole

clavate club-shaped; one end thicker than the other

clone an individual or group of individuals originating from a single parent by asexual reproduction

colluvium soil that has accumulated at the base of a hill through the action of erosion or gravity

column a floral structure characteristic of orchids, composed of the fused style and filaments
common buckthorn *Rhamnus cathartica;* a large broad-leaved deciduous shrub or small tree in the buckthorn family (Rhamnaceae); native to Europe and introduced to North America for horticultural purposes, now naturalized in native habitats throughout southern and central Minnesota
compilospecies a genetically aggressive species incorporating germplasm of related species via introgressive interbreeding
conifer a species of tree or shrub characterized by bearing cones or strobili, as in many gymnosperms, e.g. pines (*Pinus*), spruces (*Picea*), northern white cedar (*Thuja occidentalis*), and tamarack (*Larix laricina*)
coralloid having the shape or form of coral
corm the swollen base of the underground portion of the stem, used for food storage and reproduction
cortex the outer layer of the root of a plant, bounded on the outside by the epidermis and on the inside by the endodermis
cross-pollination the fertilization of the ovary of one plant with pollen from another plant, producing a progeny with a new genetic makeup distinct from either parent
cylindrical in the shape of a cylinder; a solid body longitudinally elongate and rounded in cross section
dehiscent the natural bursting open of a fruit or capsule for the release of the seeds
deltate in the shape of the Greek letter delta; an equilateral triangle
diploid with two complete sets of chromosomes in each cell
distal toward the tip or end of a structure, opposite the end of attachment
divergent diverging or spreading; inclining away from each other
ecotone the transition zone between two different plant communities or habitats
ellipsoid a solid body, elliptical in long section and circular in cross section
elliptical in the shape of an ellipse; a plane, symmetric form broadest at the middle and narrower at the two equal, curved ends
endemic occurring naturally only in a specific geographic area or habitat type
ericaceous relating to the family Ericaceae, which includes a number of evergreen shrubs
erose irregularly or unevenly notched, toothed, or indented
evergreen a plant having foliage that persists and remains green throughout a given year, in contrast with a deciduous plant that loses its leaves for part of the year
falcate hooked or curved like a sickle
fen a type of wetland strongly influenced by groundwater and occurring on saturated peat; pH circumneutral or alkaline and comparatively rich in nutrients
filiform threadlike
form (forma) a taxonomic category with a hierarchical rank below that of a variety, usually used to describe minor color variation; abbreviated f.
genet an individual plant derived from sexual reproduction
genus a taxonomic category with a hierarchical rank between that of species and family
garlic mustard *Alliaria petiolata;* a herbaceous biennial in the mustard family (Brassicaceae); native to Europe and parts of Asia, it is highly invasive in North American forests
glabrous hairless
gland an appendage, protuberance, or other structure that produces a sticky, greasy, or viscous substance
green ash *Fraxinus pennsylvanica;* a broad-leaved deciduous tree in the olive family (Oleaceae); a common native tree in mesic forests throughout most of Minnesota, reaching a maximum height of about 34 meters
hardwood a general and nonspecific term for broad-leaved trees, as in oaks, maples, ashes, and so on
herbaceous a plant with no persistent woody stem; nonwoody
herbarium a collection of dried plant specimens that are mounted and systematically arranged for study; the place where dried plant specimens are stored
hyphae any of the threadlike filaments forming the mycelium of a fungus

indian grass *Sorghastrum nutans;* a tall, clump-forming member of the grass family (Poaceae); a common native grass of mesic prairies throughout Minnesota

inflorescence the flowering portion of the plant, in particular the arrangement of flowers on an axis

internode the portion of a stem that occurs between any two nodes

isozymes also known as isoenzymes; one of several forms of an enzyme in an individual or population that differs in amino acid sequence but catalyzes the same chemical reaction

jack pine *Pinus banksiana;* a needle-leaved evergreen tree in the pine family (Pinaceae); a common native forest tree in parts of northern and central Minnesota, reaching a maximum height of about 31 meters and age of 240 years

Labrador tea *Rhododendron groenlandicum;* a broad-leaved evergreen shrub in the heath family (Ericaceae); a common native inhabitant of bogs and swamps in northern and central Minnesota, reaching a height of about 1 meter

lacustrine of or relating to lakes or a lake environment

lanceolate shaped like the head of a lance; broadest below the middle and gradually tapered to a pointed apex; much longer than wide

leatherleaf *Chamaedaphne calyculata;* a broad-leaved evergreen shrub in the heath family (Ericaceae); a common native inhabitant of bogs and swamps in northern and central Minnesota, reaching a height of about 1 meter

linear long and narrow with parallel sides; resembling a line

lip one of the three petals of an orchid flower, usually larger than and different in shape from the other two; in a normal resupinate flower, it is the lowermost of the flower parts

lobe a division or segment of an organ such as a flower petal; larger than a tooth but may have a tooth at its apex or margin, although more often rounded

loess soils a soil composed of wind-deposited silt

mesic soil condition between wet and dry; moist

metapopulation a group of spatially separated populations or subpopulations of the same species that interact at some level

moraine the accumulated earth, sand, gravel, and stones deposited by a glacier, or the landforms created by the deposits

morphology the form and structure of a plant

muck the final stage of decomposition or mineralization of peat

mycelium the vegetative part of a fungus, consisting of a mass of branching, threadlike hyphae

mycorrhiza the process or product of a close association between the underground parts of a fungus, termed *hyphae*, and the roots of higher plants; a root-fungus symbiosis

native originating or occurring naturally in a certain place; indigenous

naturalized plants introduced from elsewhere but now established in the wild and reproducing as if native

nectary a structure that produces nectar, usually associated with a flower

node a place on a stem where a leaf originates, usually seen as a hard swelling or enlargement

northern pin oak *Quercus ellipsoidalis;* a broad-leaved deciduous tree in the beech family (Fagaceae); a common native tree in savannas and early successional dry and dry-mesic forests in southeastern and central Minnesota, reaching a maximum height of about 31 meters

northern white cedar *Thuja occidentalis;* a tree in the cypress family (Cupressaceae) with scale-like leaves; a common native tree in moist or wet forests in north-central and northeastern Minnesota, reaching a maximum height of about 25 meters and an age of 1,000 years or more

oblanceolate inversely lanceolate, with the attachment at the narrow end

oblong a symmetric plane figure two to four times longer than wide, widest at the midpoint with margins essentially parallel and ends equally curved

obovate inversely ovate, with the attachment at the narrow end

obovoid inversely ovoid, with the attachment at the narrow end

obpandurate inverse pandurate

obtuse tapering evenly to a point; the sides straight or somewhat convex and forming an angle greater than 90 degrees

orbicular circular or spherical

ovary the expanded basal portion of the pistil that contains the ovules (immature seeds)
ovate a symmetric plane figure with the widest axis below the middle and with the margins evenly curved; egg-shaped in outline and attached at the broad end
ovoid ovate but in three dimensions (a solid form); egg-shaped
pandurate shaped like a fiddle in outline
paper birch *Betula papyrifera;* a broad-leaved deciduous tree in the birch family (Betulaceae); a common native tree in forests throughout Minnesota, especially northward, reaching a maximum height of about 28 meters and age of about 250 years
peat soil composed entirely of partially decomposed plant material
peatland peat-covered land; a permanent wetland
pedicel the stalk of an individual flower in an inflorescence
pedicellate having a pedicel
pendent hanging or suspended
peduncle the stalk of a solitary flower or the stalk of an inflorescence
perianth all of the sepals and petals of a flower in whatever number or form
petal an individual segment or member of the corolla
petiole the stalk of a leaf
pH the logarithm of the reciprocal of the hydrogen ions in solution, represented on a scale of 1 to 14 with 7 being neutral, numbers greater than 7 being alkaline, and numbers less than 7 being acidic
pollen the mass of developing male gametophytes produced in the anther of an angiosperm or the microsporangium of a gymnosperm
pollinium (pl. pollinia) a coherent mass of pollen grains
polyploid having three or more complete sets of chromosomes in each cell, indicative of hybridization
prairie cordgrass *Spartina pectinata;* a tall, rhizomatous member of the grass family (Poaceae); a common native grass in wet prairies, sloughs, and marshes throughout much of Minnesota
protocorm the life stage of an orchid that follows germination of the seed and precedes the first appearance aboveground
proximal toward the base or the end of the structure to which it is attached
pseudobulb a false bulb; a storage organ that is derived from the part of a stem between two leaf nodes, as in *Malaxis* and *Liparis*
purple pitcherplant *Sarracenia purpurea;* an insectivorous wetland plant in the family Sarraceniaceae; a common species in peatlands throughout much of northern and central Minnesota
quack grass *Elymus repens;* a grass native to Eurasia; a common and invasive species spreading rapidly via long rhizomes
quadrate being square or approximately square
raceme an unbranched, elongate inflorescence with pedicellate flowers maturing from the bottom upward
rachis the main axis of a structure; the axis to which the individual flowers of an inflorescence are attached
ramet an individual plant derived from nonsexual reproduction; a clone of its parent
red maple *Acer rubrum;* a broad-leaved deciduous tree in the maple family (Aceraceae); a relatively common native tree in upland and lowland forests in parts of central and eastern Minnesota, reaching a maximum height of about 29 meters and an age of 150 years
red oak *Quercus rubra;* a broad-leaved deciduous tree in the beech family (Fagaceae); a common native tree in mid- and late successional mesic forests throughout most of Minnesota, especially southward, reaching a maximum height of about 33 meters and age of 300 years or more
red-osier dogwood *Cornus sericea;* a broad-leaved deciduous shrub in the dogwood family (Cornaceae); a common native shrub in shallow wetlands throughout Minnesota, reaching a maximum height of about 4 meters
red pine *Pinus resinosa;* a needle-leaved evergreen tree in the pine family (Pinaceae); a common native tree in early and mid-successional forests in parts of northern Minnesota, reaching a maximum height of about 37 meters and an age of 400 years or more
reed canary grass *Phalaris arundinacea;* a perennial member of the grass family (Poaceae); an invasive nonnative species that has become common in wetlands throughout most of Minnesota

resupinate in the context of an orchid flower, the condition of being twisted approximately 180 degrees so that the lip, which would otherwise be uppermost of the petals, becomes lowermost
rhizome an underground stem usually producing roots and/or aerial shoots at the nodes
rosette a cluster of basal leaves arranged radially or spirally
rostellum the projecting portion of the column of an orchid flower, which by separating the male portion of the flower from the female portion commonly prevents self-fertilization
sac a bag-shaped compartment, as the cavity of an anther
secund arranged on one side of an axis
sedge any member of the sedge family (Cyperaceae), especially of the genus *Carex*
self-pollination pollination of a flower by its own pollen
semiorbicular half of a circle or sphere
senescence becoming old; becoming dried or shriveled with age
sepal an individual segment or member of the calyx
sessile attached directly by the base, without a stalk of any kind
sheath the lower part of the leaf, forming a tubular envelope around the stem or pseudobulb, present in some species, not in others; usually with an expanded blade, but sometimes without
smooth brome grass *Bromus inermis;* a perennial grass native to Eurasia, now widely naturalized in North America; a highly invasive species in grasslands throughout Minnesota
spatulate shaped like a spatula; with a rounded apex gradually tapered to the base
speckled alder *Alnus incana* subsp. *rugosa;* a broad-leaved deciduous shrub or small tree in the birch family (Betulaceae); a common native plant in shallow wetlands throughout most of Minnesota, reaching a maximum height of about 8 meters
spherical shaped like a sphere; a 3-dimensional structure round in outline
Sphagnum a genus of mosses commonly called peat mosses; their partially decomposed remains, commonly called sphagnum peat, make up the great bulk of peat in acid peatlands throughout the world
spicate having flowers that grow in spikes
spike an unbranched, elongate inflorescence with sessile flowers maturing from the bottom upward
spur a hollow tubular structure projecting roughly downward or laterally from the base of the lip of a flower; usually contains nectar
stamen the male reproductive organ of a flower
stigma the portion of the pistil that is receptive to pollen, usually supported by the style
subglobose not quite globose
suborbicular less than a full circle or sphere
subsp. standard abbreviation of *subspecies;* a taxonomic rank between species and variety; sometimes abbreviated ssp.
subtend to be immediately below
subulate slender and tapering to a point
sugar maple *Acer saccharum;* a broad-leaved deciduous tree in the maple family (Aceraceae); a common native tree in late successional mesic forests throughout Minnesota, especially southward, reaching a maximum height of about 33 meters and an age of 200 years
sundew *Drosera* spp.; a genus of small insectivorous plants in the family Droseraceae found in various wetlands across northern and central Minnesota
swamp a type of tree- or shrub-dominated wetland typically occurring on peat soil with moderate to strong groundwater influence
symbiont an organism that lives in a symbiotic relationship
symbiotic describing an intimate relationship with mutual benefit between two individuals or organisms
synsepal a floral structure formed by the partial or complete fusion of two or more sepals
tamarack *Larix laricina;* a needle-leaved deciduous tree in the pine family (Pinaceae); a common native tree in peat swamps throughout the northern two-thirds of Minnesota, reaching a maximum height of about 26 meters and an age of 300 years or more
taxonomy the classification of plants or animals according to natural relationships
temperate the climatic region immediately south of the boreal region, marked by a moderate climate with warm summers and cold or cool winters

terminal at the tip or apex
tetraploid with four complete sets of chromosomes in each cell
trailing arbutus *Epigaea repens;* a prostrate, vine-like shrub in the heath family (Ericaceae); a native inhabitant of dry, sandy pine forests in parts of northern Minnesota
trembling aspen *Populus tremuloides;* a broad-leaved deciduous tree in the willow family (Salicaceae); a common native tree in early successional forests throughout Minnesota, especially in the north, reaching a maximum height of about 32 meters and an age of 200 years
triploid with three complete sets of chromosomes in each cell
truncate with the apex or base transversely straight or nearly so, as if cut off
tuber an enlarged, underground stem that stores food and generates the aboveground stem and roots
tubercle a nodule or small knobby protuberance
undulate wavy in appearance, particularly the margin of a leaf
variety the taxonomic rank below that of subspecies; abbreviated var.
white oak *Quercus alba;* a broad-leaved deciduous tree in the beech family (Fagaceae); a common native tree in dry and dry-mesic forests in southeastern and east-central Minnesota, reaching a maximum height of about 29 meters and an age of 500 years or more
white pine *Pinus strobus;* a needle-leaved evergreen tree in the pine family (Pinaceae); a common native forest tree in parts of north-central and northeastern Minnesota, reaching a maximum height of about 41 meters and an age of 450 years
willow a species in the genus *Salix;* a genus containing approximately 450 species of deciduous trees and shrubs and occurring worldwide; at least 21 species of willow are known to occur wild in Minnesota, most prominently in shallow wetlands
yellow birch *Betula alleghaniensis;* a broad-leaved deciduous tree in the birch family (Betulaceae); a native tree occurring occasionally to infrequently in late successional mesic or wet forests throughout much of Minnesota, especially eastward, reaching a maximum height of about 28 meters and an age of 300 years or more
white spruce *Picea glauca;* a needle-leaved evergreen tree in the pine family (Pinaceae); a common native tree in late successional mesic forests in parts of north-central and northeastern Minnesota, reaching a maximum height of about 37 meters and an age of 300 years or more
xeric dry, desert-like

Bibliography

Ackerman, J. D. 1981. Pollination biology of *Calypso bulbosa* var. *occidentalis* (Orchidaceae): A food-deception system. *Madroño* 28(3): 101–110.
Ackerman, J. D., and M. R. Mesler. 1979. Pollination biology of *Listera cordata* (Orchidaceae). *American Journal of Botany* 66(7): 820–824.
Adams, M. S. 1970. Adaptations of *Aplectrum hyemale* to the environment: Effects of preconditioning temperature on net photosynthesis. *Bulletin of the Torrey Botanical Club* 97(4): 219–224.
Ames, O. 1921. Notes on New England orchids: 1. *Spiranthes*. *Rhodora* 23:73–85.
Anderson, A. B. 1991. Symbiotic and asymbiotic germination and growth of *Spiranthes magnicamporum* (Orchidaceae). *Lindleyana* 6:183–186.
Antlfinger, A. E., and L. F. Wendel. 1997. Reproductive effort and floral photosynthesis in *Spiranthes cernua* (Orchidaceae). *American Journal of Botany* 84(6): 769–780.
Auclair, A. N. 1972. Comparative ecology of the orchids *Aplectrum hyemale* and *Orchis spectabilis*. *Bulletin of the Torrey Botanical Club* 99(1): 1–10.
Bateman, R. M., K. E. James, Y. Luo, R. K. Lauri, T. Fulcher, P. J. Cribb, and M. W. Chase. 2009. Molecular phylogenetics and morphological reappraisal of the *Platanthera* clade (Orchidaceae: Orchidinae) prompts expansion of the generic limits of *Galearis* and *Platanthera*. *Annals of Botany* 104:431–445.
Bateman, R. M., A. M. Pridgeon, and M. W. Chase. 1997. Phylogenetics of subtribe Orchidinae (Orchidoideae, Orchidaceae) based on nuclear ITS sequences: 2. Infrageneric relationships and taxonomic revisions to achieve monophyly of *Orchis* sensu stricto. *Lindleyana* 12:113–141.
Baumback, N., and E. Lückel. 2009. Die Gattungen *Platanthera* L. C. Rich. und *Blephariglottis* Raf. in den USA und Kanada. *Die Orchidee* 60(1/2): 119–127.
Boyden, T. C. 1982. The pollination biology of *Calypso bulbosa* var. *americana* (Orchidaceae): Initial deception of bumblebee visitors. *Oecologia* 55:178–184.
Brown, P. M., and G. W. Argus. 2002. *Epipactis*. In *Flora of North America North of Mexico*, ed. Flora of North America Editorial Committee, 26:584–586. New York: Oxford University Press.
Bruns, T. D., M. I. Bidartondo, and D. L. Taylor. 2002. Host specificity in ectomycorrhizal communities: What do the exceptions tell us? *Integrative and Comparative Biology* 42:352–359.
Butters, F. K., and E. C. Abbe. 1953. A floristic study of Cook County, northeastern Minnesota. *Rhodora* 55:21–201.
Carlson, M. C. 1938. Origin and development of shoots from the tips of roots of *Pogonia ophioglossoides*. *Botanical Gazette*, 100:215–225.
Case, M. A. 1993. High levels of allozyme variation within *Cypripedium calceolus* (Orchidaceae) and low levels of divergence among its varieties. *Systematic Botany* 18(4): 663–677.
Catling, P. M. 1976. On the geographic distribution, ecology, and distinctive features of *Listera ×veltmanii* Case. *Rhodora* 78: 261–269.
———. 1980a. Rain-assisted autogamy in *Liparis loeselii* (L.) L. C. Rich. (Orchidaceae). *Bulletin of the Torrey Botanical Club* 107:525–529.
———. 1980b. Systematics of *Spiranthes* L. C. Richard in northeastern North America. Ph.D. thesis, University of Toronto. 550 pp.
———. 1983. Autogamy in eastern Canadian Orchidaceae: A review of current knowledge and some new observations. *Naturaliste Canadien* 110:37–53.
———. 1984. Distribution and pollination biology of Canadian orchids. In *Proceedings of the 11th World Orchid Conference*, ed. K. W. Tan, 121–135. Miami: World Orchid Conference.
Catling, P. M., and V. R. Catling. 1989. Observations of the pollination of *Platanthera huronensis* in southwest Colorado. *Lindleyana* 4(2): 78–84.
———. 1991. A synopsis of breeding systems and pollination in North American orchids. *Lindleyana* 6(4): 187–210.
———. 1994. Identification of *Platanthera lacera* hybrids (Orchidaceae) from New Brunswick and Nova Scotia. *Lindleyana* 9:19–32.

———. 1997. Morphological discrimination of *Platanthera huronensis* in the Canadian Rocky Mountains. *Lindleyana* 12(2): 72–78.
Catling, P. M., and J. E. Cruise. 1974. *Spiranthes casei,* a new species from northeastern North America. *Rhodora* 76:526–536.
Catling, P. M., and L. K. Magrath. 2002. *Malaxis*. In *Flora of North America North of Mexico,* ed. Flora of North America Editorial Committee, 26:627–632. New York: Oxford University Press.
Correll, D. S. 1950. *Native Orchids of North America North of Mexico*. Waltham, Mass.: Botanica Chronica.
———. 1938. *Cypripedium calceolus* var. *pubescens*. *Botanical Museum Leaflets, Harvard University* 7:1–18.
Curtis, J. T. 1941. Some native orchids of the Lake Superior region. *American Orchid Society Bulletin* 10:190–194.
———. 1943. Germination and seedling development in five species of *Cypripedium*. *American Journal of Botany* 30:199–206.
Dickie, G. 1872. Note on the buds developed on leaves of *Malaxis*. *Journal of the Linnean Society of London* 14:1–3.
Dieringer, G. 1982. The pollination ecology of *Orchis spectabilis* L. (Orchidaceae). *Ohio Journal of Science* 82(5): 218–225.
Dressler, R. L. 2005. How many orchid species? *Selbyana* 26:155–158.
Freudenstein, J. V. 1997. A monograph of *Corallorhiza* (Orchidaceae). *Harvard Papers in Botany* 10:5–51.
Gamarra, R., P. Galán, I. Herrera, and E. Ortuñez. 2008. Seed micromorphology supports the splitting of *Limnorchis* from *Platanthera* (Orchidaceae). *Nordic Journal of Botany* 26:61–65.
Gill, D. E. 1989. Fruiting failure, pollinator inefficiency, and speciation in orchids. In *Speciation and Its Consequences,* ed. D. Otte and J. A. Endler, 458–481. Sunderland, Mass.: Sinauer Associates.
Goldman, D. H. 1995. A new species of *Calopogon* from the Midwestern United States. *Lindleyana* 10(1): 37–42.
Goldman, D. H., L. K. Magrath, and P. M. Catling. 2002. *Calopogon*. In *Flora of North America North of Mexico,* ed. Flora of North America Editorial Committee, 26:597–602. New York: Oxford University Press.
Gregg, K. B. 2004. Recovery of showy lady's slippers (*Cypripedium reginae* Walter) from moderate and severe herbivory by white-tailed deer (*Odocoileus virginianus* Zimmerman). *Natural Areas Journal* 24(3): 232–241.
Heywood, V. H., R. K. Brummitt, A. Culham, and O. Seberg. 2007. *Flowering Plant Families of the World*. Buffalo, N.Y.: Firefly Books.
Hogan, K. P. 1983. The pollination biology and breeding system of *Aplectrum hyemale* (Orchidaceae). *Canadian Journal of Botany* 61:1906–1910.
Holm, T. 1900. *Pogonia ophioglossoides* Mitt.: A morphological and anatomical study. *American Journal of Science,* 4th ser., 9(49): 13–19.
Hultén, E. 1958. The amphi-atlantic plants and their phytogeographical connections. *Kongliga Svenska Vetenskapsakademien Handlingar,* 4th ser., 8(5): 1–275.
———. 1968. *Amerorchis* nov. gen. *Arkiv för Botanik,* 2nd ser., 7:34–35.
Jones, P. S. 1998. Aspects of the population biology of *Liparis loeselii* (L.) Rich. var. *ovata* Ridd. ex Godfery (Orchidaceae) in the dune slacks of South Wales, UK. *Botanical Journal of the Linnaean Society* 126:123–39.
Kallunki, J. A. 1976. Population studies in *Goodyera* (Orchidaceae) with emphasis on the hybrid origin of *G. tesselata*. *Brittonia* 28:53–75.
———. 1981. Reproductive biology of mixed-species populations of *Goodyera* (Orchidaceae) in northern Michigan. *Brittonia* 33(2): 137–155.
———. 2002. *Goodyera*. In *Flora of North America North of Mexico,* ed. Flora of North America Editorial Committee, 26:514–517. New York: Oxford University Press.
Klier, K., M. J. Leoschke, and J. F. Wendel. 1991. Hybridization and introgression in white and yellow ladyslipper orchids (*Cypripedium candidum* and *C. pubescens*). *Journal of Heredity* 82(4): 305–318.
Kozhevnikova, A. D., and T. N. Vinogradova. 1999. Pseudobulb structure in some boreal terrestrial orchids. *Systematics and Geography of Plants* 68:59–65.

Kull, T. 1999. Biological flora of the British Isles: *Cypripedium calceolus* L. *Journal of Ecology* 87:913–924.

Luer, C. A. 1975. *The Native Orchids of the United States and Canada, excluding Florida.* New York: New York Botanical Garden.

Magrath, L. K. 2002. *Liparis.* In *Flora of North America North of Mexico,* ed. Flora of North America Editorial Committee, 26:624–626. New York: Oxford University Press.

Magrath, L. K., and R. A. Coleman. 2002. *Listera.* In *Flora of North America North of Mexico,* ed. Flora of North America Editorial Committee, 26:586–592. New York: Oxford University Press.

Magrath, L. K., and J. V. Freudenstein. 2002. *Corallorhiza.* In *Flora of North America North of Mexico,* ed. Flora of North America Editorial Committee, 26:633–638. New York: Oxford University Press.

Malterer, T. J., D. J. Olson, D. R. Mellem, B. Leuelling, and E. J. Tome. 1979. *Sphagnum* moss peat deposits in Minnesota. St. Paul: Minnesota Department of Natural Resources.

Marschner, F. J. 1974. *The Original Vegetation of Minnesota.* Map scale 1:500,000. St. Paul, Minn.: USDA Forest Service, North Central Forest Experiment Station.

McCormick, M. K., D. F. Whigham, D. Sloan, K. O'Malley, and B. Hodkinson. 2006. Orchid-fungus fidelity: A marriage meant to last? *Ecology* 87(4): 903–911.

McMaster, R. T. 2001.The population biology of *Liparis loeselii,* Loesel's twayblade, in a Massachusetts wetland. *Northeastern Naturalist* 8(2): 163–178.

MDNR (Minnesota Department of Natural Resources). 2003. *Field Guide to the Native Plant Communities of Minnesota: The Laurentian Mixed Forest Province.* St. Paul: Minnesota Department of Natural Resources.

———. 2005a. *Field Guide to the Native Plant Communities of Minnesota: The Eastern Broadleaf Forest Province.* St. Paul: Minnesota Department of Natural Resources.

———. 2005b. *Field Guide to the Native Plant Communities of Minnesota: The Prairie and Tallgrass Aspen Parklands Provinces.* St. Paul: Minnesota Department of Natural Resources.

Mesler, M. R., J. D. Ackerman, and K. L. Lu. 1980. The effectiveness of fungus gnats as pollinators. *American Journal of Botany* 67(4): 564–567.

Mosquin, T. 1970. The reproductive biology of *Calypso bulbosa. Canadian Field-Naturalist* 84:291–296.

Mousley, H. 1925. Further notes on *Calypso. Torreya* 25(5): 54–59.

Nieuwdorp, P. J. 1972. Some observations with light and electron microscope on the endotrophic mycorrhiza of orchids. *Acta Botanica Neerlandica* 21:128–144.

Pijl, L. van der, and C. H. Dodson. 1966. Orchid flowers, their pollination, and evolution. Coral Gables, Fl.: University of Miami Press.

Pridgeon, A. M., et al. 1997. Phylogenetics of subtribe Orchidinae (Orchidoideae, Orchidaceae) based on nuclear ITS sequences: 1. Intergeneric relationships and polyphyly of *Orchis* sensu lato. *Lindleyana* 12:89–109.

Rasmussen, H. N. 1986. The vegetative architecture of orchids. *Lindleyana* 1:42–50.

———. 1995. *Terrestrial Orchids: From Seed to Mycotrophic Plant.* Cambridge: Cambridge University Press.

Rasmussen, H. N., and D. F. Whigham. 1993. Seed ecology of dust seeds *in situ:* A new study technique and its application in terrestrial orchids. *American Journal of Botany* 80(12): 1374–1378.

———. 2002. Phenology of roots and mycorrhiza in orchid species differing in phototrophic strategy. *New Phytologist* 154:797–807.

Reddoch, J. M., and A. H. Reddoch. 1997. The orchids of the Ottawa District: Floristics, phytogeography, population studies, and historical review. *Canadian Field-Naturalist* 111(1): 1–187.

———. 2007. Population dynamics and flowering synchrony of *Goodyera pubescens* (Orchidaceae) in Southwestern Quebec, Canada. *Journal of the Torrey Botanical Society* 134: 379–388.

Reeves, L. M., and T. Reeves. 1984. Life history and reproduction of *Malaxis paludosa* in Minnesota. *American Orchid Society Bulletin* 53(12): 1280–1291.

Ridley, H. N. 1930. *The Dispersal of Plants throughout the World.* Ashford, Kent: Reeve & Co.

Romero-González, G. A., G. C. Fernández-Concha, R. L. Dressler, L. K. Magrath, and G. W. Argus. 2002. Orchidaceae. In *Flora of North America North of Mexico,* ed. Flora of North America Editorial Committee, 26:490–651. New York: Oxford University Press.

Rowe, E. 2007. Elusive orchids. *Minnesota Conservation Volunteer,* July–August.

Shefferson, R. P., et al. 2007. The evolutionary history of mycorrhizal specificity among lady's slipper orchids. *Evolution* 61(6): 1380–90.
Sheviak, C. J. 1973. A new *Spiranthes* from the grasslands of central North America. *Botanical Museum Leaflets, Harvard University* 22(7): 285–297.
———. 1991. Morphological variation in the compilospecies *Spiranthes cernua* (L.) L. C. Rich.: Ecologically-limited effects of gene flow. *Lindleyana* 6(4): 228–234.
———. 1992. Natural hybridization between *Cypripedium montanum* and its yellow-lipped relatives. *American Orchid Society Bulletin* 61:546–559.
———. 1993. *Cypripedium parviflorum* Salib. var. *makasin* (Farwell) Sheviak. *American Orchid Society Bulletin* 62(4): 403.
———. 1994. *Cypripedium parviflorum* Salisb.: 1. The small-flowered varieties. *American Orchid Society Bulletin* 63:664–669.
———.1995. *Cypripedium parviflorum* Salisb.: 2. The large-flowered plants and patterns of variation: *American Orchid Society Bulletin* 64:606–612.
———. 1999. The identities of *Platanthera hyperborea* and *P. huronensis*, with the description of a new species from North America. *Lindleyana* 14(4): 193–203.
———. 2001. A role for water droplets in the pollination of *Platanthera aquilonis* (Orchidaceae). *Rhodora* 103:380–386.
———. 2002a. *Cypripedium*. In *Flora of North America North of Mexico*, ed. Flora of North America Editorial Committee, 26:499–507. New York: Oxford University Press.
———. 2002b. *Platanthera*. In *Flora of North America North of Mexico*, ed. Flora of North America Editorial Committee, 26:551–571. New York: Oxford University Press.
Sheviak, C. J., and M. L. Bowles. 1986. The prairie fringed orchids: A pollinator-isolated species pair. *Rhodora* 88:267–290.
Sheviak, C. J., and P. M. Brown. 2002. *Spiranthes*. In *Flora of North America North of Mexico*, ed. Flora of North America Editorial Committee, 26:530–546. New York: Oxford University Press.
Sheviak, C. J., and P. M. Catling. 2002a. *Pogonia*. In *Flora of North America North of Mexico*, ed. Flora of North America Editorial Committee, 26:513–514. New York: Oxford University Press.
———. 2002b. *Calypso*. In *Flora of North America North of Mexico*, ed. Flora of North America Editorial Committee, 26:622–623. New York: Oxford University Press.
———. 2002c. *Coeloglossum*. In *Flora of North America North of Mexico*, ed. Flora of North America Editorial Committee, 26:550. New York: Oxford University Press.
———. 2002d. *Galearis*. In *Flora of North America North of Mexico*, ed. Flora of North America Editorial Committee, 26:550. New York: Oxford University Press.
Smith, S. E., and D. Read. 2008. *Mycorrhizal Symbiosis*. 3rd ed. New York: Academic Press.
Smith, W. R. 1993. *Orchids of Minnesota*. Minneapolis: University of Minnesota Press.
Stevens, W. C., and F. E. Dill. 1942. *Aplectrum spicatum* in a Kansas woodland. *Transactions Kansas Academy of Science* 45:138–151.
Stoutamire, W. P. 1964. Seeds and seedlings of native orchids. *Michigan Botanist* 3:107–19.
———. 1967. Flower biology of the lady's-slippers. *Michigan Botanist* 6:159–175.
———. 1968. Mosquito pollination of *Habenaria obtusata* (Orchidaceae). *Michigan Botanist* 7:203–212.
———. 1971. Pollination in temperate American orchids. In *Proceedings of the Sixth World Orchid Conference, Sydney, Australia*, ed. M. J. G. Corrigan, 233–243. Sydney: Halstead Press.
———. 1974. Terrestrial orchid seedlings. In *The Orchids: Scientific Studies*, ed. C. L. Whitner, 101–28. New York: Wiley.
———. 1991. Annual growth cycles of *Cypripedium candidum*: Root systems in an Ohio prairie. *Lindleyana* 6(4): 235–240.
Szlachetko, D. L., and H. B. Margonska. 2006. Redefinition of the genera *Malaxis* Sol. ex Sw. and *Microstylis* (Nutt.) Eaton (Orchidaceae, Epidendroideae). *Acta Societatis Botanicorum Poloniae* 75(3): 229–231.
Taylor, R. L. 1967. The foliar embryos of *Malaxis paludosa*. *Canadian Journal of Botany* 45(9): 1553–1556.
Thien, L. B., and B. G. Marcks. 1972. The floral biology of *Arethusa bulbosa*, *Calopogon tuberosus*, and *Pogonia ophioglossoides* (Orchidaceae). *Canadian Journal of Botany* 50:2319–2325.

Thien, L. B., and F. Utech. 1970. The mode of pollination in *Habenaria obtusata* (Orchidaceae). *American Journal of Botany* 57(9): 1031–1035.

Vinogradova, T. N. 1996. The early stages of *Listera cordata* (L.) R. Br. development in natural conditions. *Moskovskoe obshchestvo i spyta telei prirody biulletin*, NS otd., 101:83–92. Summary in English.

Wallace, L. E. 2003. Molecular evidence for allopolyploid speciation and recurrent origins in *Platanthera huronensis* (Orchidaceae). *International Journal of Plant Science* 164(6): 907–916.

———. 2004. A comparison of genetic variation and structure in the allopolyploid *Platanthera huronensis* and its diploid progenitors, *Platanthera aquilonis* and *Platanthera dilatata* (Orchidaceae). *Canadian Journal of Botany* 82(2): 244–252.

———. 2006. Spatial genetic structure and frequency of interspecific hybridization in *Platanthera aquilonis* and *P. dilatata* (Orchidaceae) occurring in sympatry. *American Journal of Botany* 93:1001–1009.

Wang, B., and Y.-L. Qiu. 2006. Phylogenetic distribution and evolution of mycorrhizas in land plants. *Mycorrhiza* 16(5): 299–363.

Westwood, A. R., and C. L. Borkowsky. 2004. Sphinx moth pollinators for the endangered western prairie fringed orchid, *Platanthera praeclara*, in Manitoba, Canada. *Journal of the Lepidopterists' Society* 58(1): 13–20.

Whigham, D. F. 2004. Ecology of woodland herbs in temperate deciduous forests. *Annual Review of Ecology, Evolution, and Systematics* 35: 583–621.

Whigham, D. F., J. P. O'Neill, H. N. Rasmussen, B. A. Caldwell, and M. K. McCormick 2006. Seed longevity in terrestrial orchids: Potential for persistent in situ seed banks. *Biological Conservation* 129(1): 24–30.

Whiting, R. E., and P. M. Catling. 1977. Distribution of the auricled twayblade orchid (*Listera auriculata*) in Canada and description of new stations in southern Ontario. *Canadian Field-Naturalist* 91(4): 403–406.

Wijaja, D. G., and J. Arditti. 1983. The orchids of Krakatau: Evidence for a mode of transport. *Annals of Botany* 52:127–130.

Willems, J. H., and C. Melser. 1998. Population dynamics and life-history of *Coeloglossum viride* (L.) Hartm.: An endangered orchid species in the Netherlands. *Botanical Journal of the Linnaean Society* 126:83–93.

Willson, G. D., M. J. Page, and F. A. Akyüz. 2006. Precipitation and fire effects on flowering of a rare prairie orchid. *Great Plains Research* 16:37–43.

Zimmer, K., C. Meyer, and G. Gebauer. 2008. The ectomycorrhizal specialist orchid *Corallorhiza trifida* is a partial myco-heterotroph. *New Phytologist* 178:395–400.

Zoladeski, C. A. 1988. New station for *Malaxis paludosa*, Bog Adder's-mouth Orchid, in northwestern Ontario. *Canadian Field-Naturalist* 102(3): 548–549.

Index

Welby R. Smith is the state botanist with the Minnesota Department of Natural Resources in St. Paul. He is the author of *Trees and Shrubs of Minnesota* and a contributor to *Minnesota's Endangered Flora and Fauna*, both published by the University of Minnesota Press.

Vera Ming Wong is a natural science illustrator and artist. Her drawings of plants, animals, and habitats have been published in many books and journals.

Bobbi Angell has been drawing orchids and other plants for North American and neotropical floras and monographs since 1977. She lives and gardens in Marlboro, Vermont.